ADDING BEAUTY TO BROCADE

Expressing the reality of life through the Four Embracing Actions

ADDING BEAUTY TO BROCADE

Expressing the reality of life through the Four Embracing Actions

SHŌHAKU OKUMURA

KYOKU LUTZ

EIDO REINHART

DORYU CAPPELLI

SHOJU MAHLER

JAKUSHŌ PIGNATIELLO

REIGEN SANJUÁN

EISHŌ AMAYA

ESHO MORIMOTO

SHINKO HAGN

DENSHO QUINTERO

ONRYU KENNEDY

SHŌRYŪ BRADLEY

DŌJU LAYTON

MYOHO KENDALL

ISSAN KOYAMA

JISHO TAKAHASHI

EDITED BY HOKO KARNEGIS AND SEIGEN HARTKEMEYER

2023

Published by: Dōgen Institute, Bloomington
www.dogeninstitute.org

ISBN: 979–8-9868175–2-1
ebook ISBN: 979–8-9868175–3-8

Cover (illustration) by Michael Grossman
Cover photo by Hoko Karnegis
Publication design by Michael Grossman

The book's cover design features a brocaded *kohonbukusa*, a cloth
designed to enclose books and notes related to study and lecture
activities. This well-worn *kohonbukusa* belongs to Okumura Roshi.
Okumura Roshi's teacher Uchiyama Roshi inscribed the other side
of this cloth with the first sentence of Dogen's Fukanzazengi: 道
本圓通 *(dō moto en zū)*, or "Originally, the Way is complete and
universal."

Table of Contents

BENEFICIAL ACTION

IDENTITY ACTION

Editor's Preface

FIVE YEARS AGO, SANSHIN ZEN COMMUNITY undertook to put together a collaborative book, *Boundless Vows, Endless Practice,* in honor of our 15th anniversary. Now we're here again, this time to commemorate two decades of practice in the particular style of our family and lineage. In this volume we offer our various perspectives on the teachings found in the *Bodaisatta Shishobo (Four Embracing Actions of the Bodhisattva)* fascicle of Dōgen Zenji's *Shobogenzo.* As in the previous volume, we focus on the life and practice of the bodhisattva in the world of the here and now rather than offering an abstract or academic work. Our writing comes from our day-to-day experiences of practice and speaks to readers as they also navigate this one unified reality moment by moment.

We are all first or second generation dharma descendants of Sanshin's founder, Shohaku Okumura, and our chapters all respond in some way to his opening teachings about the four embracing actions: giving, loving speech, beneficial action and identity action. Some of us live the lives of householders and are holding down jobs and raising families in addition to carrying out our dharma teaching. Others are engaged in some form of residential practice, living in a temple and spending all day every day facilitating the practice of our sanghas and ourselves. We come from South America, North America, Europe and Japan and speak a variety of languages. We have varying levels of comfort and experience in writing for publication, and for some, English is a second or third language. When I first contacted my brothers and sisters to invite them to participate, I told them they were welcome to write in their first language rather than in English if they felt best able to say what they wanted to say in that way. Thus, this book contains dharma teachings in English, German, Italian and Spanish. Authors did their own translations into English except where noted.

As I did with our 15th anniversary volume, I've tried to preserve the authors' individual voices in their chapters, even where the English may be quirky or unusual. As long as the text was readable and understandable, I've opted not to edit with a heavy hand in order to make it possible for readers who know the writers to say to themselves, "Ah! I can just hear her saying that!"

This book would not have been possible without the linguistic expertise of Seigen Hartkemeyer, who edited all of the non-English chapters as well as their translations. In at least one case, he himself was the translator. The value of having a retired teacher of languages as part of the ordained sangha—someone who understands both the language and the dharma teaching being expressed—can't be overstated. In some instances, brothers and sisters helped each other with writing, translation and fine tuning—just another example of the ways in which the Sanshin Network is learning to create partnerships and work together to share our practice of the dharma.

Hoko Karnegis
Senior Dharma Teacher
Sanshin Zen Community

THE TEXT

.

Shobogenzo Bodaisatta Shishobo

TRANSLATED BY SHOHAKU OKUMURA AND ALAN SENAUKE

FIRST IS GIVING OR DANA. Second is loving-speech. Third is beneficial-action. Fourth is identity-action.

OFFERING

Offering means not being greedy. Not to be greedy means not to covet. Not to covet commonly means not to flatter. Even if we rule the four continents, in order to offer teachings of the true Way, we must simply and unfailingly not be greedy. It is like offering treasures we are about to discard to those we do not know. We give flowers blooming on the distant mountains to the Tathagata, and offer treasures accumulated in past lives to living beings. Whether our gifts are of the Dharma or of material objects, each gift is truly endowed with the virtue of offering, or *dana*. Even if this gift is not our personal possession, nothing hinders our practice of offering. No gift is too small, but our effort should be genuine.

When the Way is entrusted to the Way, we attain the Way. When we attain the Way, the Way unfailingly continues to be entrusted to the Way. When material things are treasured, these treasures actually become *dana*.We offer ourselves to ourselves, and we offer others to others. The karma of giving pervades the heavens above and our human world alike. It even reaches the realm of those sages who have attained the fruits of realization. Whether we give or receive, we connect ourselves with all beings throughout the world.

The Buddha said, "When a person who practices *dana* comes into an assembly, other people watch that person with admiration." We should know that the mind of such a person quietly reaches others. Even if we offer just one word or verse of Dharma, it will become a seed of goodness in this lifetime and in other lives to come. Even if we give humble things—a single penny or a stalk of grass—we plant a root of goodness in this and other ages. Dharma can be a material treasure, and a material treasure can be Dharma. This depends entirely upon the giver's vow and wish.

Offering his beard, a Chinese emperor harmonized his minister's mind. Offering sand, a child gained the throne. These people did not covet rewards from others. They simply shared what they had according to their ability. To launch a boat or build a bridge is the practice of *dana* paramita. When we understand the meaning of *dana*, receiving a body and giving up a body are both offering. Earning a livelihood and managing a business are nothing other than giving. Trusting flowers to the wind and trusting birds to the season may also be the meritorious action of *dana*. When we give and when we receive, we should study this principle: Great King Ashoka's offering of half a mango to hundreds of monks was a boundless offering. Not only should we urge ourselves to make offerings, but we must not overlook any opportunity to practice *dana*. Because we are blessed with the virtue of offering, we have received our present lives.

The Buddha said, "One may offer a gift to oneself and use one's own gift; even more, one can pass it to one's parents, wife, and children." Therefore we should know that giving to ourselves is a kind of offering. To give to parents, wife, and children is also an offering. Whenever we can give up even one speck of dust for the practice of *dana*, we should quietly rejoice. This is because we have already correctly transmitted a virtue of the buddhas, and because we practice one dharma of a bodhisattva for the first time.

The mind of a sentient being is difficult to change. We begin to transform the mind of beings by offering material things, and we resolve to continue to transform them until they attain the Way. From the beginning we should make use of offering. This is the reason why dana-paramita is the first of the Six Perfections. Both giving and receiving without attachment to either objects or our own actions is the manifestation of the virtue of dana paramita through which the wheel of dharma is turning. The vastness or narrowness of mind cannot be measured, and the greatness or smallness of material things cannot be weighed. But there are times when our mind turns things, and there is offering, in which things turn our mind.

LOVING-SPEECH

Loving speech means, first of all, to arouse a compassionate mind when meeting beings, and to offer loving, caring words. In general, we should not use any violent or harmful words when we speak. In society, there is the courtesy of asking others if they are well. Within the Buddha-way we have the practice of speaking the words "Please treasure yourself!" There is also a disciple's filial duty to ask her teacher "How are you?" To speak with a mind that "compassionately cares for living beings as if they were our own babies" is loving-speech. We should praise those with virtue and we should pity those without virtue. From the time we begin to delight in loving speech, loving speech is nurtured little by little. When we practice like this, loving speech, which is usually not known or seen, will manifest itself. In our present life we should practice loving speech without fail and we should continue this practice throughout many future lives. Whether subduing a deadly enemy or making peace, loving speech is fundamental. When a person hears loving speech directly, that person's face brightens and his mind becomes joyful. When a person hears of someone else's loving speech, that person inscribes it in his heart and soul. We should know that loving speech arises from a loving mind, and that the seed of a loving mind is a compassionate heart. We should study how loving speech has the power to transform the world. It's not merely praising someone's ability.

Beneficial-action

Beneficial action is simply creating skillful means to benefit living beings, whether they are noble or humble. For example, we care for the near and distant future of others, and use skillful means to benefit them. We should take pity on a cornered tortoise and care for a sick sparrow. When we see this tortoise or sparrow, we try to help them without expecting any reward. We are motivated solely by beneficial action itself.

An ignorant person may think that if we benefit others too much, our own benefit will be excluded. This is not the case. Beneficial action is the whole of dharma; it benefits both self and others widely. In an ancient era, a man, who tied up his hair three times while he took a bath and who stopped eating three times in the space of one meal, solely intended to benefit others. He never withheld truths from people of other countries.

Therefore, we should equally benefit friends and foes alike; we should benefit self and others alike. Because beneficial actions never regress, if we attain such a mind we can perform beneficial action even for grass, trees, wind, and water. We should strive solely to help ignorant beings.

IDENTITY-ACTION

Identity action means to be not different—neither different from self nor from others. For example, it is like the way that, in the human world, the Tathagata identifies himself with human beings. Because he identifies himself in the human world, we know that he must be the same in the other worlds. When we realize identity-action, self and others are one suchness. Harps, poems, and wine make friends with people, with heavenly beings, and with spirits. People befriend harps, poems and wine. There is a principle that harps, poems, and wine befriend harps, poems, and wine; that people make friends with people; that heavenly beings befriend heavenly beings, and that spirits befriend spirits. This is how we study identity action.

For example, "action" means form, dignity, and attitude. After letting others identify with our "self," there may be a principle of letting our "self" identify with others. Relations between self and others vary infinitely depending on time and condition. Guanzi says, "The ocean does not refuse water; therefore it is able to achieve its vastness. Mountains do not refuse earth; therefore they are able to become tall. Wise rulers do not weary of people, therefore they form a large nation."

That the ocean does not refuse water is identity action. We should also know that the virtue of water does not refuse the ocean. This is why water is able to form an ocean, and earth is able to form mountains. We should know in ourselves that because the ocean does not refuse to be the ocean, it can be the ocean and achieve greatness. Because mountains do not refuse to be the mountains, they can be mountains and reach great height. Because wise rulers do not weary of their people, they attract many people. "Many people" means a nation. "A wise ruler" may mean an emperor. Emperors do not weary of their people. This does not mean that they fail to offer rewards and punishment, but they never tire of their people. In ancient times, when people were gentle and honest, there were no rewards and no punishments in the country. The idea of reward and punishment in those days was different. Even these days, there must be some people who seek the Way with no expectation of reward. This is beyond the thought of ignorant people. Because wise rulers have clear minds, they do not weary of their people. Although people always desire to form a nation and to find a wise ruler, few of them fully understand why a wise ruler is wise. Therefore, they are glad simply to be embraced by the wise ruler. They don't realize that they themselves are embracing a wise ruler. Thus the principle of identity action exists both in the wise ruler and ignorant people. This is why identity action is the practice and the vow of a bodhisattva. We should simply face all beings with a gentle expression.

Because each of these Four Embracing Actions includes all the Four Embracing Actions, there are sixteen embracing actions. These Four Embracing Actions all embrace each other; these are not four separate items.

Written on the 5th day of the 5th lunar month in the 4th year of Ninji (1243) By Monk Dōgen who went to Song China and transmitted the Dharma[1]

The Bodhisattva's Four Embracing Actions

SHOHAKU OKUMURA

ABOUT SHISHOBO

The Connection between *Shishobo* and the *Shobogenzo*

SHOBOGENZO SHISHOBO (THE BODHISATTVA'S FOUR EMBRACING ACTIONS) is the 28th fascicle in Dōgen Zenji's 60-fascicle version of the *Shobogenzo*. The process by which the *Shobogenzo* was compiled is clear. Six different editions were hand copied before the Tokugawa period (1603–1867). These are the 75-fascicle version, the 12-fascicle version, the 60-fascicle and 28-fascicle versions, the 84-fascicle version, and the 83-fascicle version. The 75-fascicle version and the 12-fascicle version have no overlapping sections, and the 60-fascicle version and the 28-fascicle version also have none. Present-day Soto Zen scholars think that the first and second versions are one set and the third and fourth versions are another.

There are various opinions, one of which is that Dōgen Zenji himself compiled the 75-fascicle version (though some scholars think that either Ejo or Senne compiled this version rather than Dōgen Zenji, and that in his final years, Dōgen Zenji had planned to write more fascicles in order to make a 100-fascicle *Shobogenzo*). At that time, he wrote twelve more fascicles, but passed away before completion of the project. According to this opinion, the 75-fascicle version that was written before 1246 and the 12-fascicle version that was written or revised later were left as separate works. The 12-fascicle version was stored at Yokoji in Ishikawa Prefecture and was not discovered until 1930.

Traditionally, it is said that when Giun Zenji (1253–1333) became the 5th abbot of Eiheiji, following the death of the 4th abbot Gien (? –1314), no versions of the *Shobogenzo* existed at Eiheiji because of damage caused by fire. Giun tried to collect as many fascicles as possible, and this was the origin of the 60-fascicle version. Twenty-eight fascicles were stored at Eiheiji, and later, this version was called the *Himitsu (Secret) Shobogenzo*. It is said that Giun sorted the fascicles and left out the ones in which Dōgen Zenji harshly criticized certain Zen masters or schools. People who had the 75-fascicle version tried to collect the fascicles that were not included in that version, while people who had the 60-fascicle version tried to collect those fascicles that they did not have. In this way, the 84-fascicle-version and 83-fascicle version were made.

In the Tokugawa Period, Manzan Dohaku (1636–1715) searched through as many manuscripts as possible and compiled the 89-fascicle version in 1684. Kozen (1627–1693), the 35th abbot of Eiheiji, made a more thorough search and compiled a 95-fascicle version in 1690, putting the fascicles in chronological order. Kozen tried to publish this version of the *Shobogenzo*, but he passed away before completing the project. In 1722, the Sotoshu authority, supported by the government of the Tokugawa shogunate, prohibited the publication of the *Shobogenzo*. Gento Sokuchu (1729–1807) began the project of publishing the entire collection of the *Shobogenzo* when he became the 50th abbot of Eiheiji in 1795. Daigu Shunryo (? –1803) and Sodo Ontatsu (? –1813) assisted him and spent much time on the project. The 95-fascicle version of the *Shobogenzo* was published by wood-block printing in 1816, almost 100 years after Kozen first tried to do so. The compilers attempted to collect as many fascicles as possible in order to make it closer to the set of 100 fascicles that Dōgen Zenji had originally planned. Because of this, the collection of 95 fascicles included writings that were not originally included in the *Shobogenzo,* such as *Bendowa, Ji-kuin-mon, Ju-undo-shiki,* and so forth.

Up until the 1970s, when I was a student at Komazawa University, the 95-fascicle version was considered to be the most reliable collection because it had been edited by Dr. Sokuo Eto of Iwanamibunko, one of the most influential publishers for academics and intellectuals in modern Japan. In recent decades however, Dōgen scholars are now considering the 75-fascicle version and the 12-fascicle version as the basis of the *Shobogenzo* and have added some fascicles from other collections such as 60-fascicle version. *Shobogenzo Bodaisatta Shishobo* was not included in the 75-fascicle version or the 12-fascicle version. It was the 28th fascicle of the 60-fascicle version, and the 45th fascicle of the 95-fascicle version.

Shishobo was written in 1243

This fascicle was written on the 5th day of the 5th month in 1243 during the summer practice period at Koshoji, founded ten years earlier in 1233 in Fukakusa near Kyoto. (Today Fukakusa is a part of Kyoto City.) A few days after that practice period was completed on 15th day of the 7th month, Dōgen Zenji and his monks left Koshoji and went to the remote district of Echizen to establish another temple. Some scholars think that Tendai monks from Hieizan Enryakuji attacked Dōgen Zenji's sangha and burned down Koshoji. Other scholars conjecture that Dōgen Zenji moved to the deep mountains following his own teacher Tendo Nyojo Zenji's advice, accepting invitations from his patron Hatano Yoshishige, who had a property to offer in Echizen, and one of Dōgen's disciples Ekan, who had a temple named Hajakuji in Echizen. Still other scholars think he left Kyoto to avoid competition with the Rinzai master Enni Ben'nen, who had returned from China in 1242 and was supported by Kujo Michiie, a high-ranking aristocrat who built Tofukuji. This temple was located several miles away from Koshoji toward the city of Kyoto, and Kujo invited En'ni to be the abbot there.

The reason is not clear to us, but Dōgen and his disciples left Koshoji very suddenly. When they moved to Echizen, they did not have a temple of their own in which to practice and they stayed at a small old temple named Yoshimine-dera. Tettsu Gikai, who later became the third abbot of Eiheiji, was the tenzo at the time. Since there was no kitchen at the temple, Gikai prepared meals at a house at the foot of the steep hill on which Yoshimine-dera was located. He then had to carry the food up the long steep hill in the deep snow during their first winter in Echizen. If their move had been well planned, they would have stayed at Koshoji until the new temple was ready. It seems likely to me they had an urgent reason to leave Koshoji, so quickly that they had no time to make prior preparations in Echizen.

While Dōgen Zenji stayed at Yoshimine-dera and Yamashibu, another small temple in the same area, through the fall of 1243 and until the fall of 1244, he wrote 33 fascicles of the *Shobogenzo*. The construction of the new temple Daibutsuji, which Dōgen renamed Eiheiji in 1246, was started in the spring of 1244 and completed in the fall of the same year.

I think it is important to remember that this fascicle *Shishobo* was written two months before their move from Kyoto to Echizen. I suppose that Dōgen Zenji and his sangha were in a precarious situation, probably one of conflict with the Tendai establishment.

About the title: *Shobogenzo Bodaisatta Shishobo*

Shobogenzo (True Dharma Eye Treasury) is an abbreviation of the expression *Shobogenzo nehan myoshin, jisso, muso, mimyo no homon* (正法眼蔵涅槃妙心実相無相微妙の法門), as it is expressed in Japanese. This is one long word. In the traditional Zen story of the transmission of the Dharma from Shakyamuni Buddha to Mahakashapa, when Shakyamuni held up a flower, Mahakashapa was the only person in the assembly who smiled. The Buddha then said, "I have *Shobogenzo nehan myoshin, jisso, muso, mimyo no homon;* I transmit or entrust it to Mahakashapa." This *Shobogenzo* is the name of the Dharma that was transmitted from Shakyamuni to Mahakashapa, from Mahakashapa to Ananda, and from ancestor to ancestor through many generations up until the present day.

A rough translation of this expression is: True Dharma Eye Treasury (正法眼蔵), Wondrous Mind of Nirvana (涅槃妙心), True Form of Formlessness (実相無相), Subtle and Wondrous Dharma Gate (微妙法門). This is an expression of the reality of our life that is the treasury of the true Dharma eye (wisdom), the wondrous mind (life) of Nirvana, in which the true form of all beings is without form, and this reality is very subtle and inconceivable.

Dōgen Zenji gave the collection of his writings in Japanese this title. When we read *Shobogenzo*, we must understand that the topic of each and every fascicle is this reality of our life. In the *Shishobo*, the four actions (offering, loving words, beneficial action and identity action) are our actual practices in our daily lives. We need to see these practices as *Shobogenzo*, that is, the Dharma transmitted through buddhas and ancestors. These actions should be done with awakening to the true reality of emptiness and interdependent origination. In Dōgen Zenji's teachings, zazen practice itself is awakening and wisdom, and these four actions are how zazen functions in our daily lives and in relation to other people and living beings.

A bodhisattva

The word *bodhisattva* (Jp. *bodaisatta,* Pali *bodhisatta*) originally referred to Shakyamuni Buddha when he was practicing before he attained Buddhahood. Later Buddhists thought that Shakyamuni Buddha had been practicing in countless lives and in various forms in order to attain Buddhahood. In the stories of the Buddha's practice in his past lives, he was called a bodhisattva, a person who is seeking the attainment of awakening. A Buddha is one who has attained awakening.

Mahayana Buddhists thought that there are numberless buddhas in the past, present, and future, and that there are myriad Buddha-lands throughout the ten directions. This is what we chant in the dedication following each sutra that is chanted during various kinds of service in Soto Zen tradition: "*Jiho-sanshi-ishifu* (all buddhas throughout the ten directions and three times), *shison-busa-mokosa* (all bodhisattvas mahasattvas)." There are countless bodhisattvas who are practicing to attain Buddhahood in the past, present, and future in every buddha-land. In this usage, a bodhisattva is a buddha-to-be.

In Mahayana sutras there are some great bodhisattvas who could become buddhas by virtue of their practice, but they intentionally vow not to do so in order to save living beings within samsara. They are also the symbol of a certain virtue of the Buddha. They include the following three:

Manjshuri (*Monju-bosatsu* in Japanese) is considered to be the symbol of Buddha's wisdom. He sits on a lion, holding a sword to cut off all delusions. Manjshuri is enshrined at the center of the monks' hall in Zen temples.

Avalokiteshvara (*Kanzeon-bosatsu* or *Kan-jizai-bosatsu* in Japanese) is the symbol of Buddha's compassion and can transform into 33 different forms, appearing to living beings in the most suitable form to save each of them. This transformation depends upon the needs of each sentient being according to the teaching about identity action in *Shishobo.*

Ksitigarba (*Jizo-bosatsu*) took a vow to save all beings transmigrating within the six realms of samsara between the time of Shakyamuni Buddha and Maitreya Buddha, who will appear in this world 5.7 billion years later. In Japan, a set of six statues of Jizo are enshrined at the entrance of many cemeteries in order to save people who are going to be reborn in each of the six realms.

These three great bodhisattvas are actually transformations of the Buddha. They are not buddhas-to-be. However, ordinary people like us who arouse *bodhicitta* (Way-seeking mind) receive the bodhisattva precepts, take the four bodhisattva vows, and practice according to the Buddha's teachings are also called bodhisattvas. In the title of *Shishobo,* "bodhisattva" refers to all

Mahayana practitioners, including ordinary human beings like us. In this fascicle, Dōgen Zenji teaches us that these four actions are the essence of the practice for all bodhisattvas, including all of the above usages of the word.

Shishobo

Shishobo (Four embracing actions, Skt., *Catursangraha-vastu,* Pali, *sangaha vatthu*) appears not only in Mahayana sutras such as the Lotus Sutra and so forth, but also in the Pali scriptures and in commentaries. I first translated this title as "Four Embracing Dharmas" because the word *bo* (another pronunciation of *ho,* 法) is often used as a translation of the Sanskrit word *Dharma* (Pali, *Dhamma*). In English, we often use the Sanskrit word Dharma instead of using an English equivalent because there isn't any one English word that conveys its many meanings and connotations. However, when I checked the original expression in Sanskrit, the word is not *dharma* but *vastu,* so now I feel that "embracing dharma" is not the right translation. Here I've temporarily translated it as "actions," although *vastu* means "affair," "matter," or "thing." Sometimes this word was translated into Chinese as ji (事), the second part of doji (同事), and so I translated it as identity-action.

Rev. Hozan Alan Senauke provided me with translations of this expression used by other translators, such as, "Foundations for Social Unity," "Ways of Showing Favor," "Four Methods of Guidance," and "Four Integrative Methods." "Method" is another meaning of the Chinese word ho (法).

According to Menzan's *Shobogenzo Shotenroku (Collection of the Sources of Expressions Dōgen Zenji used in Shobogenzo),* *shishobo* is defined in the 17th volume of the *Sanzo Hossu (Dharma Numbers in the Three Baskets)* in this way:

Each of the four items of *shishobo* (四摂法) have the adjective *sho* (摂 "embracing, unifying, integrative"). In this case, *sho* (摂) has the meaning of *shoju* (摂受), which is "to embrace and accept." When a bodhisattva wishes to guide living beings and transform them, then without fail he or she should embrace and accept living beings and allow them to trust him or her. Then he or she guides them to the true Mahayana Way. In the Vimalakirti Sutra, it is said that first we attract living beings with what they desire and then enable them to enter the Buddha's wisdom.

The first item is *dana* embracement (布施摂, Skt. *Dana-sangraha-vastu*). A bodhisattva embraces and accepts all living beings with the two kinds of offering: material offerings and Dharma offerings. If some living beings wish for something material, a bodhisattva embraces those living beings by offering material things. When living beings seek the Dharma, a bodhisattva embraces those living beings by offering Dharma. When living beings receive the benefits of those two kinds of offerings, they arouse the mind of intimacy and love the bodhisattva. They trust the bodhisattva and accept the Way and will be able to abide in the truth. Therefore this is called offering-embracement.

The second is loving speech embracement (愛語摂, Skt. *priyavadyta-sangraha-vastu*). According to the nature of living beings, a bodhisattva comforts them with kind words. When living beings hear these affectionate words, they arouse the mind of intimacy. Then they trust the bodhisattva, accept the Way, and abide in the truth. Therefore it is called loving-words-embracement.

The third is beneficial-action-embracement (利行摂, Skt. *arthacarya-sangraha-vastu*). A bodhisattva does good activities with body, thought, and speech to benefit all living beings. Because of this the living beings arouse the intimate mind of love and trust, relying on bodhisattvas. They accept the Way and abide in the truth. It is therefore called beneficial-action-embracement.

The fourth is identity-action-embracement (同事摂, Skt. *samanarthata-sangraha-vastu*). A bodhisattva clearly sees the nature of each living being with the eye of the Dharma and then the bodhisattva manifests itself in the form depending upon what they wish. The bodhisattva shares these identity actions for their sake and because of these actions, they trust and rely on the bodhisattva, love the Way, and abide in the truth. It is therefore called identity-action-embracement."

According to this definition, these four actions are the ways a bodhisattva helps living beings to enter the Way of Buddha and abide in the truth. In this sense, the translation used by Kaz Tanahashi in *Moon in a Dewdrop,* "Methods of Guidance," is a good translation. However, when Dōgen Zenji expounds these four practices as "*Shobogenzo,*" I think he does not merely mean that these are methods guiding people to enter the Buddhist path. Dōgen teaches that these four practices allow the bodhisattvas themselves to be free from the three poisonous states of mind: greed, anger/hatred, and ignorance. These practices benefit both the person practicing and living beings at the same time. So, I don't think the translation of "guiding method" is the best one in the case of Dōgen Zenji's *Shishobo.*

Giun's capping phrase and praising verse

Giun Zenji (1253–1333), the fifth abbot of Eiheiji, wrote a capping phrase and a praising verse for each fascicle of the 60-fascicle version of *Shobogenzo*. I would like to introduce the phrase and verse he wrote for *Shishobo*.

> Giun's capping verse:
> Adding flowers on the golden brocade.

This phrase appears in a poem by the famous politician and poet of the Song dynasty China O Anseki (Wang Anshi, 1021–1086). Weaving is one of the oldest art and craft forms in human culture. All peoples in any part of the world, whether primitive or developed countries, hot or cold places, dry or wet climates, have a weaving technique for making cloth. Production of clothing allowed human beings to live in severe climates, areas where it was not possible for humans to live without clothing.

The way the warp and the woof are woven using vertical and horizontal threads has been used as a good metaphor for interdependent origination. Depending upon how the warp and the woof are woven, different patterns are created. This is like the network of life on earth. Depending upon causes and conditions, time and space, many different kinds of scenery appear. We create numberless stories on the stage of time and space and also beyond the limit of time and space that is eternity. In Japan, the warp is often compared to time and the woof is compared to space. Each and every thing that happens day to day is like the woven pattern of a tapestry.

The network of interdependent origination is the golden brocade on which many different patterns are designed and created moment by moment. In China and other East Asian countries, golden brocade is the most exquisite fabric using silk with gold or other bright colors and often has beautiful patterns. Here in this verse, golden brocade does not refer to something more valuable than other things, but it is rather something priceless and beyond any comparison or evaluation. It is something that human beings cannot create. Human activities are also part of the patterns on the golden brocade.

This capping phrase means adding beauty to the golden brocade that is already beautiful. In Zen literature, this phrase has been understood in two opposite ways. One is as a meaningless and unnecessary action. If something is already beautiful, to add more beauty is unnecessary. It is like trying to search for your own face even though you already have one. The other meaning is to keep making effort to continually refine the beauty. When Giun used this expression as the capping phrase for this fascicle of the *Shobogenzo,* he meant that to practice *shishobo* is to make the already perfect network of interdependent origination into something even more perfect. This is another expression of "practice upon enlightenment" (*shojo no shu*); bodhisattvas are born, live, and die within the network of interdependent origination. The practice of awakening to that reality of interdependence and expressing that reality is the practice of *shishobo.*

When this phrase is used in the first sense, it is used in a way that is a little paradoxical or cynical. It means that bodhisattva practice is not something special, so we should not be proud of it. We just express our reality of life in order to express the reality of life.

Wanshi and Dōgen

In *Eihei Koroku* (*The Extensive Record of Eihei Dōgen*),[1] Dōgen Zenji quotes Wanshi (Ch. Hongzhi) Zenji's Dharma Hall

Discourse on the day of the winter solstice. Wanshi said, "In a bowl, the bright pearl rolls on its own without prodding," and "For a luminous jewel without flaw, if you carve a pattern on it, its virtue is lost." He meant that if we add something artificial to the natural beauty of the bright pearl, we damage it.

Dōgen Zenji comments on Wanshi's saying, "I, old man Daibutsu (Dōgen), do not agree. Great assembly, listen carefully and consider this well. For a luminous jewel without flaw, if polished its glow increases."[2] In our practice of following the Buddha's teachings, the already beautiful jewel becomes more and more beautiful. Some Soto scholars put emphasis on the difference between Wanshi and Dōgen, or silent illumination Zen in China and Dōgen Zen, on this point.

Wanshi Zenji's statement implies that Buddha-nature is perfect as it is; we shouldn't interfere with it by adding artificial human activities. Dōgen Zenji's comment implies that even though Buddha-nature is perfect as it is, our practice can clarify and extend its manifestation. In both cases, practice and enlightenment are one, but for Wanshi the emphasis is on enlightenment that is perfect from the beginningless beginning, and practice is its natural function, like the pearl rolling on its own. For Dōgen, the emphasis is on practice, which expresses and actually deepens enlightenment. This has the same meaning as the capping phrase that Giun chose for *Shishobo*.

Giun's praising verse:
The great gate of offering is open and enriches the nine heavens.
Going beyond love and hatred expressed in speech is the wheel of the Dharma.

Beneficial actions for beings and the wind of identity actions reach far beyond a thousand miles.

On the rootless tree, the spring of four seasons has come.

The first three lines are Giun's summary of the *Shishobo*. The bodhisattva practice of offering will enrich all living beings including the bodhisattva himself. When bodhisattvas go beyond love and hatred, their speech can turn the Dharma wheel. This is Giun's definition of "loving words." In this case, love is not in dualistic opposition to hatred. Usually, our love is directed toward certain people as objects, and that love can then become hatred toward another group of people depending on causes and conditions. To speak true loving words, we need to go beyond love and hatred. This is Buddha's compassion. One word of the Buddha's compassion is the Dharma wheel.

Beneficial action benefits all beings and the wind of identity-action reaches beyond the 1000 miles that is the human realm of duality.

Timeless spring on the rootless tree

This final line of Giun's verse shows that this practice of *shishobo* is the practice of emptiness that brings about eternal or timeless spring. The literal translation of Giun's expression is "the spring of four seasons." This means that all four seasons become the timeless, unconditioned spring of Nirvana. The rootless tree is a symbol of emptiness used in Buddhist literature, the same as a bamboo or a banana tree. These four practices of the bodhisattva bring Nirvana to the human world, where we are always creating pain and suffering. We human beings often stain, pollute or even destroy the beauty of the golden brocade by our actions based on the three poisonous states of mind. In this sense, the four embracing actions are practices enabling us to awaken to the preciousness of the network of interdependent origination and to heal ourselves and others from the damages caused by our deluded actions.

At the end of *Shobogenzo Genjo-koan,* Dōgen Zenji said, "To say we should not use a fan because the nature of wind is ever present, and that we should feel the wind even when we don't use a fan, is to know neither ever-presence nor the wind's nature. Since wind's nature is ever present, the wind of the Buddha's family enables us to realize the gold of the great earth and to transform the [water of] the long river into cream."

Our practice of zazen and daily activities actualizes the everlasting nature of wind and causes the actual wind that makes our life and world into cream and gold. What Giun says here has the same meaning. Our practice adds beauty to an already beautiful golden brocade.

Giun's capping phrase and praising verse provide us a good preparatory understanding for our study of Dōgen Zenji's *Shobogenzo Shishobo.*

Offering
Offering means not being greedy

> Offering means not being greedy. Not to be greedy means not to covet. Not to covet commonly means not to flatter. Even if we rule the four continents, in order to offer teachings of the true Way, we must simply and unfailingly not be greedy. It is like offering treasures we are about to discard to those we do not know. We give flowers blooming on the distant

mountains to the Tathagata, and offer treasures accumulated in past lives to living beings. Whether our gifts are of the Dharma or of material objects, each gift is truly endowed with the virtue of offering or *dana*. Even if this gift is not our personal possession, nothing hinders our practice of offering. No gift is too small, but our effort should be genuine.

Dōgen Zenji's definition of offering (*dana*) as "not to be greedy" is a wonderful explanation. The basic teaching of the Buddha is that our life is suffering and we transmigrate within the six realms of samsara because we live and act based on three poisonous states of mind: greed, anger/hatred and ignorance. All Buddhist practices are about ending the suffering of samsara by being released from these three poisonous minds. This basic structure is also true in the case of the four embracing actions. Offering is a way to be released from greed. Practicing loving speech is a way not to be caught up in anger and hatred. Beneficial action is a treatment for both greed and anger. Engaging in identity action is a way to be free from the ignorance of self-centeredness through the wisdom of seeing the heart of being that is empty of self and interconnected with all beings.

As we've seen, commonly the four embracing actions are considered to be methods of guidance used by bodhisattvas to lead people to become Buddhists. However, in Dōgen Zenji's teaching, as explained in the section on beneficial action, the practice of *shishobo* is not only the way to lead others, but also the way for the person practicing it to be free from the three poisonous states of mind. "Ignorant people may think that if we benefit others too much, our own benefit will be excluded. This is not the case.

Beneficial-action is the whole of Dharma; it benefits both self and others widely."

> Not to be greedy means not to covet. Not to covet commonly means not to flatter.

"To be greedy" and "to covet" have almost the same meaning. To English speaking people, this sentence may sound like a repetition of the same word. In the original text, Dōgen Zenji uses the Chinese word *fu-ton* (不貪) and he put the Japanese equivalent using hiragana (one of the two Japanese phonetic alphabets made by simplifying Chinese characters), *musaborazarunari* (むさぼらざるなり). Structurally, this is the same as the English sentence "*Dana* is offering." Because *dana* means offering in Sanskrit, to say "*Dana* is offering" seems repetitive. When we study *Shobogenzo,* however, it is important to understand that Dōgen Zenji was writing in two different languages and sometimes playing with the Chinese words and expressions in a way only a non-native speaker can. Unfortunately, when we translate his writings into English, we cannot show his subtle use of both Chinese and Japanese. Sometimes his sentences don't make any sense, and sometimes they look like childish repetition.

According to Dōgen, "to flatter" is another expression of our greed. Typically, when we have enough power to get the things we want by ourselves, we covet them and just take them. When we don't have enough power to get things we want, we flatter someone who has the power to give them. By flattering the superior person, we try to satisfy our personal desires.

I think it's interesting that Dōgen Zenji uses the negative expression in order to define *dana* instead of using a positive one like "*Dana* is generosity. To be generous means such and such." By doing this, I think he's urging us to reflect on our deeper motivation when being generous to others. Even when we are giving something to someone who is in need and the action looks really generous on the surface, if we take a close look at our minds we almost always see that greed is still working there. We may expect some return from the receiver or we covet the receiver's gratitude. We may want to think we are generous or expect others to think that we are great people. Of course on the level of social morality, it's good to do good things. However, Buddhism is not merely a teaching of social morality. If the deeper motivation is greed, no matter how much we give, it cannot be *dana paramita,* the perfection of offering. To practice *dana* is to be free from greed.

Traditional practice of *dana* in *takuhatsu* (begging)

In India, since the time of Shakyamuni Buddha, Buddhist monks were required to relinquish the bonds with their families, give up their livelihood and property and live with three robes and one bowl. Monks begged in nearby villages for food, eating only once a day before noon. Their begging was a practice of being free from desire for possessions and essentially from ego attachment. This tradition still continues in the Theravada Buddhism in South Eastern Asia.

As I mentioned earlier, there are two sorts of offering in Buddhism: the offering of materials and the offering of Dharma. Lay people offer materials such as food, clothing, medicine and other requirements to temples or monks and offer things as charity to the needy people in society. Monks offer Dharma, the spiritual teachings they study and practice. Monks and laity support each other through the practice of these two kinds of offering.

Takuhatsu at Antaiji

In modern Japan, almost all Buddhist temples are supported by temple members. Clergy don't commonly practice *takuhatsu* except while they're in training or on certain special occasions. Usually, people these days offer money instead of food, except when *takuhatsu* is done specifically for rice or some vegetables.

During the time I was practicing at Antaiji, because the temple had no members, our practice was supported solely by our *takuhatsu.* We monks did it a few times a month. We walked on the market streets in Kyoto, Osaka, Kobe and other smaller cities and towns in the area. When we did *takuhatsu,* three to five of us walked together. Since most of us were in our early 20s, it was fun, like taking a hike.

It was also very meaningful practice. At Antaiji, we focused on zazen practice and Dharma study, mainly of Dōgen Zenji's teachings. When we practice in this way, we tend to feel like we're living a much more meaningful and higher way of life than the people who are working hard in society to earn money day after day. We may even look down on people by seeing them from our lofty position. When we practice *takuhatsu,* we are just beggars on the street. We have a chance to see society from the bottom.

When doing *takuhatsu,* we walk on the street wearing the traditional monks' black robe, straw sandals and a bamboo hat. We hold a begging bowl and intone "*Ho-o-o*" in a loud voice (*ho* refers to the bowl). We usually stop in front of each house or shop on the street for a short while until the shop owner or other people give a donation or express their rejection with words or a gesture. If no one is there or people do not react, we continue on to the next shop.

When people make a donation, we recite the praising verse of *dana*: *Zaiho nise kudoku muryo danbaramitsu gusoku enman naishi hokkai byodo riyaku* (The virtue of two kinds of offering; the offering of materials and offering of Dharma, is boundless. The perfection of generosity [*dana paramita*] is completed and it benefits all living beings in the entire dharma world). When we are rejected or ignored, we simply and sincerely make a bow and walk to the next door. Some people make a bow with gassho like they do to the Buddha when they put their donation into our begging bowl. Some people look down on us and put money in our bowls like they would with a beggar. Some people shout, "Go away!" Some people decline to make an offering by saying, "I'm sorry, but..." Some people just ignore us. Some people make fun of us. We encounter many different reactions from many different people: rich, mediocre or poor, tough, gentle or pious, etc. We just see people's reactions and keep the same respectful attitude toward everyone. We walk in this way about five to six hours a day.

When we first go on *takuhatsu,* we are taught several important principles of that practice. The most important point is to keep the same respectful attitude toward all people. We should not skip any single house or shop on the street. Whether rich or poor, kind or not kind, we should not have any preferences toward people. We should not change our attitude depending upon the amount of donation or their way of treating us. We should be mindful not to disturb people working at a shop, people shopping or people walking on the street. *Takuhatsu* is a practice of equanimity, freeing us from self-centeredness and our discriminating minds. Through *takuhatsu,* our practice is connected with everyone in society.

Takuhatsu as a koan

In my early 30s, while I was living on *takuhatsu,* I had a question regarding this definition of *dana* by Dōgen Zenji. From 1981 to 1984,

I lived in a small nunnery in Kyoto as a caretaker. A friend of mine looked after the temple and because he had another temple, he generously allowed me to live there and practice. I also worked on translation of Dōgen Zenji's and my teacher's books from Japanese to English with my American Dharma brother Daitsu Tom Wright. I had daily zazen and monthly five-day sesshin. Because I became a monk while I was a university student studying Buddhism and Zen and entered a temple directly from school, I had no skills to make an income at all. All I knew was zazen practice and something about Zen Buddhism. However, to be mature as a zazen practitioner takes a really long time, and in my 20s and 30s I felt I had nothing to offer anyone. A few times a month, I practiced *takuhatsu* in the market streets in Kyoto, Osaka, Kobe and other places just as I did while I was at Antaiji. In that manner, I received approximately 30,000 Yen ($300), just enough income to keep my practice and translation work going.

Although I had practiced at Antaiji doing *takuhatsu* together with other monks and enjoying it as a hike, doing *takuhatsu* alone was completely different. I was often intimidated and felt as if I was just a meaningless beggar.

Once I did *takuhatsu* alone in a market place in Osaka. Osaka and Kyoto are quite different cities. In Kyoto, since there are many temples, people know about *takuhatsu* and respect Buddhist monks. Osaka, however, has been a city of merchants from the Tokugawa era, so there is much less sympathy for monks. Actually, my family had been merchants in Osaka for the last six generations, about 300 years, and I knew the people's attitudes towards monks there.

Once when I was begging, a boy about ten years old asked me, "You want money, don't you?" I thought what he was really asking was whether I did *takuhatsu* for the sake of Dharma or for the sake of money to live on. I couldn't give him an answer. It was a big and difficult koan for me. If I didn't need money, I wouldn't do *takuhatsu,* so I couldn't say I didn't want money. But if money was really what I wanted, there are much better ways than *takuhatsu* to get it. *Takuhatsu* is not an easy way to make money. It was hot walking along in summer wearing four layers of clothing—underwear, juban, kimono, and koromo. In the winter, walking with bare feet and hands was really hard practice. However, mentally it was even more difficult. I often felt I was a meaningless, valueless person in society and sometimes I really didn't want to go. There were days when I felt so guilty living on alms that I quit begging and returned to the temple. I knew it would be much easier to do some work to make money. At this time, I thought of many good reasons to quit not only doing *takuhatsu,* but being a monk altogether. *Takuhatsu* practice makes it very clear whether we do things for the sake of Dharma or for the sake of ourselves.

My question regarding Dōgen's definition of offering

Eventually my koan regarding Dōgen Zenji's definition of *dana* became clear to me: by trying not to be greedy, I felt like I had nothing to offer. As Sawaki Roshi taught, zazen is good for nothing. Although I was working on translation, Japanese people were naturally not interested in English translations of Zen texts. I really felt I just received money from people without offering them anything. As I have said before, to be mature as a zazen practitioner takes really a long time. As long as we are half baked, zazen practitioners are really good for nothing. Until we are quite ripe, we are simply not edible, like an astringent persimmon.

Because I wanted to live without greed, I did zazen and *takuhatsu;* because of that, I felt I had nothing to offer. I simply received donations from people. I often felt guilty, and my sense of unworthiness made me feel small and ashamed. I thought that my condition was totally contrary to Dōgen Zenji's definition of offering.

Ryokan the beggar

In my 20s, I wanted to live like Dōgen Zenji and I devoted myself completely to zazen practice. In my early 30s, I thought I could not live like Dōgen anymore, and further, I found that I didn't want to do so. During that period, Ryokan (1758–1831) became my hero instead of Dōgen. Ryokan was trained at a Soto Zen temple and received Dharma transmission from his teacher, but after his teacher's death he never lived in a temple. He traveled all over Japan for many years, went back to live in his hometown, built a hermitage on a mountain and simply practiced *takuhatsu*. He never acted like a Zen master. He wrote poems both in Japanese and in Chinese, made calligraphy, and played with children while on his begging rounds.

Ryokan also wrote many poems about his *takuhatsu*. When children found Ryokan doing *takuhatsu* in their village, they gathered together around him and urged him to play with them. Ryokan often did so and forgot about begging. Ryokan's famous *waka* poems on *takuhatsu* show his attitude.

Playing ball
With the children in this village
Spring day, never let the shadow fall!

I was on my way to beg
But passing by a spring field
Spent the whole day
Picking violets.

In my begging bowl
Violets and dandelions are mixed together
Let's make an offering
To all the buddhas in the three times.[3]

On a spring day, while he was doing *takuhatsu,* children asked him to play with them. Ryokan played with the children tossing a ball or picking the wild spring flowers in the field. Sometimes he forgot about *takuhatsu* completely, as in these two poems.

Oh! My poor begging bowl!
I left it behind
Picking violets by the roadside.

I left my begging bowl behind
And yet no one took it.
No one took it! My poor begging bowl!

My *takuhatsu* was not like Ryokan's. I never played with children. During the day while I did *takuhatsu,* children were in school except on Sundays. At Ryokan's time there were no schools or daycare for the children in a farming village. Playing with children was Ryokan's offering.

Also, to me, *takuhatsu* was the way to support my zazen practice and translation work. I needed to do *takuhatsu* efficiently; otherwise, I lost my time to sit and work on translation. I tried to do *takuhatsu* only a few times a month, just enough to support my practice. But for Ryokan, *takuhatsu* was not a method to support his practice—*takuhatsu* itself was his practice.

In the poem above which begins with, "In my begging bowl / Violets and dandelions…," the begging bowl used to receive offerings from people became a container to make offerings of flowers from the spring fields to all buddhas in the past, present and future. This is because Ryokan has no desire to get anything for himself. He was completely free from any greed to gain anything for his own sake. His *takuhatsu,* playing with children and talking with the villagers were all his offering, and even after his death his way of life itself was an offering to people in later generations. Many people have been inspired and encouraged by his way of life.

Although this poem is without a title, I'm pretty sure Ryokan wrote it about his *takuhatsu.*

> With no mind, the flower invites the butterfly.
> With no mind, the butterfly visits the flower.
> When the flower opens, the butterfly visits.
> When the butterfly visits, the flower opens.
> I am the same
> I do not know the people
> And the people do not know me.
> Without knowing
> we follow the heavenly emperor's law

I understood through Ryokan that receiving an offering can itself be an offering only when it is done without selfish concern. Once while I was begging in Kobe, a middle-aged man riding a bicycle stopped in front of me and offered a 1,000 yen (about $10) bill, an exceptionally large donation to receive for *takuhatsu,* saying, "My wife died a few days ago. This offering is for her."

During *takuhatsu,* we don't speak much with people, but in this encounter I felt a deep and powerful communication. I felt the virtue of *takuhatsu* was not only for me but also for the people making the offering. To receive offerings, I had to keep my attitude toward life free from my selfishness. I had to live and practice for the sake of Dharma, not for myself personally. To keep this attitude is extremely difficult. Doing *takuhatsu* is a hard yet wonderful opportunity to examine one's way of life and life in society. It's a terribly difficult koan.

In studying Dōgen Zenji's teaching that offering is not being greedy, I found a deeper meaning of offering. We exist only within the network of offering. We receive offerings from air, water, plants, animals, mountains and rivers and people. Our practice of offering is just to keep this cycle of offering circulating instead of only receiving and using things to satisfy our personal desires. The spring flower offers nectar to the butterfly. The butterfly carries pollen for the flower. Each is helping and supporting without calculating how much it gets as a reward. To keep the network of interdependent origination pure is the true meaning of practicing *dana paramita.* We really don't need to gain things in order to offer them to others. Living without greed is itself an offering. The best example of this was Shakyamuni Buddha's life. He gave up his position as a prince and all family wealth and became a beggar. That was the greatest offering, not because someone else could have his position and wealth, but because people who came after him could see from his example that we can live without greed. This is what Dōgen says later, in the second paragraph of *Shobogenzo Shishobo:* "When the Way is entrusted to the Way, we attain the Way. When we attain the Way, the Way unfailingly continues to be entrusted to the Way. When material things are treasured, these treasures actually become *dana.*"

Dana is an offering made and received without greed. When we are truly free from the three poisonous minds of greed, anger/hatred, and ignorance, our activities of either giving or receiving are *dana.* If we act based on the three poisonous minds, even charity, an act of justice, or act of love can create twisted karma. Offering benefits both giver and receiver, and the gift is also free from the three poisonous minds. Thus, our activities simply become one with the circulation of the myriad dharmas that are always coming and going within the Dharma world. We simply refrain from blocking such a circulation by ceasing to create a wall between ourselves and all others.

> Even if we rule the four continents, in order to offer teachings of the true Way, we must simply and unfailingly not be greedy.

The ideal king in Buddhism, Chakravarti-raja (the Wheel Turning King with the golden wheel), governs the four continents located in the four directions around Mt. Sumeru. Everything in the world belongs to the king and if he wishes to give, he can give anything he wants. However, Dōgen said that not being greedy is the best and greatest offering to give as a teaching of the Way of true Dharma, the Buddha Way or the Bodhisattva Way. Here the word "Way" also has a connotation of awakening or enlightenment inherited from the Chinese Buddhist use of *dao* as a translation of the Sanskrit word *bodhi.* So, to give a gift to someone we love or to someone in need is, of course, a good thing. Yet such a gift does not necessarily help us to wake up to the reality of emptiness and impermanence but may rather strengthen our ego clinging and make us arrogant. In such a case the gift is not an offering of the true Way.

It is like offering treasures we are about to discard to
those we do not know.

Here Dōgen Zenji shows us a concrete example of the kind of attitude we should maintain if we wish to practice *dana* as a *paramita*.
Here's an example of this practice from my own life. When my
family and I moved to Minneapolis from Japan, my daughter was
five years old and my son was one-and-a-half years old. Since we
couldn't bring a lot of things from Japan, members of the sangha
gave us many things as gifts. One of the sangha members gave us
a rocking horse for our children. The rocking horse stayed in our
home for ten years and our children became too big to ride it. During
those ten years the horse experienced many difficulties as a result of
the children's playing and two family moves. Some parts of it were
broken, and when we moved from Minneapolis to Bloomington, we
felt that it was not worth giving to someone else. We decided to put
the rocking horse on the sidewalk in front of our apartment, and
within 10 minutes someone had taken it. We didn't need the horse
and we didn't think it was even worth giving away. We just put it on
the sidewalk by a street in order to discard it. We had no attachment
to it and we didn't expect anything in return from the unknown
person who took it. The person who took it didn't know who put the
horse on the street, and there was no need for the person to pay us
or even say "thank you." Still, the rocking horse moved from one
family to another and served other children.

It's not so difficult to offer with such an attitude of nonattach-
ment and non-expectation in the case of a broken rocking horse or
something we don't really need. However, Dōgen Zenji urges us not
to offer only unimportant things with such an attitude. He says that
all activities of offering, giving, or donation, whether of the Dharma

or of material things, should be made in this way. If we closely examine our minds, we see that when we make an offering we almost always have some expectation of return from the action. This expectation might be of a material return, some gratitude from the recipient, a good reputation with other people, or a better image of oneself.

In light of this point, *takuhatsu* is a very precious practice. The people who give donations to monks don't really know who the monks are or whether they are really sincere practitioners of Buddha's teachings. Although there are some fake monks practicing begging in Japan simply to make money, people on the street, many of them merchants who are making money to support themselves, make donations without making such judgments. They simply trust the monks' robes. When I practiced *takuhatsu,* my fellow monks and I felt people were giving to the Buddha rather than to us as individuals.

> We give flowers blooming on the distant mountains
> to the Tathagata...

Those flowers blooming on the distant mountains are not ours. We have no sense of possession of those flowers. They grow by themselves and by blooming they decorate the mountains and make us feel good. The beauty of the flowers on the distant mountains is a generous gift from nature, yet we don't cling to the flowers or their beauty. If we keep the same attitude towards the flowers inside our garden that have received a lot of our time and energy, our time and effort spent helping those flowers grow can be true *dana*—but it's very difficult to practice in this way. We usually want to enjoy the flowers we help to grow by ourselves, or we want to share our joy in them with only our loved ones.

When a woman asked Ryokan to give her a poem as a keepsake, he wrote this verse:

What have I to leave as a keepsake?
In spring, the cherry blossoms
In summer, the warbler's song
In autumn, the maple's crimson leaves.

There is another of Ryokan's poems about *takuhatsu:*

Clouds billow upward
Skies are clear
I go out to beg
And receive heaven's gifts.

Ryokan was living truly without greed, and therefore he was one with everything within the entire world. He had nothing to which he was attached and nothing to covet. He lived within the network of the offerings of heaven and earth. The flowers in the distant mountains are keepsakes of Ryokan and he offers them to those of us who appreciate his poems and his way of life. He received the gifts of heaven and earth, and his poems as well as his way of life are his gifts to us.

...and offer treasures accumulated in past lives to living beings.

Bodhisattvas arouse bodhi-mind to attain buddhahood and to save all living beings. They practice throughout many lifetimes. Because of the power of their vows and the practices on which they base those vows, we can practice in this lifetime. Our lives are the result of our efforts in past lives. Even if one doesn't believe in the reincarnation of individuals, she knows that the air was created by primitive living beings, that soil is a mixture of sand and the residue of living beings, and that petroleum and coal are also gifts from living beings that lived billions of years ago. Languages we study and use in our cultures are gifts from people who previously lived in our societies. Various rich cultures are also legacies of people of the past. We cannot live without all these gifts from the first most primitive living beings on the earth, and if we awaken to this reality, we cannot avoid trying to offer something to benefit other beings. *Dana* as a practice of *paramita* comes from such an awakening.

> Whether our gifts are of the Dharma or of material objects, each gift is truly endowed with the virtue of offering, or *dana*.

Each and every thing in the universe is within the network of interdependent origination. Each being is connected with all other beings. Therefore, by simply being as it is, each thing is participating in the network of offering. Still, human beings try to take only good things into "my" territory and make them "my" possessions. We use all beings in nature as resources to satisfy our desires and make us happy. Even when we try to help others, our intention may have some subtle defilement created by some underlying self-centeredness. Even so, when we live in such an ego-centered way, we are still knots in Indra's net of interdependent origination. Awakening to interconnectedness and making efforts to live peacefully with other beings allow us to live in harmony. Such awakening allows us to take the bodhisattva vow, "Beings are numberless, we vow to free them." In order to free other beings we need to free ourselves, and the practice of *dana* is a practice that frees us and other beings simultaneously.

In addition to the offering of material things and the dharma, there is the offering of fearlessness. Within the Buddhist sangha, laypeople usually offer material things to support the Buddha, dharma and sangha, and the practice of offering to people in need has been encouraged in order to benefit society. The Buddha and monks offer Dharma in order to benefit people's practices and culti- vate their spirituality. Also, Buddhists practice offering fearlessness by avoiding harming others and by taking good care of others with a compassionate heart.

> Even if this gift is not our personal possession, nothing hinders our practice of offering.

In the very beginning of the Heart Sutra it says, "Avalokiteshvara Bodhisattva when deeply practicing *prajna paramita,* clearly saw that all five aggregates are empty and thus relieved all suffering." *Dana paramita* is a practice of offering that is based on the insight or wisdom (*prajna*) that the five aggregates are empty. The five aggre- gates are form (*rupa,* or material), sensation, perception, formation and consciousness. These five aggregates are the elements of all beings. Avalokiteshvara saw that there is nothing that exists other than the five aggregates, and he also clearly saw that even those five aggregates are empty. "Empty" means there is no inherent nature that makes things fixed, substantial, or permanent. Things are only collections of the five aggregates that are coming and going, arising and perishing, and gathering and scattering. The five aggre- gates themselves are also empty and have no self nature. When we see the reality of the emptiness of the five aggregates, that is (in the case of human beings), of our bodies and minds, we can be free from attachment to them. The body is composed of *rupa* and the other four elements constitute the functioning of our minds. Nothing exists other than the body and mind that are conditioned and always changing.

We suppose that there is something that does not change within or outside of our bodies and minds. Since I was born, my physical condition has been always changing, and my mental condition is also always changing, but we assume there is something that is not changing and we call it identity. When I was a baby, my body was much smaller than it is now, and in my twenties, my body was much stronger. Now I am getting older and my body is losing strength. Some of the things I could once do easily are now difficult for me. Still, when I was a baby, when I was a teenager, when I was in my twenties, when I was in my thirties, and when I was in my forties, Shohaku was always Shohaku, as he will be when I reach my eighties and nineties. Although both my physical and mental conditions are changing, it seems there is something that continues without change as I age. In Buddhism this something that does not change is called *atman,* and the Buddha taught that there is no such thing. He said that the *atman* is merely a product of our minds, that is, a concept. If we see ourselves and all other beings thoroughly in light of this *prajna paramita,* we cannot say that there is an "I" that possesses "this thing." We therefore cannot say that because "I" am the owner of "this thing," I have authority to give "it" to "that person." In reality there is no such thing called "I," "my possession," or "that person." Still, we can make our offerings. In fact, it is precisely because we possess nothing that things can be endowed with the virtue of offering.

No gift is too small, but our effort should be genuine.

The worldly value of things has no significance when we practice *dana.* Whether or not our intention to offer is sincerely for the benefit of others is most important. For example, Ryokan and his child playmates picked spring flowers like violets and dandelions and placed them in his begging bowl. In the same way that Ryokan made this offering to the Buddhas of the past, present, and future, a baby's smile can sometimes be the most precious *dana.*

In his book *Awakening to Prayer,*[4] a Japanese Catholic priest, Father Ichiro Okumura, introduces a story he found in a newspaper about a four-year-old-girl. The heading of the article, written by the little girl's aunt, was "*Kami sama, gomen-ne*" ("Dear God, pardon me").

One day my little four-year-old niece came to visit me. Since there were only boys in my family, the visit of this little girl was like a ray of sunshine, or the opening of a flower. The public gardens are nearby, so I brought her there, and when the time came to return home I took her by the hand and showed her how to cross the park, in which there is a small temple in honor of Jizo Bodhisattva, protector of children and the poor. My niece noticed it and led me there saying, "Let's go and pray." Since the door was closed, I thought we would pass by, but to my shame, the little girl opened it herself and began to pray fervently. I prayed too, and then asked her, "What did you say?" "I said, '*Kami sama,* pardon me; I have nothing to offer.'" I was deeply moved, since all I think of saying

to the God or the Buddha is, "Give me this; do that...."
Happily, I did not tell this child to ask Jizo Bodhisattva
to make her good, or other such things. If I had been that
clumsy I would never have felt the purity of the innocent
heart. I just squeezed her little hand.[5]

Father Okumura comments on this story: "Unless you change and
become like children, you will never enter the kingdom of heaven"
(Mt. 18:3). A story like this should awaken the hearts of adults who
no longer know the meaning of pure prayer. 'Pardon me, I have
nothing to offer.' As St. John of the Cross said, 'This awareness
of our nothingness (nada), of our poverty, at the very moment we
come emptyhanded before God who is all (todo), is possible only if
we take time out for reflection during the day."

Usually people bring some offerings to an enshrined Buddha
or bodhisattva of a temple and pray for their wishes to be fulfilled.
Such an offering is a kind of trade or "give-and-take" offering.
The person offering says, "I give offerings to the Buddha and
then the Buddha will give me something I want in return." The
girl in this story had nothing to offer and she just apologized
instead of asking God to give her something she wanted. The
little girl's prayer was her precious offering to her aunt and all
the people who read this story. Father Okumura interprets her
prayer as expressing her awareness of the nothingness of the self
before God.

This is the same spirit of Ryokan's offering to the Buddhas of
wildflowers in his begging bowl. He and the children had nothing to
offer except those wildflowers that were not theirs. Ryokan's empty
begging bowl that was made to receive offerings from other people
became a bowl for him to make an offering to the Buddhas.

When the Way is entrusted to the Way, we attain the Way. When we attain the Way, the Way unfailingly continues to be entrusted to the Way. When material things are treasured, these treasures actually become *dana*. We offer ourselves to ourselves, and we offer others to others. The karma of giving pervades the heavens above and our human world alike. It even reaches the realm of those sages who have attained the fruits of realization. Whether we give or receive, we connect ourselves with all beings throughout the world.

I think this first sentence is the same thing that Dōgen said in the Genjokoan; "Conveying oneself toward all things to carry out practice/enlightenment is delusion. All things coming and carrying out practice/enlightenment through the self is realization." When the Way is entrusted to the Way, the person refrains from making judgments and controlling all things according to his personal view and system of values. This is what we do in our zazen by letting go of thought, or to use Uchiyama Roshi's expression, by "opening the hand of thought." When we try not to deal with all things based on our personal views and desires, the reality of all things as they are is made manifest. This is the same as the four-year-old girl saying, "I am sorry I have nothing to offer." When we practice with an empty hand, the Way manifests itself. This is what Dōgen meant when he said, "we attain the Way." Actually, when the Way is attained, we hold nothing. We simply continue to entrust all things, including ourselves, to the Way. In this sense, Ryokan's practice of offering, the little girl's prayer, Dōgen Zenji's zazen, and St. John of the Cross's awareness of the nothingness of the self, are all the same thing. Only with an awareness of the reality that we have nothing to offer, or even more radically, that there is nothing to grasp as "me," can we practice *dana* as a *paramita.*

> When material things are treasured, these trea-
> sures actually become *dana*. We offer ourselves to
> ourselves, and we offer others to others.

A more literal translation of this sentence is, "When material treasures are entrusted to the material treasures, the material treasures without fail become *dana.*" As is so with the Way that is awakening or enlightenment, when material things are entrusted to themselves, that is, when we do not deal with them with our personal and selfish views and desires, all things become *dana.* Air as it is is an offering. Water as it is is an offering. Trees' being as they are is an offering. Flowers' being as they are is an offering. Butterflies' being as they are is an offering. Ryokan expresses this truth, I think, in his poem about begging which begins, "With no mind, the flower invites the butterfly," earlier in this chapter.

When we don't deal with things according to our personal desires and try not to use things only for fulfilling these desires, all things appear as they are. Otherwise, we only see the image created in our minds by our own conditioned thoughts and desires. That realm of letting go of thoughts and desires is the common ground of interdependent origination in which all things are sustaining each other. Simply being a knot in the network of interdependence is already an offering.

We offer ourselves to ourselves, and we offer others to others. This means we entrust ourselves to ourselves and entrust others to others. We refrain even from controlling ourselves as well as others.

This is what we do in our zazen. In zazen, the self settles down within the self and others become as they are. This is much different from our usual way of seeing ourselves with greed and anger or hatred. Zazen allows us to give up our usual struggle between who we are and who we want to be, and it frees us from our expectations of how others should behave.

> The karma of giving pervades the heavens above and our human world alike. It even reaches the realm of those sages who have attained the fruits of realization. Whether we give or receive, we connect ourselves with all beings throughout the world.

"The karma of giving" is a translation of *in-nen-riki,* or *dana. In* is cause, *en* is conditions and *riki* is power. Thus *in-nen-riki* literally means "the power of causes and conditions." "Causes and conditions" in this case is one of the "ten suchnesses" mentioned in the second chapter of the Lotus Sutra. The ten suchnesses are the suchness of (1) form, (2) nature, (3) body, (4) power, (5) function, (6) primary cause, (7) secondary cause (conditions), (8) effect, (9) recompense, and (10) the complete fundamental whole. Each and every thing is endowed with these ten suchnesses.

My understanding is that the first five suchnesses indicate the uniqueness of each thing. The next four show us that each thing occurs and exists within a relationship to everything else in both time and space. The suchness of primary cause (6) and the suchness of effect (8) are relationships within time. Cause (6) is a relationship with the past, while effect or result (8) is a relationship with the future. For example, a flower has a relationship in the past with its "parent's" seed as the flower's "cause," and its own fruits

or seeds give it a relationship in the future with the next generation of flowers. The suchness of secondary cause (7) and the suchness of recompense (9) are relationships within space at the present
time. Flowers can bloom because of numberless conditions that
sustain them, such as moisture, sunlight, and insects like butterflies
and bees. The recompense or secondary result (9) in this illustration may be, for example, that the flower gives butterflies or bees
nectar and brings joy to human beings. Finally, the suchness of the
complete fundamental whole (10) expresses the truth that all of the
previous nine elements in this list are actually one unified whole
rather than nine independent items. Thus, each thing is connected
with everything else within time and space and within a network of
causes and conditions.

The Lotus Sutra doesn't discuss the ten suchnesses in order
to teach principles of nature; it aims to teach us the principles
of bodhisattva practice. Each action we perform as a practice
of the bodhisattva vows is connected to everything in the past,
present and future. Therefore, even our small offerings given
with sincere hearts have a connection with all beings in all the
six realms, including heaven realms, human realms, and the
realms of all sages such as buddhas and bodhisattvas. This is what
Dōgen means when he says, "Whether we give or receive, we
connect ourselves with all beings throughout the world." When
either giving or receiving, by letting go of egocentricity and being
giving or receiving, we go beyond the separation of self and all
other beings. We then actively participate in the network of interdependent origination.

> The Buddha said, "When a person who practices
> dana comes into an assembly, other people watch

that person with admiration." We should know that the mind of such a person quietly reaches others. Even if we offer just one word or verse of Dharma, it will become a seed of goodness in this lifetime and in other lives to come. Even if we give humble things—a single penny or a stalk of grass—we plant a root of goodness in this and other ages. Dharma can be a material treasure, and a material treasure can be Dharma. This depends entirely upon the giver's vow and wish.

In this paragraph Dōgen Zenji says that our practice of *dana* influences our personality and creates a peaceful and supportive atmosphere for other people's practice. If we have a tendency to take advantage of others and to try to gain something from everyone we meet, our greed and aggressiveness will make others feel defensive in our presence. Yet one who practices *dana* allows others to feel safe and peaceful in his presence. "We should know that the mind of such a person quietly reaches others" means that people will respect one who practices *dana,* and her practice will quietly influence others, allowing them to be friendlier. This happens because the virtue of *dana* is boundless, reaching beyond the separation of self and other.

In Buddhist philosophy, "perfuming" (Jap. *Kunju,* 薫習, Skt. *vasana*) is an important concept that refers to the influence of our actions on our personality. It is a key word in the philosophy of the Yogacara school and is used in the teachings of Mahayana Buddhist texts such as *The Awakening of Faith in Mahayana* (大乗起信論 *Daijo-kishinron*).

In D.T. Suzuki's translation of *The Awakening of Faith* (the version translated into Chinese by Cikshananda) we read:

By "perfuming" we mean that while our worldly clothes [viz., those which we wear] have no odor of their own, neither offensive nor agreeable, they acquire one or the other according to the nature of the substance with which they are perfumed.

Now suchness is a pure dharma free from defilement. It acquires, however, a quality of defilement owing to the perfuming power of ignorance. On the other hand, ignorance has nothing to do with purity. Nevertheless, we speak of its being able to do the work of purity, because it in its turn is perfumed by suchness.[6]

According to this text, perfuming is the way suchness and ignorance influence each other and either defile or purify our lives. In quoting an ancient, Dōgen Zenji says in *Shobogenzo Zuimonki 4–4,* "Associating with a good person is like walking through mist and dew; though you will not become drenched, gradually your robes will become damp." Here Dōgen is talking about the equivalent of "perfuming." He is saying that if we keep practicing the four embracing actions, we become influenced by these actions and become "damp" with the "moisture" of our own activities. Our own activities as well as the activities of others perfume self and other, and in this way our lives and this world evolve together. Together we may create for ourselves either samsara, which includes heaven and hell, or nirvana.

The Awakening of Faith also explains how suchness, in a concrete way, perfumes ignorance and in turn reduces the delusive desires of the three poisonous minds, which are the root of the suffering experienced in samsara:

All beings since their first aspiration (cittotpada) till the attainment of Buddhahood are sheltered under the guardianship of all Buddhas and bodhisattvas who, responding to the requirement of the occasion, transform themselves and assume the actual forms of personality.

Thus for the sake of all beings Buddhas and Bodhisattvas become sometimes their parents, sometimes their wives and children, sometimes their kinsmen, sometimes their servants, sometimes their friends, sometimes their enemies, sometimes reveal themselves as devas or in some other forms.

Again Buddhas and bodhisattvas treat all beings sometimes with the four methods of entertainment, sometimes with the six paramitas, or with some other deeds, all of which are the inducement for them to make their knowledge (bodhi) perfect.

Thus embracing all beings with their deep compassion (mahakaruna), with their meek and tender heart, as well as their immense treasure of blissful wisdom, Buddhas convert them in such a way as to suit their [all beings'] needs and conditions; while all beings thereby are enabled to hear or see Buddhas, and, thinking of Tathagatas or some other personages, to increase their root of merit (kucakamula).[7]

In saying that buddhas and bodhisattvas transform themselves to appear as our parents, friends, enemies, etc., the text tells us that all activities of all beings in our lives are the functioning of buddhas and bodhisattvas. These activities are intended to help us awaken to the reality of all beings and to help us see and hear the Dharma so that we may be liberated from the suffering of samsara. From the other point of view, when we engage in practices that are in accordance with the bodhisattva vows, we can help others to reduce their pain and sorrow and to be liberated from delusion. Practices such as offering dharma teachings can become the functioning of buddhas and bodhisattvas and help those around us to attain the Buddha Way. Thus we can all help each other by participating in the buddhas' and bodhisattvas' liberating work for all beings. In a sense, all people and all beings are working to liberate each other, and all people and all beings are constantly revealing the reality of life to each other in order to liberate all people and all beings. This is what Dōgen Zenji describes in his Jijuyu-zanmai as the function of our zazen practice.

The words "four methods of entertainment" in the text above are Suzuki's translation of shishobo. These practices are not simply intended to help and guide other people, but they also help to liberate us as we work together with all beings.

Even if we offer just one word or verse of Dharma, it will become a seed of goodness in this lifetime and in other lives to come. Even if we give humble things—a single penny or a stalk of grass—we plant a root of goodness in this and other ages.

Depending upon our vow, we can be either full-time practitioners or lay practitioners. However, today many lay people are well educated and can therefore share their knowledge of the Dharma. Such offerings can be *dana* if given as part of the practitioner's bodhisattva vow, and even a practitioner's most simple actions can be *dana* as well. Even if we don't have formal knowledge of the Dharma or if we don't have material goods to offer, a simple offering such as a smile can be very helpful *dana* in certain situations.

For example, the second of the four embracing actions is loving-speech. Loving-speech can be a great practice of *dana,* as I once learned in the 1970s when I was practicing at Pioneer Valley Zendo and working at a tofu shop in a nearby town. We worked in the evening, and since I didn't have a driver's license I had to sleep at the shop after work rather than going back to the zendo. Because it was the warmest spot in the shop, I slept next to the furnace on a pile of bags containing soybeans. This spot was warm but noisy, and consequently I could not sleep well. One cold winter morning I awoke and decided to stop by a coffee shop before beginning to hitchhike home. I did not feel particularly bad, but I had not slept well the night before. The waitress at the coffee shop, a woman in her sixties, looked at my face as she served me coffee and said, "Smile! It's a beautiful day!" For a while I did not understand why she had said such a thing. I just said, "Thank you!" Later, because of the waitress's words. I noticed that although it was very cold, it really was a beautiful day. When I started to walk after having the coffee, I thought, "When she looked at my face, she thought I was desperate." Now I feel that her words were one of the greatest offerings of *dana* that I ever received. Whenever I am having a hard time and forget to smile, I remember the kind words of that waitress.

Offering by a Chinese Emperor

Offering his beard, a Chinese emperor harmonized his minister's mind. Offering sand, a child gained the throne. These people did not covet rewards from others. They simply shared what they had according to their ability. To launch a boat or build a bridge is the practice of *dana-paramita*. When we understand the meaning of *dana*, receiving a body and giving up a body are both offering. Earning a livelihood and managing a business are, nothing other than giving. Trusting flowers to the wind and trusting birds to the season may also be the meritorious action of *dana*. When we give and when we receive, we should study this principle: Great King Ashoka's offering of half a mango to hundreds of monks was a boundless offering. Not only should we urge ourselves to make offerings, but we must not overlook any opportunity to practice *dana*. Because we are blessed with the virtue of offering, we have received our present lives.

Here Dōgen gives examples of the practice of *dana*. The first is a story of Taiso, the second emperor of the Tong Dynasty [597–649]. He was the second son of the founding emperor of Tong, who with the help of Taiso united China. Taiso skillfully governed his country with benevolence for twenty-three years, and later generations considered his administration to be an ideal model of Chinese sovereignty. Dōgen Zenji refers to stories of Taiso four times in *Shobogenzo Zuimonki*. For example, in section 2–3 of that text we read:

> During the reign of Taiso of the Tang dynasty, Gicho (Wei Zheng), one of the ministers, remarked to the emperor, "Some people are slandering your Majesty." The emperor replied, "As a sovereign, if I have virtue, I am not afraid of being slandered by people. I'm more afraid of being praised despite the lack of it."

Dōgen commented on this passage saying, "Here is an example of how even a lay person had such an attitude (about virtue). Monks should, first of all, maintain this attitude."

According to another story, when one of Taiso's ministers was sick a doctor recommended roasted bear to cure him. Hearing this, the emperor slaughtered his own bear and gave it to the minister. I am not sure if roasted bear is truly a good medicine, but in this story it is probably a symbol of the emperor's authority. Even if the roasted bear did not really cure the minister's body, the fact that it was the emperor's bear, prepared by the emperor himself, touched the minister and increased his loyalty.

Offering by the Indian King Asoka

Dōgen Zenji also refers to two stories from the Sutra of King Asoka[8] about the offerings of the king. One is the story of a boy who offered a handful of sand to Shakyamuni Buddha, and the other tells of King Asoka's offering half of a mango to the sangha.

According to Japanese scholarly references, King Asoka was the grandson of Candragupta, the king of India who fought against Seleukos, the retainer of Alexander the Great. Alexander invaded India in 326 B.C.E. and conquered its northwestern region before returning to the West in 325. Alexander died in the year 323 B.C.E. in Babylon, but Seleukos who established his empire in Syria in 306 B.C.E., invaded India in 305. After the war with Seleukos ended, Candragupta destroyed the kingdom of Magada and founded the Maurya Dynasty in its place. King Asoka, the grandson of Candragupta, reigned between 268–232 B.C.E. He fought against his brothers to become king after his father's death, and after he was enthroned he conquered many kingdoms. It is said that he was a very violent ruler who was good at making war.

In the 9th year of his reign, he defeated Kalinga in a battle that united most of India but produced more than 100,000 casualties and caused much suffering for many people. The king experienced great sadness upon witnessing such vast suffering, and as a result he came to believe that war was wrong. He is said to have come to the realization that only the truths of Buddhist teachings (*dharma-vijiya*), rather than war and competition, can produce real victories in life. After he took refuge in Buddhism, he lived near a Buddhist sangha for more than a year and practiced enthusiastically. The king worked to spread Buddhism by ordering the building of stone pillars inscribed with Buddhist teachings, and many of these carvings have been discovered. He declared that he would govern his kingdom based on the paramita teachings of the Dharma: affection (*daya*), few delusive desires (*alpasrava*), generosity in giving (*dana*), truth (*satya*), purity (*sauca*), and gentleness (*mardava*).

King Asoka sent Buddhist envoys to Syria, Egypt, Macedonia, and other countries, and his son, Mahinda, and daughter, Sanghamitta, established Buddhism in Sri Lanka. Thus Buddhism traveled to many places outside of India because of King Asoka's support. Yet the king's Buddhist policies and excessive financial support of Buddhist orders eventually caused the decline of his government. His son and ministers eventually turned against him, and his empire disappeared shortly after his death.

The following are stories about King Asoka that Dōgen Zenji introduces from the Sutra of King Asoka. Of course these stories are merely traditional images of the great benevolent king (*cakravarti-raja*) who supported Buddhism rather than presentations of historical facts. The first story from Section One of the sutra creates a connection between King Asoka and Shakyamuni Buddha by relating an event from a past life of the king:

While the World-honored One was begging for food on a big street, he met two boys there playing with sand. The boys saw the 32 features on the Buddha's body, and the first boy took a handful of sand and put it in the Buddha's begging bowl as an offering. The second boy did a gassho and joyfully composed a verse about the Buddha; "With natural boundless compassion, a circle of light ornaments my body. Having already departed from life-and-death, now I wholeheartedly concentrate my mind." And of the first boy he recited, "Because I think of the Buddha, I offer this sand with reverence."

At that time, the first boy made a vow saying, "I vow to do Buddha's work within Buddha's dharma. Because of this root of goodness, please make me the king of a country."

Shakyamuni Buddha penetrated the boy's mind and saw that the boy's vow would bear excellent fruit because it was a seed planted in Buddha's field of happiness (*fukuden*). Shakyamuni then accepted the sand with compassion and said to Ananda, "One hundred years after my entering Nirvana, this boy will be born in the city of Pataliputra and be named Asoka. He will be the Quarter Wheel-Turning King. He will take refuge in the true Dharma, make offerings to Buddha's relics, build eighty-four thousand stupas, and be beneficial to numberless people."

Then Shakyamuni Buddha handed the sand to Ananda saying, "Mix this sand together with cow dung and put it on the ground where the Buddha practices walking meditation."

This was King Asoka's first practice of *dana* for the Buddha, dharma and sangha. Although he only offered a handful of sand, because of his wholehearted vow he received an excellent reward in being reborn as the wheel-turning king.

The second story is from Chapter 5 of the sutra:

When King Asoka was an old man, a minister said to the prince, "The great King Asoka will pass away soon. Now the king wants to donate forty thousand gold pieces to the Rooster Temple. For all kings, their source of power is their material wealth. Prince, you should prevent the king from wasting such a huge amount of money." The prince accepted this advice and seized control of government money from the king, who was then forced to cancel his donation to the temple.

Now King Asoka's only remaining valuable was a golden plate he used for dining. After finishing his meal, the king sent the golden plate to the Rooster Temple, leaving himself with only half of a mango as his last possession. At that time the King summoned his ministers and said, "On behalf of all people in this country, tell me who is the lord of this land!" A minister stood up, did a gassho and said, "Heaven is the only lord of the land. No particular person can be lord." Upon hearing this, King Asoka shed tears like rain.

The king then called one of his close attendants and said to him, "Now I have lost my power and my freedom. Please do a final favor for me now—do just this one thing; take this mango half to the Rooster Temple and tell the monks, "King Asoka prostrates himself at the feet of the monks of the assembly. In the past he owned all the land of the continent; now he only owns half of a mango. This mango is his last offering; monks, please accept this offering. It is small but this offering's virtue will benefit the monks' assembly boundlessly."

The monks accepted the mango half from the king, cut it into tiny pieces, and put the pieces into a stew to serve the assembly. At that time, the aging King Asoka was nearing death. From his bed his attendants propped him up so that he could look around in all four directions. Then the king faced the direction of the temple, did a gassho and said, "Now, in addition to the treasures I have given, I offer the entire Earth and its great oceans to the sangha."

These two offerings of the great King Asoka, the first made as a boy and the final made as a dying man, were worthless by the standards of society's market value. But because these small offerings were made with purity of heart, Dōgen Zenji praised them more than the incalculable number of offerings the king made as a powerful ruler. We can also find praise for this spirit of offering in the teachings of Jesus Christ:

He sat down opposite the treasury, and watched the crowd putting money into the treasury. Many rich people put in large sums. A poor widow came and put in two small copper coins, which are worth a penny. Then he called his disciples and said to them, "Truly I tell you, this poor widow has put in more than all those who are contributing to the treasury. For all of them have contributed out of their abundance; but she out of her poverty has put in everything she had, all she had to live on."[9]

Shishobo continues:

> These people did not covet rewards from others. They simply shared what they had according to their ability. To launch a boat or build a bridge is the practice of *dana paramita*. When we understand the meaning of *dana*, receiving a body and giving up a body are both offering. Earning a livelihood and managing a business are nothing other than giving.

When I read the story about King Asoka, I think that when he had great power he gave Buddhist temples more than was required and more than he was capable of. Because of his immeasurable donations, Buddhist temples became wealthy and prosperous and Buddhism spread throughout India and beyond. However, as a result of the king's contributions, the genuine spirit of practice began to decline in his kingdom because many people joined the sangha seeking wealth and status rather than true spiritual practice. The financial condition of his government and of his nation also suffered as a result of the king's actions. Since he had responsibility as a ruler to govern the nation, he should have managed his country's resources more carefully. If he had governed the nation according to the teachings of the Dharma, his work as a benevolent ruler would have been the practice of *dana*. This is what Dōgen Zenji meant when he said, "To launch a boat or build a bridge is the practice of *dana-paramita*." To make those very large material donations to the Buddhist order may have been excessive or even contrary to the genuine spirit of the Dharma. If the king wished to make contributions to the Dharma beyond his means as a ruler, he should have resigned the throne and became a Buddhist monk. It must be very difficult for a person with great power and wealth to know his own limitations, and this is why King Asoka "shed tears like rain" when his ministers turned against him in his final days. But the king truly rose to excellence when he kept his faith in the Dharma after losing his power as a ruler. I feel fortunate, as Ryokan did, that I do not have such a problem. In Ryokan's keepsake poem which begins, "What have I to leave as a keepsake?" earlier in this book, the final three lines were inspired by Dōgen's poem entitled "Original Face" (*Honrai no memmoku*):

In spring, the cherry blossoms,
In summer, the cuckoo's song,
In autumn, the moon, shining,
In winter, the frozen snow:
How pure and clear are the seasons!

This is what Dōgen meant when he said, "Trusting flowers to the wind and trusting birds to the season may also be the meritorious action of *dana*." Just living together with all beings without trying to possess them is the meritorious action of *dana*. It is truly important to understand that Dōgen Zenji did not praise King Asoka as the great patron of Buddhism simply because of the king's great monetary contributions. There are many examples of great patrons of Buddhism who, like Asoka, hindered the Buddhist sangha with their excessive donations while creating problems for their societies. That is why Dōgen says that Asoka's offering of a handful of sand and his giving half of a mango were the king's greatest practices of *dana*.

The Buddha said, "One may offer a gift to oneself and use one's own gift; even more, one can pass it to one's parents, wife, and children." Therefore we should know that giving to ourselves is a kind of offering. To give to parents, wife, and children is also an offering.

Initially I had difficulty understanding what Dōgen was saying here, but on December 20th, 1975, I came to the US for the first time with my dharma brother and a few American friends. I was twenty-six years old. We stayed with our friend John in Los Angeles, and then Michael, another friend, came to pick us up to take us to San Francisco. On our way, we stopped in Santa Barbara to visit another friend, Paul who had practiced at Antaiji, and then we went to UC Santa Barbara on New Year's Eve. We talked with Paul and his roommates regarding our trip to Massachusetts.

A dharma brother who had gone to Massachusetts one year before us had bought a piece of wooded land in the woods in the western part of the state, intending to build a zendo. Speaking among ourselves, we noted that there was nothing there other than a small house built by practitioners the previous summer. It was going to take a lot of work to establish a practice center. When he heard us, Michael gave me a pair of working boots. He said, "I am happy if these boots are useful for you." The pair of boots did fit my feet quite well. My English was very poor, so I could only say, "Thank you" and receive his offering. At the same time, I was uncomfortable. I appreciated his kindness and generosity to a stranger who had come from Japan, but some deeper part of my mind said, "I don't want to receive it." I didn't really understand what this feeling was.

The next day was New Year's Day, 1976. Taking a walk by myself early in the morning along the nearby streets that had big beautiful trees on both sides, I tried to figure out what that feeling was. The sky was so blue, a color that was rare in Japan. After a while, I found that the feeling had something to do with the teaching of Sawaki Roshi, "Gaining is delusion, losing is enlightenment."

My teacher, Kosho Uchiyama Roshi, retired from Antaiji in the winter of 1975. Right before he left the temple, he gave his last lecture as the abbot on February 23. In the lecture, he talked on the seven points he kept in mind in order to educate his disciples and maintain sincere practice while he was the abbot. His wish was that his disciples would observe these points and continue his vow in our activities.

The third of those seven points was "Zazen must work concretely in our daily lives as the two practices (vow and repentance), the three minds (magnanimous mind, nurturing mind, and joyful mind), and as the realization of the saying 'Gaining is delusion, losing is enlightenment.'"

Uchiyama Roshi talked about the saying as an essential point of practice based on buddhadharma:

> To recognize true zazen, we have to look at our practice from an absolute perspective. If you are caught up in one of the limited kinds of Zen of the six realms, you can no longer see the essential point of buddhadharma. And what is that? As I said before, Buddhism teaches impermanence and the quality of non-ego. Letting go and opening the hand of thought is the foundation of Zen based on the buddhadharma.

The saying "gaining is delusion, losing is enlightenment" has very practical value. In our ordinary human life, we are always trying to fulfill our desires. We're satisfied only when all our desires are met. In Buddhism, though, it's just the opposite: it is important for us to leave our desire alone, without trying to fulfill them. If we push this one step further - gaining is delusion, losing is enlightenment - we're talking about active participation in loss.

Let me be clear that I am not saying, "Losing is important, so go help people out by collecting what you can from them." That just makes you the "someone" who gains. Rather, apply this saying just to yourself and give something up. For breaking the ego's grip, nothing is more effective than giving something up.[10]

Originally this saying was Sawaki Kodo Roshi's unique colloquial Japanese expression of Dōgen Zenji's phrase *mushotoku* (冥徐橡), or no gaining. *Mushotoku* originates in the Mahayana teaching of the emptiness of subject and object: there is no one to gain and nothing to be gained.

In the Heart Sutra, we find the expression, "There is neither ignorance nor extinction of ignorance—- neither old age and death, nor extinction of old age and death; no suffering, no cause, no cessation, no path; no knowledge and no attainment (冥橡, *mutoku*). With nothing to attain (冥徐橡, *mushotoku*), a bodhisattva relies on prajnaparamita, and thus the mind is without hindrance."

Uchiyama Roshi said that someone criticized Sawaki Roshi saying, "Neither gaining nor losing, neither enlightenment nor delusion is in accord with buddhadharma. 'Gaining is delusion and losing is enlightenment' is still incomplete." What Uchiyama Roshi said in the last paragraph of the above quote was his refutation against that criticism. Because we all have a tendency to gain something desirable and not to lose anything we possess, we need to actively practice not to gain and to lose. This was a very important teaching to me since from the beginning, I studied and practiced following Sawaki Roshi and Uchiyama Roshi's teachings.

Since Uchiyama Roshi retired and I began to make preparations to come to the US to work on establishing the zendo in Massachusetts, many people, including my teacher, parents, dharma brothers, and various friends, helped and supported me. Some of them were so generous that they made offerings of money to help me buy the necessary things to travel and to live in the US. Without their help, I could not have moved to the US. I was almost overwhelmed by those offerings. Although I was very grateful for all such gifts, in some part of myself I felt as if the donors had some expectation of me and I had some obligation to them. I didn't think that I had some desire to gain something for myself from my practice or that I saw going to the US as a means to get some benefit. When I received so many offerings from so many people, I felt uncomfortable and yet I could not reject them. That was the feeling I had had when Michael gave me the pair of working boots in Santa Barbara.

The teaching of "gaining is delusion, losing is enlightenment" is about being free from the ego-centered mind that is always calculating how much we gain and how much we lose. When what's coming in is larger than what's going out, we think our lives are in good shape. It's very difficult for us to be free from this kind of basic desire for gaining even when we practice the buddhadharma. We always ask, "What I can get from this?" Our expectation from Buddhist practice is usually so-called enlightenment. We practice as if we can expect some kind of benefit that makes us better or makes our lives easier and more comfortable.

Basic Mahayana teachings of egolessness and no-gaining warn against this kind of mental framework, but when we try to study and apply it, we can have a rather complicated problem. Because gaining is delusion, I don't want to gain. Because losing is enlightenment, I want to lose. When I am offered something from others or when I don't have anything to lose (offer), I feel small and guilty. When I can offer something, I feel good. When we understand this teaching in this way, we simply create another standard to measure gaining and losing. We are still in the framework of gaining and losing. That was what was happening in my mind on the New Year Day of 1976. I did not want to gain, because gaining was losing.

At the time, I made up my mind to receive the working boots with gratitude and use them not for the sake of my desire but for the sake of Dharma. After arriving at Pioneer Valley Zendo, I put on the pair of working boots when I worked on cutting trees, clearing land to make a vegetable garden, chopping wood to make firewood, etc. The pair of working boots was really helpful both in the summer and winter. They protected my feet. People taught me how to take care of the leather. The pair of boots became a very good friend, and after two years of hard work in the woods of western Massachusetts, they were completely broken. In colloquial Japanese, we say that they had become Buddha.

In *Shobogenzo Gyoji* (*Continuous Practice*), Dōgen Zenji wrote,

Now that we today have become people who see and hear the true Dharma, we should unfailingly repay our debt of gratitude to the (Second) Ancestor. Extraneous methods of repayment will not do: bodies and lives are not sufficient, and nations and cities are not important. Nations and cities can be plundered by others, and bequeathed to relatives and children. Bodies and lives can be given over to the impermanent; they can be committed to a lord, or entrusted to false ways. Therefore, to intend to repay our gratitude through such means is not the way. Simply to maintain the practice day by day: only this is the right way to repay our gratitude. The principle here is to maintain the practice so that the life of every day is not neglected, and not wasted on private pursuits. For what reason? [Because] this life of ours is a blessing left over from past maintenance of the practice; it is a great favor bestowed by maintenance of the practice, which we should hasten to repay.[11]

Here Dōgen Zenji discussed his debt of gratitude to the Second Ancestor of China for having succeeded in Bodhidharma's teachings and enabling the Dharma to survive in China through successive generations of the tradition. I believe we can include not only our ancestors but also all other people who support and help our practice as the source of our debt of gratitude. How can we repay the debt of gratitude? Since the number of people who support us is literally numberless, we cannot do something good for them in return one by one. We cannot even say thank you to them. The only way we can repay the debt of gratitude is to live an unselfish way and try to be helpful to other people we encounter. That is, we offer the same support as we received to others. In the case of Buddhist practitioners, we practice buddhadharma for the sake of buddhadharma. This is what Dōgen Zenji means when he says, "The principle here is to maintain the practice so that the life of every day is not neglected, and not wasted on private pursuits."

As Dōgen Zenji said in the beginning of the section of offering in *Shishobo,* "Offering means not being greedy." We are born, live and die within the network of interdependent origination. Within this network, things are interconnected, moving and changing, giving and receiving, supporting and helping. To be greedy means to make a wall between ourselves and other beings and trying to make desirable things our possessions and keep them inside the wall and undesirable things outside the wall. This is done by the three poisonous minds; greed, anger/hatred, and ignorance. To be free from these three poisonous minds, especially greed, is the actual practice of offering as a *paramita.* Within this network, each one of us is included. Unless we take good care of ourselves and our family, we cannot help others. This is why Dōgen Zenji quotes the Buddha's saying, "One may offer a gift to oneself and use one's own gift; even more, one can pass it to one's parents, wife, and children."

Bodhisattva practice is not the way of self-sacrifice. The goal of our practice is to find a way we and other beings can live together without causing suffering to each other. This is the middle way between pursuing only one's own interests and sacrificing oneself. Offering is a practice of not disturbing the movement of all beings in the network in which we and our families are included.

Whenever we can give up even one speck of dust for the practice of *dana,* we should quietly rejoice. This is because we have already correctly transmitted a virtue of the buddhas, and because we practice one dharma of a bodhisattva for the first time.

Because of our self-centered tendency influenced by the three poisonous minds, it is difficult to give up even small things. We'd like to make our situation secure not only today but also for the rest of our lives. We can't be completely satisfied even when our stomachs are full now because we can think of the future. We want to accumulate wealth not only for ourselves but also for our children. Understanding these principles of social life, if we give up even one speck of dust for the practice of *dana,* we transmit and manifest one of the virtues of the buddhas. This is the first step of entering into the way of a bodhisattva. Even if our offering is as small as a glass of water to someone who's thirsty or directions to someone who's lost, our small gift can be the first practice of *dana paramita.* We can quietly rejoice for that.

> The mind of a sentient being is difficult to change. We begin to transform the mind of beings by offering material things, and we resolve to continue to transform them until they attain the Way. From the beginning we should make use of offering. This is the reason why *dana*-paramita is the first of the Six Perfections. Both giving and receiving without attachment to either objects or our own actions is the manifestation of the virtue of *dana* paramita through which the wheel of dharma is turning.

Both giving and receiving without attachment to either objects of our own actions is the manifestation of the virtue of *dana paramita* through which the wheel of dharma is turning. Although the mind of a living being is difficult to change, active offering is the most powerful way to change living beings and create a friendly, harmonious condition. Common sense tells us that offering material things might be easier, offering kind and friendly sympathy might be more difficult, and offering dharma might be the most difficult. We should offer whatever we can offer. The action of offering changes our own minds and the minds of those receiving the offering. Dōgen Zenji encourages us to continue this practice until both we and others attain the Way, awakening to the reality of all beings together.

Offering is the first of the six *paramitas,* the others being, once again, precepts, patience, diligence, meditation and wisdom. These six *paramitas* are a bodhisattva's practice to help all living beings to cross from this shore of samsara to the other shore of nirvana. One of the English translations of the Sanskrit *paramita* is "perfection." Another translation is "reaching [from this shore of samsara] to the other shore [of nirvana]." Dōgen Zenji says that *dana paramita* is the first of the six *paramitas* because it's the most powerful in terms of changing the minds of living beings.

> The vastness or narrowness of mind cannot be measured, and the greatness or smallness of material things cannot be weighed. But there are times when our mind turns things, and there is offering, in which things turn our mind.

This is the conclusion of Dōgen Zenji's comments on the practice of offering. He discusses the relation between our minds and things as the objects of our minds. Depending upon how the mind and its objects interact, we create either samsara or nirvana. Dōgen Zenji wrote in *Shobogenzo Genjokoan,* "Conveying oneself toward all things to carry out practice/enlightenment is delusion. All things coming and carrying out practice/enlightenment through the self is realization." According to him, delusion and enlightenment lie within the relation between oneself and myriad things. It's not that we contain delusion that can be surgically removed like a cancerous tumor, resulting in enlightenment.

In the *Sutta-Nipata,* one of the oldest Buddhist scriptures, we find the older version of the Buddha's teaching about dependent origination, which contributed to the development of the teachings about the twelve links of causation. *Sutta-Nipata* is a collection of short *sutta* (Skt. *sutra*). In this collection there is a *sutta* called *Kalahavivada Sutta (Disputes and Contention).* This *sutta* begins with someone's question to the Buddha:

> "Sir, whenever there are arguments and quarrels there are tears and anguish, arrogance and pride and grudges and insults to go with them. Can you explain how these things come about? Where do they all come from?"
>
> The Buddha replied, "The tears and anguish that follow arguments and quarrels, the arrogance and pride and grudges and insults that go with them are all the result of one thing. They come from having preferences, from holding things precious and dear. Insults are born out of arguments and grudges are inseparable from quarrels."[12]

The question and answer sequence continued. The Buddha pointed to the causes of the problems we have in our daily lives at the source, that is, preferences, impulse of desire, pleasant and unpleasant sensation, action of contact and the compound of mind and matter. These are number eight and number four of the twelve links of causation. Finally the Buddha said, "There is a state where suffering ceases to exist. It is a state without ordinary perception and without disordered perception and without any perception and without any annihilation of perception. It is perception, consciousness, that is the source of all the basic obstacles."

Consciousness is number three of the twelve links. In this short *sutta,* six of the twelve links are mentioned, although the words are different from the final version that appears in various part of the *Nikaya.*

I believe that what Dōgen Zenji says in *Genjokoan,* what we actually practice in our zazen, and what the Buddha said are the same things. By letting go of thoughts coming up from our karmic (conditioned) consciousness, and refraining from any action based on our thoughts, we are illuminated and verified by all beings. All beings cease to be the objects of our consciousness (*namarupa,* compound of name and form) and appear as they are. In Dōgen Zenji's teachings, zazen itself is awakening.

The practice of offering in its true sense as a *paramita* comes from this liberation and awakening. This is what Uchiyama Roshi meant when he said, "Zazen must work concretely in our daily lives as the two practices (vow and repentance), the three minds (magnanimous mind, nurturing mind, and joyful mind), and as the realization of the saying 'Gaining is delusion, losing is enlightenment.'"

LOVING SPEECH
Words from a compassionate mind

Loving speech means, first of all, to arouse a compassionate mind when meeting beings, and to offer loving, caring words. In general, we should not use any violent or harmful words when we speak.

Sango, which means "the three actions" or "the source of karma," refers to body, speech and thought (or mind). Depending upon how we use the body, speech and thought, we can create healthy and happy relationships or we can generate pain in our dealings with others. Since early in the history of Buddhism, it has been considered very important to carry out wholesome activities using these three aspects of human life. For example, in the *Mahavacchagotta Sutta* (*The Great Discourse to Vacchagotta*) found in *Majjhima Nikaya,* Shakyamuni Buddha presents the Ten Unwholesome Actions when he teaches about the Path of the Ten Wholesome Actions carried out through body, speech and thought. The following are unwholesome actions: (1) killing living beings, (2) taking what is not given (stealing), (3) misconduct in sensual pleasures, (4) false speech, (5) malicious speech (speaking words which cause enmity between two or more persons, or speaking with a "double tongue"), (6) harsh speech, (7) gossip (idle talk, flowery language, or speaking defiled words), (8) covetousness, (9) ill will, and (10) wrong view.

Abstaining from these ten unwholesome actions is wholesome. The first three are actions of the body, the next four are actions of speech, and the final three items describe karmic results produced from thought or mind. The Buddha taught that these ten unwholesome actions arise from the three poisonous minds of greed, anger/hatred, and ignorance. The final three items of the list are thoughts that arise as direct expressions of the three poisonous minds; greed gives rise to covetousness, anger/hatred gives rise to ill will, and ignorance gives rise to wrong views. When we engage in any of the ten unwholesome actions, we create suffering within the cycle of samsara for ourselves and for others. Avoiding these actions is the path that leads to the cessation of suffering.

Within the ten major precepts we receive in the Soto Zen tradition, there are three precepts regarding speech: (4th) not speaking falsehood, (6th) not speaking of faults of others, and (7th) not praising oneself or slandering others. From these examples we can see that right speech, one of the items of the Noble Eightfold Path, is a very important part of Buddhist practice. In *Shobogenzo Zuimonki,* Dōgen Zenji repeatedly admonished his assembly regarding speech.[13]

In *Shishobo,* loving speech is the second of the four embracing actions. Here Dōgen Zenji says that loving speech arises from the compassionate mind. Compassion, along with wisdom, is one of the aspects of Buddha mind. Wisdom shows us that we are living together with all other beings within the network of interdependent origination, and we see that we can exist only through the support of relationships with others. Without many different kinds of support from other beings, we could not live even for a moment. We need air to breathe, water to drink, food to eat, etc. in order to maintain our physical lives. Since human beings are born helpless, they can't survive without being taken care of for many years until they mature. Children must receive food, shelter, and education from their parents and society, and it takes almost 20 years for them to become mature, fully independent people. To become independent members of society, we need much support from others.

Connections with others are not the only important relationships in our lives. On a deeper level, each individual is simply a collection of relationships. We are like bubbles. A bubble is simply a pocket of air inside some water; it is simply a relationship between some water and some air. Similarly, clouds are simply water floating in air. In reality there are no such things as bubbles and clouds that are independent and substantial entities; they are just names for certain relationships between water and air. We human beings are the same. There is no fixed independent entity named Shohaku Okumura;

Shohaku is simply a collection of the five aggregates. Shohaku is a bit more complicated than a bubble or a cloud, but not at all essentially different from them. Awakening to the reality that every being is empty and totally interconnected is the source of compassion.

These relationships within and between beings are also always changing. Things are therefore always moving, arising and perishing; living beings are continually being born, growing, aging and dying. There is nothing we can hold onto. When we awaken to these realities of life, we find sympathy and compassion for others. This happens because we realize that for a time we share the same time, space, and essential life conditions with every other living being. I think awakening to this reality of life allows wisdom to guide our lives. Wisdom is the source of the compassionate heart, and this compassionate heart is in turn the source of loving speech.

Ryokan wrote several poems about a pine tree he saw each time he practiced *takuhatsu*. Actually, these are not poems written about the pine tree; they were written for and dedicated to the pine tree. One of them is as follows:

A lone pine stands
In the fields of Iwamuro
And how miserably soaked
It was in the rain
When I looked at it today.
Oh, Solitary Pine,
How gladly would I have
Protected you with my paper-umbrella
Or with my straw-coat
Were you only flesh and blood.
What a pity – to see you drenched so![14]

In this poem Ryokan reveals his compassionate heart for the pine tree with loving speech.

Ryokan was very sensitive in his manner of speech. He wrote lists of admonitions to himself and to others regarding correct speech. Eighteen of these lists remain and are included in his collected writings. The following list of admonitions is from *Ryokan: Zen Monk-poet of Japan:*[15]

Beware of:

talking a great deal

talking too fast

volunteering information when not asked

giving gratuitous advice

talking up your own accomplishments

breaking in before others have finished speaking

trying to explain to others something you don't understand yourself

starting on a new subject before you've finished with the last one

insisting on getting in the last word

making glib promises

repeating yourself, as old people will do

talking with your hands

speaking in an affectedly offhand manner

reporting in detail on affairs that have nothing to do with anything

reporting on every single thing you see or hear

making a point of using Chinese words and expressions

learning Kyoto speech and using it as though you'd known it all your life

> speaking Edo dialect like a country hick
> talk that smacks of the pedant
> talk that smacks of the aesthete
> talk that smacks of satori
> talk that smacks of the tea master

When we reflect on our manner of speaking, we may find that we often unknowingly break the bodhisattva precepts; it is really difficult to practice loving speech. Language is a way to create connections between people through communication, but it can become a means to sever connections if used unskillfully or maliciously. Although the ability to use language makes us human beings and enabled us to develop our civilization, we have the ability to speak words that are contrary to reality. Language can be used as a sword to take life, create enmity, and cut off the sense of connection between people.

> In society, there is the courtesy of asking others if they are well. Within the Buddha-way we have the practice of speaking the words "Please treasure yourself!" There is also a disciple's filial duty to ask her teacher "How are you?" To speak with a mind that "compassionately cares for living beings as if they were our own babies" is loving-speech.

When we speak with a kind and compassionate heart, even a daily greeting becomes loving speech. We say "Good morning!" "How are you today?" "Are you OK?" This kind of greeting is often spoken insincerely, without an actual compassionate heart, but even so, it's better to respond to people when they greet us rather than to just stay silent. Even when we feel we can't help someone, just asking how they are can be a support to them if we do so with deep sincerity; in this way we can help them feel they're supported as a part of the network of interdependent origination.

In Zen temples, on certain occasions such as New Year's Day, at the beginning of the practice period and the end of practice period, monks exchange formal greetings with their teachers, seniors and fellow monks. Dōgen refers to these traditions as examples of loving speech.

"Compassionately cares for living beings as if they were our own babies" (慈念衆生、猶如赤子) is an expression from *Devatatta,* the 12th chapter of the Lotus Sutra. This is from the famous story of the eight-year-old dragon daughter who attained awakening instantaneously. In a passage describing her virtue we read, "She has unembarrassed powers of argument and a compassionate mind for all the living as if they were [her] children; her merits are complete and the thoughts of her mind and explanations of her mouth are both subtle and great. Kind and compassionate, virtuous and modest, gentle, and beautiful in her disposition, she has been able to attain Bodhi."[16]

When I go back to Japan with my children, we sometimes visit a fast food restaurant or a family restaurant. The training for employees in the service industry in Japan is very strict and very well done. Even young people of both genders who look twenty-years-old or younger speak very politely and courteously to every customer, but often their speech is not natural; they speak like tape-recorders. They just insincerely repeat the words that they were taught in their training. Sometimes I see their lines posted on the cash register they are using. Their speech is polite but it is obvious that their words are not spoken from the heart. Such polite language is artificial; it is not loving speech.

We should praise those with virtue and we should pity those without virtue. From the time we begin to delight in loving speech, loving speech is nurtured little by little. When we practice like this, loving speech, which is usually not known or seen, will manifest itself. In our present life we should practice loving speech without fail and we should continue this practice throughout many future lives.

As Buddhist practitioners we should develop our ability to use language in a way that is encouraging to others, promoting peace and harmony and maturation in the bodhisattva way. To do this we can praise the virtuous traits we see in others and we can have compassion for them when we see their weaknesses and mistakes. This can help others to improve and nurture their virtue.

I have been a very shy person since my childhood. I learned to use language primarily by reading books rather than by talking with others. When I was a boy I was frightened to speak in front of other people, but I have been making an effort to talk with others since I was a teenager. Even now, unless it is really necessary for me to speak, it is easier for me to be silent and it's almost unbelievable to me that I now give lectures in English. Before a lecture, sometimes I feel terribly uneasy and upset, my heart beats quickly, and I want to escape, until I actually start to talk. This kind of practice is very difficult for me; to me, to communicate using language seems almost like magic.

When we intentionally look for virtuous and praiseworthy traits in others, little by little we will find these traits and our ability to appreciate people's actions will grow. On the other hand, if we try to find fault in others, we can find many things to criticize in any person. To practice loving speech we need to find a way to recognize the good points of others. Depending upon whether we try to see the virtues of others or the shortcomings of others, our way of speech and even our entire personalities can become either supportive or non-supportive to others.

> Whether subduing a deadly enemy or making peace, loving speech is fundamental. When a person hears loving speech directly, that person's face brightens and his mind becomes joyful. When a person hears of someone else's loving speech, that person inscribes it in his heart and soul.

In *Shobogenzo Zuimonki,* Dōgen Zenji relates the story of a Chinese minister named Lin Xiangru (Jp., Rin Shojo) who lived in the country of Zhao. Although Xiangru was of humble birth, he was very wise and the king of Zhao therefore took him into service as an administrator of the country's affairs.

Dōgen Zenji tells the story of Xiangru being sent as an envoy to the king of Qin in order to exchange a very precious piece of jade for 15 cities. When the king of Qin did not honor his part of the exchange, Xiangru took the jade and sent it back to his own country. This action made Xiangru famous, and he later became the prime minister. Since Xiangru had never fought in battle, another minister in Zhao who was a military general became envious of Xiangru's higher political position. The general tried to kill Xiangru, but Xiangru fled to various places in avoidance of the general. Since Xiangru purposely avoided any encounter with the general, even at the imperial court, it appeared that he was afraid of the general.

One of Xiangru's retainers asked, "It would be easy to kill that general. Why do you hide from him in fear?"

Xiangru said, "I am not afraid of him. With my eyes I have defeated the general of Qin, and I took back the jade from the king himself. Of course I can kill the general, but gathering troops to raise an army should be reserved for defending our country against our enemies. As ministers we are in charge of protecting the country. If the two of us quarrel and fight with each other, one of us will die and half of the country's strength will be lost. If this happens, neighboring countries will take heart and surely attack us. I therefore wish for the two of us to remain unharmed so that we may protect our country together. For this reason I will not fight him."

Upon hearing this, the general was ashamed that he had tried to kill Xiangru and called upon the prime minister in order to express his regret. The two of them then cooperated in the task of governing the country.

After relating this story, Dōgen Zenji said, "Xiangru forgot himself and carried out the Way. Now, in maintaining the Buddha-way, we should have the same attitude. It is better to die for the Way than to live without it."

It seems Dōgen Zenji studied many stories such as this one in the Chinese classics before he became a monk at the age thirteen. In *Shobogenzo Zuimonki* he often used this kind of story from ancient China to illustrate a point from the Dharma. In this story, Dōgen showed how Xiangru's thoughtful words spoken to his retainers changed the general's heart and fostered peace in the country.

We should know that loving speech arises from
a loving mind, and that the seed of a loving mind is

a compassionate heart. We should study how loving speech has the power to transform the world. It's not merely praising someone's ability.

In *Gakudo-Yojinshu* (*Points to Watch in Practicing the Way*), Dōgen Zenji admonishes us to practice the way when truth comes to us in the form of words:

> Honest advice given by a loyal minister often has the power to change the emperor's will. There are none who fail to change their minds when the Buddhas and ancestors offer a single word.

The phrase translated as "power to change the emperor's will" and "power to transform the world" is the same Chinese expression, *kaiten-no-chikara* (回天の力). The literal translation of this expression is "power to turn over heaven." The word *ten* (heaven) can mean "the world under heaven" and it can refer to the Chinese emperor, who was called the "son of heaven." In ancient China, a change in the emperor's will could change the entire world since the emperor had absolute power.

This expression, "power to change the emperor's will," came from another Chinese story. During the reign of Taizong in the Tang dynasty, the emperor wanted to have the palace repaired. Zhang Xuansu advised him not to do so, and the emperor accepted his advice. Wei Zheng, another minister, admired Xuansu and said, "When Mr. Zhang discusses matters of state, his words have the power to change the emperor's will."

Our minds are like the emperor's will. We think we have absolute power to make decisions, at least in those decisions that regard our own lives. But in reality, we cling to our own opinions and judgments. However, if we listen to the words of the Dharma with an open mind, our minds become changed and therefore our world becomes changed. Although it can be difficult, it is part of our bodhisattva work to try to offer kind words as Dharma, words that can have the power to transform people's lives.

BENEFICIAL ACTION
Transformation of human consciousness

> Beneficial action is simply creating skillful means to benefit living beings, whether they are noble or humble. For example, we care for the near and distant future of others, and use skillful means to benefit them. We should take pity on a cornered tortoise and care for a sick sparrow. When we see this tortoise or sparrow, we try to help them without expecting any reward. We are motivated solely by beneficial action itself.

Dana is the foundation of all of the Four Embracing Actions. Loving speech is an offering that uses language, and beneficial action is a form of offering using body and mind. Identity action is a method we can use to make our offerings acceptable to others.

Bird and Tortoise
In this section Dōgen introduces two examples of beneficial actions that are directed towards small living beings. He shows that these helping activities arise solely from a compassionate heart rather than a calculating mind, emphasizing that a beneficial action should be

performed for its own sake. According to Dōgen, beneficial actions will return to those who perform them without any expectation of reward, yet here is a paradox: when a person performs a beneficial action without expecting any reward, that person receives some benefit in return for that action. However, if a person helps others with some expectation of a reward, such actions essentially become a means of barter, therefore producing no reward. Dōgen says that actions can be either defiled or pure, depending upon the motivation of the person performing them. If a person performs a generous act without any expectation of personal gain, although rewards for the action are not important to that person, the person does receive a reward. If the person has even the slightest expectation of any reward, however, the action is defiled and the person definitely is not rewarded. What strange logic!

Kongyu (Jp. Koyu), who lived in Jin (Shin) Dynasty China, met a person on the road who was carrying a basket on his shoulder that contained a captured tortoise. Kongyu, seeing that the poor tortoise was suffering, aroused a compassionate heart and gave the person some money for the tortoise. When Kongyu released it to the river, the tortoise turned its head to the left to look back at Kongyu in a gesture of gratitude as it headed to its home. Many years later, Kongyu became the governor of the region in which he released the tortoise. As was the custom, shortly after being installed to the position, Kongyu designed the governor's official stamp. The stamp was to bear the head of a tortoise, but the finished image inexplicably showed the tortoise with its head turned to the left. Kongyu had the stamp remade three times, but each time the head of the tortoise was turned in the same way. Then he remembered that the tortoise he released many years before had looked back to him three times, turning its head to the left. He realized that he had become governor as a result of the tortoise's aid and protection.

Another story about Yangbao (Yoho) of the Later Han Dynasty (Gokan) contains a similar theme. When he was nine years old, Yangbao found a sick sparrow on the ground that was being attacked by ants. Yangbao took the bird home, and after nursing it back to health he released it. Later when Yangbao was an adult, the sparrow came to him in a dream. It appeared to him in the form of a yellow-robed boy offering four white rings. According to the story, Yangbao's family enjoyed prosperity for four generations as a result of the sparrow's protection.

In order to present the Buddhist teaching of beneficial action more understandably to Japanese people, Dōgen Zenji used such stories from Chinese classic literature because they were well known among the educated people of his day. There are many such tales to be found in Chinese as well as Japanese classic story collections.

From the Perspective of the Tortoise and the Sparrow

As I indicated when I wrote about offering, throughout my life my position has been more similar to the tortoise's and the sparrow's in these stories than the position of the people who helped them. Since I became a monk as a young university student and then entered directly into a monastic life at Antaiji, for much of my life I have had no particular skill or knowledge with which to help others. My knowledge of Buddhism and experience of zazen weren't useful in helping others until I became a mature practitioner many years later. I had no money to offer to needy people either; in fact, I was often in need of help myself.

When I was young I traveled quite a lot, crossing the USA twice. Soon after I first came to this country in 1975, I made a cross-country car trip with several friends. After driving from San Francisco to Los Angeles, we made our way across the USA by way of the South and then headed north to Massachusetts. During my second cross-country trip, I traveled from San Francisco to Boston by bus. During both of those trips I never had to stay at a hotel. I always stayed with someone who offered food and shelter to "the traveling monk with no money." I also did a lot of hitchhiking in the 70s.

In Japan, for many years I lived on the offerings I received from *takuhatsu*. Thousands of people gave support to me without expecting anything in return. They didn't even know who I was or what I was doing; they made offerings simply because I was wearing Buddhist robes. Since I could not offer anything in return that was directly helpful to those people, I have been trying to be gentle and kind to others in order to pay back some tiny part of my debt to the many people who helped me.

While I was living in Kyoto I did *takuhatsu* in Kobe several times a year. At that time I was giving on-going lectures on the *Shobogenzo* and *Heart Sutra* to a Catholic study group. Members of that group transcribed the *Heart Sutra* lectures and made a book from that material after I revised it. The book was completed in 1995, the year an earthquake in Kobe killed several thousand people. I was in Minneapolis at the time, and I was certain that many of the people who gave me offerings were killed, injured, or otherwise suffering from the loss of family members or posses-sions. For that reason I asked that any money raised from the sale of the book composed of my *Heart Sutra* lectures be offered to help needy people in Kobe. The Catholic study group members donated the money through their church in Kobe, and although the amount of money donated must have been small, I nonetheless was very happy that I could make even a tiny offering to the people in Kobe.

Friends and Enemies

> An ignorant person may think that if we benefit others too much, our own benefit will be excluded. This is not the case. Beneficial action is the whole of dharma; it benefits both self and others widely.

When we vow to adopt beneficial action as a bodhisattva practice, we must try to do what is best for all living beings without discriminating between noble or humble, rich or poor, friends or enemies.

The Buddha said in *Dhammapada,* "Through hatred, hatreds are never appeased; through non-hatred are hatreds always appeased—and this is a law eternal."

Jesus Christ said, "You have heard that it was said, 'You shall love your neighbor and hate your enemy.' But I say to you, love your enemies and pray for those who persecute you, so that you may be children of your father in heaven; for he makes his sun rise on the evil and on the good, and sends rain on the righteous and on the unrighteous. For if you love those who love you, what reward do you have?"[17]

Jesus said that we should love our enemies; to love families, relatives, and friends is a matter of course. In Buddhism, our ability to love our enemies determines our ability to be bodhisattvas.

Buddha's teaching and Christ's teaching are the same on this point. Can we carry out these teachings? Of course it's usually very difficult for us to do so. In fact, if we can love someone, that person is not our enemy; people become our enemies because we cannot love them, so each of us must transform our consciousness and go beyond discriminations between friends and enemies. Buddha and Christ were people who could make that transformation. There have been other people who could do so as well, such as India's Mahatma Gandhi. Dōgen Zenji taught in the *Shishobo* that we should act in accordance with what is best for the sake of all beings. To do this, we must act without concern for whether people are noble or humble, whether they're people we love or strangers, or even whether they are considered to be our friends or our enemies.

Bodhisattva Never-Disparaging

In the Lotus Sutra there is a chapter called "Bodhisattva Never-Disparaging." This chapter is a story about a bodhisattva who made prostrations to everyone he met saying, "I will never disparage you because in the future you will attain Buddhahood." Other monks and lay people were arguing about Buddhist teachings, each trying to prove their own understanding was best, but Bodhisattva Never-Disparaging did not study systems of doctrine or meditation; he just walked the streets and made prostrations to whomever he met, saying he would never disparage them because they would someday become Buddhas. Those who were arguing did not like this bodhisattva because he would not choose sides in arguments; he said he respected everyone involved in any argument since all were bodhisattvas. From the perspective of the people arguing and fighting, a person who respected all points of view in their conflicts could not be a friend. Sometimes people even beat or threw stones at Bodhisattva Never-Disparaging, but as long as he lived he did not stop his practice of honoring everyone he met.

According to the story, when he was dying he was able to see the reality of all beings, even though he had never studied any system of Buddhist teachings. He accepted, upheld, and expounded this reality and attained eternal life. People who had despised him became his followers.

Human History

Throughout actual human history, things have been difficult for people who have taught us to go beyond discriminations between friends and enemies and to love all beings. Shakyamuni Buddha could not keep his clan from being conquered by the strong neighboring kingdom of Kosala. Christ was crucified. Gandhi was assassinated. Dōgen had to leave the capital of Japan to live deep in the mountains.

Buddhist teachings emphasize seeing all things equally, without greed, anger/hatred, and ignorance. Buddha's wisdom, prajna, is the wisdom beyond discrimination that sees the emptiness and equality of all things. To see this reality is the goal of all the various styles of Buddhist meditation. In our meditation practice we can become one with prajna, but it is very difficult to realize such wisdom in our daily lives.

Shortly after September 11th in 2001, I had a chance to read a Japanese scholar's article about the person who assassinated Mahatma Gandhi. According to the author, the person was a Hindu fundamentalist who thought he had good reason to kill Gandhi. In the assassin's mind, if his family members were attacked and killed, justice demanded that he carry out revenge, but Gandhi forbade Hindu people to carry out such revenge, asking them to forgive their enemies. Because this was contrary to the assassin's concept of justice, he killed Gandhi.

When the American government responded to the 9–11 tragedy with military action, I remembered this article. When

I learned that the majority of American people supported the government's decision to use military force in seeking revenge, I felt they were supporting the same concept of justice held by Gandhi's assassin. Many of my American Buddhist friends were against the war. In San Francisco, where I lived at that time, thousands of people demonstrated against the war and some of them were arrested. I admired them but they were in the minority; on almost every block of each street we saw a sign saying, "God bless America." I wondered if that God was the same God of Jesus Christ, the God whom Jesus taught wishes us to love our enemies. To me, the signs saying "God bless America" seemed to refer to a guardian god of the nation, a type of god that almost all countries have. Of course, Japanese Buddhists did something similar during World War II. During that time, Buddhism was used for nationalist means in persuading young people to fight for Japan in the war.

Transformation

How can we transform our consciousness and go beyond this sense of separation from other human beings? This is an especially important question at this time in human history. As a result of developments in science, technology, transportation and communication, the world of human beings has become one community. People from different racial, religious, and cultural backgrounds must communicate and interact with each other. Unless we find some common ground, one on which people can live knowing they are connected to each other, human beings will not be able to live together peacefully.

Many people from many spiritual traditions have put forth much effort in this area. In my case, I have been practicing zazen and sharing Buddhist teachings with American people for many years. Even though my activity is limited, my hope is that I can contribute at least a small drop into this stream of transformation that aims to change the consciousness of human beings.

I am from Japan, and for me the USA has been a special country. Japan and the USA are the only two countries I have lived in. I was born three years after World War II ended, and in my parents' time Japan and the USA were enemies. The first time I ever heard anything about the USA was when I was probably four or five years old. It was raining and my mother and some neighborhood women were idly talking beneath the eaves of a house. I was running around in the rain and one of the women said to me, "Don't run around in the rain. You might lose your hair." That was near the time the US government had performed a nuclear experiment in the Bikini Islands. A Japanese fishing boat, the *Daigo Fukuryumaru,* was exposed to nuclear radiation that eventually killed one of the boat's crewmembers and made many others sick. In Japan the ash from nuclear weapons was called *shi-no-hai* (ash of death). It was probably on that occasion, the time the woman said, "You might lose your hair," that I first heard that Japan had fought and lost a war against the USA. My family had been merchants in Osaka for several generations, but in just one night in March of 1945 we lost all of our family wealth during a US Air Force bombing. I also heard that my uncle was killed during the war and that his wife had died of TB (my parents raised one of my uncle's orphaned children as part of our family). After hearing these things, I had some negative feelings about the USA. I did not see US soldiers in Japan on many occasions, but when I did see them, I was afraid.

When I entered elementary school, our principal told us that Japan had a very difficult time after losing the war. People were hungry, but they were saved from starvation by food and other aid offered by the USA. He also said that we needed to study and work hard to restore the prosperity we had before the war. I was taught that the USA had brought democracy to Japan and that all good things such as electronics, science, technology, movies, and music came from the USA. The USA was the great teacher of democracy and of scientific and technological civilization; it seemed like a paradise of materialistic culture. So, my view of the USA became confused. Later I also learned that from the end of the 19th century until the end of World War II, Japan did terrible things to other Asian countries such as Korea and China. As I studied history, my fear turned to sadness.

When I became a teenager, my view of the USA took another twist. During the Vietnam War, some Japanese newspapers presented American military action as imperialist activity that was close to being the enemy of humanity. Newspaper cartoons depicted President Johnson's face as the face of a demon.

When I began practicing at Antaiji in the late 60s, I met some Americans from my own generation. Those people, who were so-called "hippies;" were the first American people I had actually met. I found that many of them were not so different from me; they were just ordinary human beings. They had the same questions I had and were trying to find the answers to those questions. In fact, very good friendships, ones that continue to this day, developed between some of those Americans and me.

In 1975, I went to Massachusetts to live and to create a small Zen community. There I again found that American people are not so different from Japanese people. Some were extremely kind and friendly and some were not so kind. Of course, I found many cultural differences between Japanese and American people, but overall I saw that we are all simply human beings who must live through many different conditions in this life; sometimes those conditions are happy and sometimes they are not so happy.

I found that the views I held in Japan before I had been in the USA reflected only partial truths; my views of this country and its people did not contain a complete perspective. My knowledge, understanding, and experiences of the USA and its people are still limited because I have been living only in Buddhist communities since I have been here. Seeing that my views were limited and distorted enabled me to let go of my preconceptions of other nations. In addition to studying our own history and culture and the cultures of other countries, living and working with people from other countries is the best way to go beyond our stereotypes.

Thirty years have passed since I went to Massachusetts, and I now practice in a small Zen Buddhist sangha with Americans as well as people from other countries. My zazen practice and study of Buddhist teachings have helped me in my effort to go beyond my fixed views of others, views that are a product of my limited karmic consciousness. This small broadening of my own perspective is a source of hope for me. My hope is that we will make a transformation of consciousness and let go of our prejudices against those who differ from us according to national origin, race, religion, and other characteristics.

In an ancient era, a man, who tied up his hair three times while he took a bath and who stopped eating three times in the space of one meal, solely intended to benefit others. He never withheld truths from people of other countries.

This example is from the Chinese classic *Shiji* (Jp. *Shiki*). When the lord Zhougong (Shuko) sent his son to govern the country of Lu (Ro), his son came to say farewell. At that time Zhougong admonished him saying, "I am a son of King Wen (Bun), the younger brother of King Wu (Bu), and the uncle of King Cheng (Jo), and I therefore am not a person of humble birth. Yet I tied up my hair three times while bathing and stopped eating three times in the space of one meal in order to meet with gentlemen [who wished to offer me their opinions in person]. I am fearful that we will lose wise people in this country; when you arrive in the country of Lu, be careful not to disparage its people even though you will be the governor."

Zhougong sent his son to a neighboring country that was a dependent of his own more powerful country. He told his son that even though his son would be governor, he should not miss any opportunity to meet and listen to any wise people of Lu.

> Therefore, we should equally benefit friends and foes alike; we should benefit self and others alike. Because beneficial actions never regress, if we attain such a mind we can perform beneficial action even for grass, trees, wind, and water. We should strive solely to help ignorant beings.

As I mentioned, *Shishobo* was written two months before Dōgen Zenji and his assembly abruptly moved from the then capital city of Kyoto into the deeply remote mountains of Echizen. He was likely not living in a peaceful environment when he wrote of the four embracing actions of bodhisattva practice. At this time, the Japanese Buddhist establishment was trying to oppress Dōgen's newly introduced Chinese style of Zen Buddhism. It was in this condition of great conflict that Dōgen Zenji wrote, "Therefore, we should equally benefit friends and foes alike; we should benefit self and others alike." One of the reasons Dōgen moved from Kyoto was to avoid conflict with the established religious institution. When we study the background of *Shishobo,* we can more clearly understand the significance of these words of Dōgen: "Because beneficial actions never regress, if we attain such a mind we can perform Beneficial Action even for grass, trees, wind, and water. We should strive solely to help ignorant beings." This was Dōgen's faith and wish. He did not think it meaningful to fight against the religious establishment; rather, he practiced the bodhisattva vow to help all beings that suffer within the cycle of transmigration in samsara. His enemies, the Tendai monks who held religious and political power, were not excluded from his vow.

IDENTITY ACTION
Benefiting self and others simultaneously

Identity action means to be not different—neither different from self nor from others. For example, it is like the way that, in the human world, the Tathagata identifies himself with human beings. Because he identifies himself in the human world, we know that he must be the same in the other worlds. When we realize identity-action, self and others are one suchness. Harps, poems, and wine make friends with people, with heavenly beings, and with spirits. People befriend harps, poems and wine. There is a principle that harps, poems, and wine befriend harps, poems, and wine; that people make friends with people; that heavenly beings befriend heavenly beings, and that spirits befriend spirits. This is how we study identity action.

As we saw in the first section, "identity-action" is an English translation of the Chinese expression *doji* (同事), which is in turn a translation of the Sanskrit word *samanarthata-sangraha* (Pali, *samanattata-samgaha*). *Samana* means "identical," "same," "equal," or "common." *Artha* in Sanskrit means "business," "purpose," "meaning," or "benefit," as in the Sanskrit word *arthacariya* (beneficial action), the third of the Four Embracing Actions. The compound word *samanartha* can be translated as "sharing the same purpose or goal."

Thus *samanarthata* means "an action taken for the common benefit" or "an action that benefits both those who act and those receiving the action." In Gudo Nishijima's and Thomas Cleary's translation of *Shobogenzo Shishobo*, *samanarthata* is translated as "cooperation," and in *Eihei Dōgen: Mystical Realist*, Hee-Jin Kim translates it as "identity with others." Following the example of Tanahashi's translations in *Moon in a Dewdrop*, my colleagues and I use "identity action" in our translations because we think it expresses a deeper reality that gives people the ability to cooperate. Identity action is a practice for benefiting both self and others simultaneously, and this is possible because all of us are interconnected with all beings within True Reality. The Four Embracing Actions (offering, loving speech, beneficial action, and identity action) are practices that are based on awakening to the True Reality that exists before we conceptually separate reality into subject and object. Dōgen Zenji's statement,

"Beneficial-action is the whole of Dharma; it benefits both self and others widely," expresses an idea that he also applied to identity action. Here he teaches that bodhisattva practice includes making an effort to practice in a way that simultaneously benefits both self and others. Practicing the Four Embracing Actions is not simply a method to guide others; it also helps us to awaken and mature. Through the practice of sincere offering, we become more generous; through the practice of loving speech, we cultivate our own compassion. As Dōgen said, beneficial action benefits both self and other simultaneously, and as we will see in the following discussion, identity action shows us how and why this benefit happens.

In the same way that each of the five fingers of a hand have different names, shapes, and functions, each one of us has our own uniqueness, beauty and dignity that can never be exchanged with any other person. We actually are different from others, so what did Dōgen mean when he wrote in the first sentence of this section, "Identity action means to be not different—neither different from self nor from others"? Perhaps it's more clear and understandable to say "not to be separate" rather than "not to be different" in such a statement. Here Dōgen is saying that as bodhisattvas, we strive to carry out identity action that benefits both self and others. Bodhisattva practice is not self-sacrifice, yet we can't sacrifice others for the sake of our own personal benefit either. To practice as bodhisattvas means we must find the best way to benefit both self and others.

For example, it is like the way that, in the human world, the Tathagata identifies himself with human beings. Because he identifies himself in the human world, we know that he must be the same in the other worlds.

The Tathagata of the Dharmakaya has no particular form; it's beyond all form. However, in the human world the formless Dharmakaya of the Tathagata appears as the form of a human being. All statues and paintings of the Tathagata, such as Shakyamuni, Amitaba, and Mahavairocana, take the form of a human being within this human world.

When Dōgen Zenji wrote the above sentences, he was probably thinking of a Tendai Buddhist teaching called *jukkai-gogu* (十界互具) which states that all of the ten realms of existence include all of the other nine realms. The ten realms include the realms of hell dwellers, hungry ghosts, animals, asuras (fighting spirits), human beings, heavenly beings, sravakas, pratyekabuddhas, bodhisattvas, and buddhas. The first six of these realms are usually referred to as the six realms of samsara, and the other four are named after categories of spiritual practitioners within the Buddhist tradition. Tientai Chiyi (Japanese pronunciation: Tendai Chigi), the great master who established the system of Tendai teachings, said that each of these ten realms contain all of the other nine realms. For example, the hell realm includes the realms of hungry ghosts, animals, asuras, etc., as well as the realm of buddhas. Therefore, even in the hell realm one may experience the awakening of Buddha or find the compassion of Buddha. This also means that even within the buddha realm the hell realm exists, and this is the reason a buddha is able to help all beings, even those dwelling in hell. Buddhas appear not only in our human realms but also in all other realms (the original Chinese words for "world" and "realm" are identical). When a buddha appears in the human realm, that buddha therefore takes the form of a human being, and when a buddha appears in the animal realm, that buddha may therefore take an animal form. This is an example of an identity action that a buddha performs for the sake of helping all beings.

Tientai Chiyi said that since all ten realms contain all other realms, there are actually one hundred realms (10x10=100). We find a similar way of thinking in the final sentence of Dōgen Zenji's *Shobogenzo Shishobo:* "Because each of these four embracing dharmas include all the four embracing dharmas, there are sixteen embracing dharmas."

> When we realize identity action, self and others are one suchness.

In this sentence it is clear that Dōgen Zenji is saying that through our practice of identity action, the basic reality of the network of interdependent origination manifests. In other words, no true reality exists for us if we do not actually practice identity action; we actualize true reality within our practice. This is another way of expressing Dōgen Zenji's teaching, "practice and verification are one."

> Harps, poems, and wine make friends with people, with heavenly beings, and with spirits. People befriend harps, poems and wine. There is a principle that harps, poems, and wine befriend harps, poems, and wine; that people make friends with people; that heavenly beings befriend heavenly beings, and that spirits befriend spirits. This is how we study identity action.

I think it is true even today that "harps, poems, and wine make friends." Dōgen Zenji takes these examples from Chinese classic literature. If melodious music is played and suitable, harmonious poetry is recited at a party where wine is being served, people attending really will become friends without separation. This phenomenon is like the performance of a symphony. Each musical instrument has a different shape, sound, and function, but a collection of instruments played together in a certain way will create one body of harmonious music. Awakening to the reality of non-separation allows us to practice identity action, and identity action creates the music of interdependent origination. Realizing that all beings are players in this symphony allows us to study and understand identity action in our lives. Identity action is not simply some technique used to establish a good social relationship, and I don't think that the word "cooperation" adequately expresses Dōgen Zenji's insight concerning this teaching. For this reason we decided to use the term "identity action" in our translation, even though it is not a common English expression.

> For example, "action" means form, dignity and attitude. After letting others identify with our "self," there may be a principle of letting our "self" identify with others. Relations between self and others vary infinitely depending on time and condition.

This is an explanation of *ji* (事, action). To actualize the reality of the network of interdependent origination, a person must use certain forms in practicing with his or her whole body and mind. A form of action such as this that is inspired by awakening, wisdom, and compassion has dignity. If we take this attitude as we deal with our own lives and interact with others, Buddha's awakening is manifested.

> After letting others identify with our "self," there may be a principle of letting our "self" identify with others.

There are also many other ways to practice with this aspect of identity action. We may first identify with others and then let others identify with us, for example, and this is just one of many possible variations.

In the Lotus Sutra, for example, there is a story of a son who ran away from home, leaving his father. The son lived in various other countries for a long time, and the older he grew, the needier he became. By chance he happened upon his father's house, and although the father recognized the poor, destitute son, the son did not recognize his father. When the son ran away in fear after seeing the wealth and dignity of his father, the father sent servants to hire his son as a laborer, and they put him to work cleaning the wealthy man's home. While the son was doing his job, the rich father removed his strings of jewels and ornaments, took off his fine clothing, and put on a coarse, torn, dirty garment. Then he smeared his body with dust, took a dustpan in his right hand, and with an intimidating voice and countenance said to the laborers: "Get on with your work, don't be lazy!" The father used this and other devices to gain more and more contact with his son, and he gradually trained his son to be a mature and suitable heir to his fortune. This story is an example of how, in practicing identity-action, it is possible to first identify with others and to then allow others to identify with us. In the story, the rich father first identified compassionately with his son and then worked with him gradually. Eventually the son came to identify with his wealthy benefactor and accepted him as his father.

There are numberless variations of interactions between teachers and students, parents and children, doctors and patients, etc. Sometimes we are like the destitute son in the story, and sometimes we take a role like the wealthy father. Although the relationship between self and others differs in every situation, we must find some way to identify with others and permit others to identify with us in each case. This becomes possible when we awaken to the common ground of interconnectedness where we live together with all beings.

Guanzi says, "The ocean does not refuse water; therefore it is able to achieve its vastness. Mountains do not refuse earth; therefore they are able to become tall. Wise rulers do not weary of people, therefore they form a large nation."

That the ocean does not refuse water is identity action. We should also know that the virtue of water does not refuse the ocean. This is why water is able to form an ocean, and earth is able to form mountains. We should know in ourselves that because the ocean does not refuse to be the ocean, it can be the ocean and achieve greatness. Because mountains do not refuse to be the mountains, they can be mountains and reach great height. Because wise rulers do not weary of their people, they attract many people. "Many people" means a nation. "A wise ruler" may mean an emperor. Emperors do not weary of their people. This does not mean that they fail to offer rewards and punishment, but they never tire of their people.

Here Dōgen Zenji quotes from a Chinese classic, *Guanzi* (管子, Jp. *Kanshi*) attributed to Guanzhong (管仲, Jp. Kanchu) who was a minister of Qi (斉, Jp. Sei), a country existing in the Chunqiu Era (春秋, Spring and Autumn; Shunju 722–481 BCE). This book is a collection of essays primarily about politics, economics, military affairs, and education. Before he became a Buddhist monk, Dōgen Zenji probably studied this text as part of a childhood education designed to prepare him to be a politician.

In the above passage the text is discussing the attitude of a good ruler. According to the quote, to become a wise ruler one must accept and embrace all of the nation's people without discrimination. One should do this in the same way that the ocean accepts all kinds of water from different rivers or the way that a mountain does not reject even tiny bits of dirt or small stones.

Every drop of water is a part of the ocean, and all kinds of dirt, mud, soil, sand, stones, and rocks are elements of a mountain. The ocean does not refuse any form of water and the mountain does not reject any form of earth. For this reason, the ocean can be the vast ocean and a mountain can be a great mountain. When a wise ruler embraces all people living in the nation, the country becomes a great country. When Dōgen Zenji speaks of the ocean and mountains in this analogy, he is referring to the entire network of interdependent origination. When he speaks of a drop of water and tiny pieces of dirt and stone, he is referring to individuals within the network in the same way that we speak of knots within Indra's net. In ancient China the emperor was considered to be the nation itself, and all people belonged to the emperor. Here Dōgen Zenji considers identity action in terms of the relationship between the self and the myriad dharmas. He discusses this relationship in the same way he discusses practice/enlightenment in *Shobogenzo Genjokoan,* teaching that the self is a part of the vast network of the myriad dharmas.

Identity action is practice based upon the realization of this interconnectedness of all things. We can illustrate this interconnectedness by again taking the example of the five fingers of a hand. Each finger has it own unique name, shape, and function, yet all of the fingers are connected in functioning as part of a single hand. Without its connection with the other fingers of the hand, a finger cannot properly function and exist as a finger. In this example, "identity" refers to the unity of the fingers that manifests as one hand. This does not mean that each finger is alike. All of the fingers of a hand are different, but each different finger can exist only in interconnectedness with the other fingers that function as part of the hand. There is no hand that exists outside of the five fingers. The hand and the five fingers are exactly the same thing, so when we touch any single finger, we automatically touch the entire hand. This is the same as saying that when we touch one knot of Indra's net we indeed touch the entirety of the whole net. Our attitude toward our lives and our attitude toward all other beings should therefore be the same as our attitude would be toward a wise ruler. We can then wholeheartedly play our own designated role within the orchestra and at the same time keep sight of the conductor who has responsibility for the entire symphony. This is Dōgen Zenji's insight concerning identity action.

Dōgen Zenji also said that because of their virtue, water also embraces the ocean, earth embraces the mountain, and subjects embrace their ruler. Without the virtue of each drop of water, there can be no ocean, and without the virtue of sand and stones, the mountain cannot exist. The greatness of the ocean and mountain is the greatness of each drop of water and each bit of sand and stone. In other words, each tiny drop of water is as vast as the ocean because without the drops, there is no ocean. In the same way, each finger is the entirety of the whole hand it belongs to. This is the wondrous way that all beings exist together within the network of interdependent origination.

> We should know in ourselves that because the ocean does not refuse to be the ocean, it can be the ocean and achieves greatness. Because mountains do not refuse to be the mountains, they can be mountains and reach great heights.

This is the *jijuyuzanmai* (samadhi of self accepting and utilizing) of the ocean and the mountain. The ocean accepts being the ocean. The mountain accepts being the mountain. The ocean allows all water to be within it and the mountain allows all earth to be part of it. All of us are also the ocean, mountain, and wise ruler, and we are simultaneously a drop of water, a speck of dirt, and an individual person.

> Because wise rulers do not weary of their people, they attract many people. "Many people" means a nation. "A wise ruler" may mean an emperor. Emperors do not weary of their people. This does not mean that they fail to offer rewards and punishments, but they never tire of their people.

It would be unrealistic to say that we can't have expectations of reward or punishment for our efforts and activities, because we couldn't otherwise find the motivation to do anything. Sometimes our expectations are fulfilled and we feel happy and satisfied, and sometimes we fail and we feel terrible, as if we were being punished in hell. Yet throughout all of these conditions, just as the wise ruler does not weary of his people, bodhisattvas do not tire of making the effort to live and walk together with all beings.

> In ancient times, when people were gentle and honest, there were no rewards and no punishments in the country. The idea of reward and punishment in those days was different. Even these days, there must be some people who seek the Way with no expectation of reward. This is beyond the thought of ignorant people.

In ancient China, people viewed human history differently than we do in modern times. Chinese people thought that the quality of the world and its people was progressively declining with time. They thought that ancient people before them were superior to the people inhabiting the Earth in their own day. This is the opposite of what I was taught during my education. I was taught that the world is better than it was in ancient times because of improvements developed through scientific knowledge and technological advances. I was told that we still have many difficulties and problems because we are still in the process of development, but once human civilization is fully developed, we will be released from all difficulty. Today there are probably not many people that are still naïve enough to agree with this. We have begun believe that technological development and economic growth are injuring nature and the network of interdependent origination; in other words, we have begun to think we have been injuring ourselves during the course of our "progress." Yet what I learned as a child contrasts sharply with the ancient Chinese belief that society had been much more peaceful and harmonious in former times. Ancient Chinese people thought that people in prior times engaged only in wholesome activity without expectation of reward, and they believed their predecessors refrained from all unwholesome activities even though there was no social penalty for undesirable behavior.

> Even these days, there must be some people who seek the Way with no expectation of reward. This is beyond the thought of ignorant people.

Here Dōgen Zenji says that even in his own day there must have been some eminent people who engaged in wholesome activity without expectation of reward. Such people would refrain from unwholesome things not because of fear of punishment, but because they were practicing in accordance with reality. Such people are called bodhisattvas, according to Mahayana Buddhism. Bodhisattvas do not avoid unwholesome activity out of fear of punishment and they do not engage in wholesome activity out of expectation. They do so because their behavior is in itself awakening to the true reality of interdependent origination.

In *Eihei Shingi* (*Pure Standards for Eiheiji*), Dōgen Zenji gives concrete instructions on how to practice in a Zen community with this attitude of awakening. For example, in *Tenzo-kyokun* (*Instruction for the Cook*) he wrote the following passage:

As I observed the people who were devoting themselves for a year to the jobs of temple administrators or heads of monastic departments in the various temples of Song China, each of them maintained the three essential attitudes of an abbot whenever they performed their jobs, encouraging themselves to strive at their tasks. Benefit others, which simultaneously gives abundant benefit to the self. Make the temple thrive and renew its high standards. Aspire to stand shoulder to shoulder and respectfully follow in the heels of our predecessors. Clearly know that there are fools who treat themselves as indifferently as others, and there are honorable people who consider others as themselves.

Dōgen Zenji vowed to create a community of practitioners that lived with this boundless attitude. This vision of the practice community came from the traditional Buddhist teachings of the Four Embracing Actions. Is such an attitude still possible in this modern society? Dōgen Zenji said that even "these days" there must be such people who hold this attitude, although this attitude was "beyond the thought" of ignorant people. Was he successful in fulfilling his vow? Was his vision fully actualized? "These days" for Dōgen Zenji is now eight hundred years ago for us, and we are living in an age that is a very different from his world. How can we apply this teaching to our own lives in this time?

Because wise rulers have clear minds, they do not weary of their people. Although people always desire to form a nation and to find a wise ruler, few of them fully understand why a wise ruler is wise. Therefore, they are glad simply to be embraced by

the wise ruler. They don't realize that they themselves are embracing a wise ruler. Thus the principle
of identity action exists both in the wise ruler and
ignorant people. This is why identity action is the
practice and the vow of a bodhisattva. We should
simply face all beings with a gentle expression.

We are like people who, though they don't know what a nation
truly is and what a wise ruler truly is, nonetheless wish to form
a nation and find a wise ruler. Other than the network of ordinary
people like ourselves, there is no nation and there is no wise ruler,
yet we must indeed find a way to embrace a nation and embrace
a wise ruler. In other words, if none of us does anything to embrace
the entire network of interdependent origination, there is no such
network for us. The network's existence for us depends entirely upon
our actions, and this is the guiding principle of bodhisattva practice.

As the conclusion to this piece Dōgen Zenji urges us to simply
face all beings with a gentle expression. We can do this without any
special training, wealth or status, yet this is a most difficult practice
that we must practice endlessly.

Because each of these Four Embracing Actions
includes all the Four Embracing Actions, there are
sixteen embracing actions. These Four Embracing
Actions all embrace each other; these are not four
separate items.

Written on the 5th day of the 5th lunar month in the
4th year of Ninji (1243) By Monk Dōgen who went to
Song China and transmitted the Dharma

Shohaku Okumura, founder and abbot of Sanshin Zen Community, was born in Osaka, Japan, in 1948. In 1970, he was ordained by the late Kosho Uchiyama Roshi, one of the foremost Zen masters of the twentieth-century. He received Dharma transmission from his teacher in 1975 and, shortly after, became one of the founding members of Pioneer Valley Zendo in Massachusetts. He returned to Japan in 1981 and began translating the works of Dogen Zenji, Uchiyama Roshi and other Soto masters from Japanese into English. In 1993, he moved back to the United States with his wife, Yuko, and their two children. He has previously served as teacher at the Kyoto Soto Zen Center in Japan and at the Minnesota Zen Meditation Center in Minneapolis, and was Director of the Soto Zen International Center in San Francisco for thirteen years.

Today, Okumura Roshi is recognized for his unique perspective on the life and teachings of Dogen Zenji derived from his experience as both practitioner and translator, and as a teacher in both Japanese and Western practice communities. He gives frequent lectures on the Shobogenzo and other foundational texts; transcriptions have appeared in Buddhadharma: The Practitioner's Quarterly, Dharma Eye, and Buddhism Now. He has also written or contributed to a number of books; the complete publication list is available from the Dogen Institute.

GIVING

Bäume und Menschen

Kyoku Lutz

Unser Praxiszentrum Frühlingsmond Zendo liegt in direkter Laufnähe zum Stadtwald Hannovers, der *Eilenriede*. Die *Eilenriede* ist ein großer, überwiegend naturbelassener Buchenwald. Auf einer grasbewachsenen Lichtung dieses Waldes sitzt ein Teil unserer Praktizierenden regelmäßig sonntagvormittags Zazen, das Gesicht dem Waldrand zugewandt, einen Meter von den ersten Bäumen entfernt. Der Stadtwald und seine Lichtungen werden von zahlreichen Spaziergängern, Radfahrern, Yogagruppen und spielenden Kindern genutzt. Es ist kein einsames Sitzen auf dieser Lichtung; gleichzeitig wird unser Tun vollständig respektiert und erfährt keine Störung. Die letzten Jahre der Corona-Pandemie hatten es zudem mit sich gebracht, dass angesichts des damals hier in Deutschland herrschenden Pandemie-Lockdowns dieses Zazen im Freien die einzige Möglichkeit war, Zazentreffen in physischer Präsenz abzuhalten.

Die Praxis unter freiem Himmel hat ihre Eigenheiten. Bei denen, die sich darauf einlassen können auch außerhalb eingrenzender, vor Blicken bewahrender Mauern Zazen zu sitzen, vermag die Praxis das Erleben eines Koexistierens mit allen Wesen zu fördern. Wir sitzen als Teil des grenzenlosen Lebensraums, unbehaust, direkt Wind und Wetter ausgesetzt. Die Lebensäußerungen von Pflanzen und großen und kleinen Tieren sind unmittelbar gegenwärtig; die Blicke der anderen, friedlich die Waldwiese Nutzenden streifen uns beim Anordnen und Einsammeln unserer Sitzutensilien. Ohne mit all diesen Lebensgeschehnissen aktiv zu interagieren, lassen wir uns nieder und öffnen die Hände des Denkens. Diese Situation lässt erfahren, dass es immer unser Niederlassen auf dem Meditations-kissen ist, das einen Ort zum Praxisort für Zazen werden lässt, und nicht das Errichten und Ausstatten spezieller Räumlichkeiten.

Kurz bevor Hoko die Einladung zum Schreiben eines *Textes zu Shobogenzo: Bodaisatta Shishobo,* auf Deutsch „Die vier Arten des sozialen Handelns eines Bodhisattvas"[1], mailte, fand an einem Sonntagvormittag ein weiteres reguläres Zazen auf der besagten Waldwiese statt. Bei diesem Zazentreffen kam es zu einer Begeben-heit, die mich beim Eintreffen der Mail sofort für einen Text zum Aspekt *GEBEN* entscheiden ließ.

Es war ein herrlicher Morgen im frühen europäischen Herbst. Ich breitete meine wasserfeste Plane aus, ordnete die Sitzmatte und das Sitzkissen darauf an und stellte unsere kleine Glocke auf. Dann hing ich das Banner des *Frühlingsmond Zendo* Hannovers, das unsere Zugehörigkeit signalisiert, an seiner Schnur in die Zweige der Buche, vor der wir immer sitzen. Danach verneigte ich mich vor dem Baum.

Eine Praktizierende, die zum ersten Mal mit auf die Wiese kam, trat neben mich, betrachtete die Buchenzweige, deren sämt-liche Blätter von Insekten völlig zernagt und zerfressen waren, und fragte lächelnd: „Habt ihr keinen schöneren Baum, vor dem ihr sitzen könnt?!"

Sie hatte durchaus recht: Wer diese Buche nach gängigen ästhetischen Maßstäben anschaute und beurteilte, konnte wirklich nur den Kopf schütteln. Diese Buche war von oben bis unten komplett zernagt und zerlöchert. Gerademal soviel Blattgrün war übriggeblieben, dass der Baum überlebte. So gesehen war diese Buche wahrlich keine Zierde des Waldes. Gleichzeitig ließen mich diese leichthin lächelnd geäußerten Worte „Habt ihr keinen schöneren Baum, vor dem ihr sitzen könnt?!" aufhorchen.

Diese jedes Jahr immer wieder aufs Neue zerfressene Buche begleitet unser Wiesenzazen, seit wir dort begonnen haben, Zazen zu sitzen. Sie lässt uns das Banner an ihr aufhängen, spendet Schatten, hält Wind und leichten Regen von uns ab und sorgt für frische Luft. Ihre Blätter haben zahllosen Tierchen als lebensspendende Nahrung gedient. Genau davon legen die immensen Fraßspuren Zeugnis ab. Ungezählte Bucheckern hat sie trotzdem produziert, Bucheckern, die ihrerseits nicht nur für weiteren Buchennachwuchs sorgen, sondern zum Teil auch umgehend weiteren Lebewesen als Nahrung dienen. Da ging und geht überhaupt nichts verloren: Eine Buchecker muss gar keine Buche werden, um ihre Bestimmung zu erfüllen. Die einen Bucheckern werden zu Buchenbäumen, die anderen werden sofort von größeren Tieren gefressen und noch andere verwandeln sich durch kleinste Lebensformen in fruchtbare Walderde. Keine Buchecker geht verloren. Es gibt keinen Bucheckern-Erfolg und kein Bucheckern-Scheitern. Einfach alles hat in Zusammenhang mit dieser Buche seine Bewandtnis. Tief wie eins verwoben mit dem gesamten Geflecht des Waldes ragt sie nicht nur in den Himmel, sie kooperiert über ihre Wurzelanteile auch mit allen unterirdisch existierenden Wesen. Von der obersten Baumkrone bis in die kleinsten Wurzelspitzen fügt sich die Buche ohne Wenn und Aber in das lebendige Miteinander des Waldes ein.

Und trotz ihres Aufgehens im gesamten Funktionieren des Waldes gibt es die einzelnen Buchen in den ihnen ganz eigenen Erscheinungsformen: Buchenbäume mit grauer Rinde, ovalförmigen Blättern und schwerem, hartem Holz, mal mächtig, mal winzig, mal aufrecht, mal schief und verbogen. Und wie für ihre Bucheckern gibt es auch für sie weder Erfolg noch Scheitern. Wenn sie älter werden, ziehen sie sich allmählich zurück. Ihre Kronen lichten sich, Äste brechen und stürzen zu Boden, sie beginnen zu wanken. In ihrem Wandel verschaffen sie mit ihren ausgelichteten Kronen der jungen Buchengeneration das notwendige Licht: Die nächste Generation muss ihre Chance erhalten, nachwachsen zu können. Darüber müssen alte Buchen natürlich nicht nachdenken; die Unterstützung des Nachwachsenden ergibt sich ganz natürlich aus ihrem Sein als Buchen.

Wenn sie dann endgültig fallen und der Länge nach auf dem Waldboden zu liegen kommen, findet ihr Wirken dennoch kein Ende. Auch in ihrem Zerfall fördern sie nahtlos über- wie unterirdisch viele Existenzen. Sie stellen die in ihnen gebundenen Nährstoffe, die ihnen selbst zusammen mit Wasser, Licht und Luft einst bedingungslos gegeben wurden und sie existieren ließen, wieder zur Verfügung. Jedes noch so kleine ihrer Teilchen dient sang- und klanglos dem Wohlergehen des Waldlebens.

Das ist für mich *GEBEN* in seiner reinsten Form: So, wie es unter den jeweiligen Umständen gerade möglich ist, wechselwirkend gebend und empfangend mit allen Mitwesen kooperieren, ohne Gier, Neid und eigennützige Überlegungen. Ohne irgendeinen Gedanken an Scheitern, Erfolg oder sozialen Status funktionieren, leben: einfach, natürlich, absichtslos, ohne Kalkül. Was für verehrungswürdige Vorbilder diese Buchen doch sind!

Und so erwiderte ich auf die lächelnd gestellte Frage „Habt ihr keinen schöneren Baum, vor dem ihr sitzen könnt?!" ebenso lächelnd: „Nein, ganz gewiss nicht!"

Ist diese Art des Existierens von Buchen so außergewöhnlich, dass sie besonders erwähnt werden muss? Selbstverständlich nicht. Alle Lebensformen dieser Erde existieren ohne großes Aufhebens genau auf diese Weise. Das ist völlig normal und nichts Besonderes. Die Welt existiert als unzählige, sich wechselwirkend nährende Wesen und Energien. Sie vollzieht sich quasi als eine Gesamtheit natürlicher Bodhisattvas, die die Begriffe *Bodhisattva* und soziales Handeln weder kennen noch brauchen.

Warum hinterließ uns dann Dōgen Zenji den Text *Shobogenzo: Bodaisatta Shishobo, „Die vier Arten des sozialen Handelns eines Bodhisattvas"*? Das liegt wohl daran, dass es *eine* Lebensform auf dieser Erde gibt, der es sehr schwer fällt, ohne Aufhebens normal und natürlich mit anderen Wesen wechselwirkend zu existieren: Menschen.

Buchen werden von allen möglichen Lebensformen zerfressen und man kann es ihnen leicht von außen ansehen. Menschen werden von Gier, Neid, Hass, Verblendung und den seltsamsten Ideen von Erfolg und Scheitern zerfressen und dies kann man ihnen nicht unbedingt sofort von außen ansehen. Die durch Gier, Neid, Hass und Verblendung entstandenen Fraßspuren manifestieren sich überwiegend den Blicken entzogen in wirren Gedankengängen und irregeleiteten Grübeleien und legen ganz und gar nicht Zeugnis für die Unterstützung anderer Lebensformen ab. Ganz im Gegenteil: Wo diese Geistesgifte nagen, sind alle möglichen Arten von schädlichen, zerstörerischen Verhaltensweisen oftmals nicht weit.

Die Buchen schicken ihr riesiges, feines Wurzelnetzwerk durch den fruchtbaren Waldboden, verbinden sich in wechselseitigem

Austausch mit dem endlosen Netzwerk der Pilze und anderen Lebenwesen und kommunizieren über diese Kanäle mit den Buchen um sie herum. So verschmelzen sie über ihr einzelnes Baumsein hinaus mit ihrem Umfeld und helfen den Kreislauf des gesamten Waldlebens in Gang zu halten.

Das eben häufig auf wirren Fantasien und irregeleiteten persönlichen Annahmen beruhende Verhalten von Menschen hingegen dringt im alltäglichen Leben Stück für Stück wie eine Art außer Rand und Band geratenes geistiges Wurzelwerk in das soziale Umfeld und die weitere Gesellschaft ein. Dort stößt dieses Verhalten vielfach keinen lebensspendenden Kreislauf und konstruktive Kommunikation an, sondern immer wieder aufs Neue nicht enden wollende Spiralen von Unfrieden, Hass und Gewalt. Wenn sich menschliches Leben zu stark auf selbstzentriertem Eigennutz gründet und die Befriedigung der eigenen Interessen und Begierden ständig im Vordergrund steht, werden alle Menschen, Mitwesen und Dinge, die nicht diesen Begierden dienen oder diesen im Weg stehen, zu Hindernissen, die im Falle des Falles auch schon mal radikal beseitigt werden.

Buchen überlegen und planen nicht auf die Art und Weise wie wir Menschen. Wir erwarten deshalb nicht, dass sie sich ihres Tuns und der daraus folgenden Konsequenzen bewusst sind, und wir kommen deshalb auch nicht auf die Idee, sie für irgendetwas belohnen oder bestrafen zu wollen.

Im Umgang mit Menschen hegen wir sehr wohl die Erwartung, dass diese wissen, was sie tun, und dass sie versuchen, sich soweit wie möglich der Konsequenzen ihres Handelns bewusst zu werden. Deshalb sind in den verschiedenen Erziehungssystemen dieser Welt, die ausgeklügelt werden, um menschliches Verhalten in einer jeweils erwünschten Weise zu regulieren, Belohnungen und

Strafen vorgesehen. Man kommt jedoch nicht umhin zur Kenntnis zu nehmen, dass alle bisherigen Bemühungen um die Erziehung und Bildung von Menschen überwiegend *nicht* zu einer friedlich kooperierenden und konstruktiv kommunizierenden Menschengemeinschaft geführt haben.

An dieser Stelle ergibt sich nun ganz von selbst die Antwort auf die Frage, warum Dōgen Zenji es wohl für notwendig hielt, über das Handeln von *Bodhisattvas* zu schreiben und uns diesen Text zu hinterlassen: Menschen müssen nach Kräften erforschen, was sie zerfrisst, warum es sie zerfrisst, wer eigentlich zerfressen wird, welche Konsequenzen das nach sich zieht und wie man aus dieser verfahrenen Situation herauskommt. Denn die meisten Menschen haben das Erleben der Verbindung mit der eigentlich für alle Wesen gleichermaßen geltenden, ganz normalen Wirklichkeit, die also wirklich „nichts Besonderes" ist, verloren.

Gier, Neid, Hass, Verblendung und die uns ankonditionierten Vorstellungen von Erfolg und Scheitern sitzen tief. Sie sind in unserer Leiblichkeit als Motivatoren menschlichen Seelenlebens und physischen Verhaltens real verankert und richten Schaden an. Die nach Belieben zu erweiternde Liste der Schäden ist umfangreich: Stress, Größenwahn, Minderwertigkeitskomplexe, Depressionen, Gewaltfantasien, Suizidgedanken, Essstörungen, psychosomatische Beschwerden jeglicher Couleur, Drogen-, Alkohol- und Medikamentenmissbrauch. Buchen sind von Schäden dieser Art frei.

Aber als Menschen können wir natürlich nicht wie Buchen werden, indem wir unser Gehirn abgeben. Es bleibt uns nichts anderes übrig als herauszufinden, wie wir mit unserem Gehirn und seinen Funktionsweisen leben und wie wir uns wieder einer wahrhaft sozialen, wirklichen Normalität annähern können: weder Buche noch zerfressener, leidender Mensch.

Deshalb lehren uns Dōgen Zenji und die Vor- und Nach-
fahren unserer Tradition *shikantaza, einfach sitzen:* Wir lassen uns
auf dem Sitzkissen nieder, nehmen eine physiologisch korrekte,
aufrechte Zazenhaltung ein und öffnen die Hände des Denkens. Wir
lassen alle fabrizierten Hirngespinste abfallen. Wir manifestieren
das, was auf dem Sitzkissen übrig bleibt, wenn alles engführende,
gierende, neidende, vergleichende, habenwollende, ablehnende
und aktiv mit Sinnesreizen interagierende Denken nicht mehr
aufgegriffen und genährt wird. Dann ereignet sich in durch nichts
begrenzter Weite etwas jenseits von „Buche" und „zerfressenem,
leidendem Mensch". Dann kann ohne Engführung und egozen-
triertes Verdrehen unbewusst und natürlich ein Mitschwingen und
Mitfühlen mit allen Existenzen auftauchen: Bodhisattva-Geist.
Durch ihn erst öffnet sich uns der Weg der Annäherung an die Welt
des absichtslos, wechselwirkend unterstützenden Funktionierens
aller fühlenden und nichtfühlenden Wesen: nichts Besonderes,
sondern die ganz normale Wirklichkeit dieses Universums. Erst dies
legt die tiefe Quelle frei, aus der GEBEN in seiner reinsten Form
hervorsprudelt: ohne Hintergedanken, Erwartungen oder Kalkül.

Dieses *shikantaza, einfach sitzen,* Körper und Geist abfallen
lassen, müssen wir, solange wir dazu in der Lage sind, bis ans Ende
unseres Lebens tun und dürfen dabei keine Anstrengung scheuen:
ganbarimashō! (Jap.), „Lasst uns unser Bestes geben!". Unser
menschliches Gehirn wird solange wir leben nicht damit aufhören,
neue Hirngespinste zu produzieren. Und wir können aufgrund
unserer menschlichen Natur auch nicht einfach damit aufhören,
an diesen Hirngespinsten zu klammern. Sie sind einfach Teil und
Grundlage unseres menschlichen Seins. Da helfen weder exzellente
Bildung noch gute Absichten. Da hilft nur, beharrlich immer wieder
aufs Neue loszulassen. Dieses Loslassen führt in eine Weite jenseits

von „Buche" und „zerfressenem, leidendem Mensch". So ist es paradoxerweise das menschliche Gehirn, das nicht nur die Hirngespinste hervorbringt, sondern auch den Weg eröffnet wie mit ihnen verfahren werden kann.

Für eines der verhängnisvollsten Hirnfabrikate halte ich das Bestreben vieler Menschen, etwas Besonderes darstellen und hervorstechen zu wollen. Mit Tunnelblick wird dabei die Nähe vermeintlich besonderer Menschen gesucht und der Besitz scheinbar besonderer Dinge angestrebt, die die ersehnte, eigene Besonderheit unterstreichen sollen. Buchen können nicht einmal von der Idee träumen, so einen Unfug in Betracht zu ziehen.

„Nichts Besonderes" ist die wahre Kostbarkeit. „Nichts Besonderes" wertzuschätzen, bedeutet zu erkennen, dass uns ganz natürlich die Präsenz und Energie unzähliger Bodhisattvas zu allen Zeiten unterstützen und begleiten. Wir Menschen können nur als Teil des wechselwirkend unterstützenden Funktionierens aller fühlenden und nichtfühlenden Wesen existieren. Wir existieren nicht aus uns selbst heraus, sondern weil dieses universale Funktionieren die Existenz der Erdkugel samt Wasser, Luft, Licht, Nahrung und unzähligen Kleinst- und Großlebewesen - ohne erkennbares Kalkül - ermöglicht. Der Mensch ist aus dieser Gemeinschaft des „nichts Besonderes" nicht herauslösbar.

Die Praxis des GEBENS, gebend und empfangend zu leben, braucht nicht angestrengt bemüht angestrebt zu werden. Es ist im Grunde ein sehr stilles und friedvolles Akzeptieren der Tatsache, ganz natürlich etwas „nichts Besonderes" zu sein. Es bedeutet ohne Wenn und Aber in der Gemeinschaft der unendlich ungezählten Bodhisattvas aufzugehen und sich wie all diese, ohne Hintergedanken nach den je eigenen, bescheidenen Kräften nützlich zu machen. Dieses „nichts Besonderes" ergibt sich nicht aus der

Unterscheidung zwischen „besonders" und „nicht besonders". Es ist einfach Sosein, Soheit.

Man darf sich eine Welt, die Gier, Neid, Hass und Verblendung etwas entgegenzusetzen weiß, durchaus als einen lebenswerteren Ort vorstellen. Ungebremste menschliche Geisteswirren sind wie Vogelkacke, die bei einer Geburtstagsfeier im Freien auf der Geburtstagstorte landet. Vogelkacke ist unabdingbar natürlicher Teil der Szenerie im Freien und dennoch möchte niemand mit ihr in Kontakt kommen, geschweige denn sie aufessen.

Da wir Menschen aber nun einmal so sind wie wir sind und häufig „den Wald vor lauter Bäumen nicht sehen"[2], brauchen wir auf sehr lange Sicht Anleitung und viele Arten von Hilfestellung, um dem Zerfraß durch unsere Geistesverwirrungen, vor dem ausnahmslos niemand gefeit ist, Einhalt zu gebieten. Man steht auf verlorenem Posten, wenn man denkt, dies alleine bewerkstelligen zu können. Um so mehr sollten wir unsere authentischen Vorfahren und Lehrer zu schätzen wissen, die den Buddha-Weg ohne Abweichung offenhalten, uns geduldig *shikantaza* lehren und uns beim Studium authentischer Texte zu *shikantaza,* der Einheit von Praxis und Erwachen, begleiten.

Und wie alle Bäume ganz natürlich eine sich wechselseitig nährende Waldgemeinschaft bilden, die keine Lebensform ausschließt, finden sich alle ernsthaft Praktizierenden ganz natürlich zu sich wechselseitig unterstützenden Gemeinschaften zusammen. Aus diesen Gemeinschaften und ihren Zentren erwächst ein durch den großzügigen, warmherzigen und freudvollen Bodhi-Geist genährtes, geistiges Wurzelwerk, das sich nicht aufhalten lässt. So, wie es Wurzelwerk eben ganz selbstverständlich tut, sprießt es in Form großzügigen, freudvollen und mitfühlenden Verhaltens seitens der Praktizierenden aus den Zentren hinaus. Es verbindet sich mit Familienangehörigen und Freunden, den Nachbarn, dem weiteren sozialen Umfeld und sorgt sich auch um alle nichtmenschlichen Lebensformen. Dann manifestiert sich *dana, GEBEN,* ohne großes Trari und Trara in all unseren Alltagsaktivitäten. Soweit jedenfalls die Theorie. Und nun?!

Einfach sitzen; studieren und lernen; den Alltag wertschätzen.

Ganbarimasho!
Legen wir uns ins Zeug!

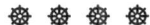

Rev. Kyoku Barbara Lutz, Jahrgang 1957, verheiratet, zwei Kinder, ist eine Dharma-Nachfolgerin von Rev. Hoko Karnegis, Sanshinji, Bloomington, und hat sowohl in Deutschland als auch den USA und Japan praktiziert. Jetzt leitet sie das Praxiszentrum Frühlingsmond Zendo Hannover, im Norden Deutschlands. Sie hat in Erziehungswissenschaften promoviert und verfügt über weitere anerkannte Ausbildungen: Krankengymnastik, Bobath-Therapie, Systemische Therapie und Beratung, Begleitung Schwerstkranker und Sterbender, Vinyasa-Yoga etc.

Trees and Human Beings

Kyoku Lutz

OUR FRÜHLINGSMOND (SPRING MOON) ZENDO PRACTICE CENTER is located within walking distance of Hannover's city forest, the *Eilenriede*. The Eilenriede is a large predominantly natural beech forest. In a grassy clearing by this forest, some of our practitioners regularly sit zazen on Sunday mornings, facing the edge of the forest, a meter away from the first trees. The urban forest and its clearings are used by numerous walkers, cyclists, yoga groups and playing children. It is not a solitary sitting in this clearing; yet at the same time, our actions are fully respected and experience no disturbance. The last years of the coronavirus pandemic had also imposed a limitation such that, in view of the pandemic lockdown prevailing here in Germany at that time, this outdoor zazen was the only possibility for holding in-person zazen gatherings.

Open-air practice has its own peculiarities. For those who are able to sit zazen outside of the enclosing walls that usually protect us from view, the practice can foster the experience of coexistence with all beings. We sit as part of the boundless habitat, unhoused and directly exposed to wind and weather. The life expressions of plants and large and small animals are directly present; the glances of others who are peacefully using the forest meadow brush against us, as we set up and gather up our sitting utensils. Without actively interacting with all these life events, we settle down and open the hand of thought. This situation allows us to experience the reality that it is always our settling down on the meditation cushion, and not the setting up and equipping of special premises, that makes any place a zazen practice place.

Shortly before Hoko emailed the invitation to write a text on *Shobogenzo Bodaisatta Shishobo,* in German "Die vier Arten des sozialen Handelns eines Bodhisattvas,"[1] another regular zazen event had taken place on a Sunday morning in the aforementioned forest meadow. At this zazen meeting, an incident occurred that made me immediately decide on a text on the aspect of GIVING when I received the email.

It was a glorious morning in the early European autumn. I spread out my waterproof tarp, arranged the seat mat and cushion on it, and set up our little bell. Then I hung the banner of the Frühlingsmond Zendo Hannover, signaling our affiliation, by its string in the branches of the beech tree in front of which we always sit. After that, I bowed to the tree.

A practitioner who had come along to the meadow for the first time stepped up beside me, looked at the beech branches, all of whose leaves were completely gnawed and eaten away by insects, and asked with a smile, "Don't you have a more beautiful tree to sit in front of?!"

She was quite right: anyone who looked at and judged this beech according to common aesthetic standards could really only shake their head. This beech was completely gnawed and pitted from top to bottom. Only enough leaf green remained for the tree to survive.

Seen in this way, this beech was truly no ornament of the forest. At the same time, these slightly smiling words "Don't you have a more beautiful tree to sit in front of?" made me sit up and take notice.

This beech tree, eaten away again and again, has accompanied our meadow zazen since we began sitting zazen there. It lets us hang the banner on it, provides shade, keeps wind and light rain off us, and provides fresh air. Its leaves have served as life-giving food for countless little animals. The immense feeding marks bear witness to this very fact. Nevertheless, it has produced countless beechnuts, beechnuts that not only provide for further beech growth, but also serve as food for other creatures. Nothing at all was and is lost: a beechnut does not have to become a beech tree in order to fulfill its purpose. Some beechnuts become beech trees, others are immediately eaten by larger animals, and still others are transformed into fertile forest soil by the smallest life forms. No beechnut is lost. There is no beechnut success and no beechnut failure. Simply put, everything has its meaning in connection with this beech. Deeply interwoven as one with the entire network of the forest, it not only rises into the sky, but also cooperates through its root parts with all beings that exist underground. From the top of the tree down to the smallest root tips, the beech—without any ifs, ands or buts—fits into the living symbiosis of the forest.

And despite their immersion within the overall functioning of the forest, the individual beech trees exist in their own unique manifestations: beech trees with gray bark, with oval-shaped leaves, or with heavy, hard wood, sometimes mighty, sometimes tiny, sometimes upright, sometimes crooked and bent. And as for their beechnuts, there is neither success nor failure.

As they grow older, they gradually retreat. Their crowns thin out, branches break and fall to the ground, they begin to sway. As they change, their thinned-out crowns provide the young generation of beech trees with the light they need: the next generation must be given its chance to grow back. Of course, old beech trees don't have to think about that, since supporting regrowth comes naturally from their being beech trees.

When they finally fall and come to rest lengthwise on the forest floor, their work nevertheless does not come to an end. Even in their decay, they seamlessly support many existences above and below ground. They once again make available the nutrients bound up in them, ones which were once unconditionally given to them along with water, light and air, and which allowed them to exist. Every one of their particles, no matter how small, silently serves the well-being of forest life.

For me, this is GIVING in its purest form: cooperating with all fellow beings in an interactive way, giving and receiving, inasmuch as it is possible under the respective circumstances, without greed, envy and selfish considerations. Functioning, living without any thought of failure, success, or social status: simply, naturally, unintentionally, without calculation. What admirable role models these beeches are! And so, to the smiling question, "Don't you have a more beautiful tree to sit in front of?!" I replied, just as smilingly, "No, certainly not!"

Is this mode of existence of beeches so extraordinary that it needs special mention? Of course not. All life forms on this earth exist exactly in this way without much fuss. It is completely normal, and nothing special. The world exists as innumerable beings and energies feeding each other interactively. It more or less takes place as a collection of natural bodhisattvas who neither know nor need the terms bodhisattva and social action. Why, then, did Dōgen Zenji leave us the text *Shobogenzo Bodaisatta*

Shishobo (*Four Embracing Actions of the Bodhisattva*)? Probably because there is a life form on this earth that finds it very difficult to exist normally and naturally by interacting with other beings without any fuss: humans.

Beech trees are eaten away by all kinds of life forms, and this is easy to see from the outside. Humans are eaten away by greed, envy, hatred, delusion and the strangest ideas of success and failure, but this cannot necessarily be seen immediately from the outside. The gnawing marks caused by greed, envy, hatred, and delusion manifest themselves predominantly out of view in confused trains of thought and misguided musings, and they do not show any evidence at all of the support of other life forms. On the contrary, where these mental poisons gnaw, all kinds of harmful, destructive behaviors are often not far away.

The beech trees send their vast, fine root network throughout the fertile forest floor, connecting in mutual exchange with the endless network of fungi and other life forms, and communicating through these channels with the beech trees around them. In this way, they merge with their environment beyond their individual treehood and help keep the cycle of all forest life going.

The behavior of people, on the other hand, based as it often is on confused fantasies and misguided personal assumptions, penetrates the social environment and the wider society bit by bit in everyday life like a kind of mental root system that has gone out of control. There, this behavior often triggers not a life-giving cycle and constructive communication, but again and again never-ending spirals of discord, hatred and violence. When human life is too strongly based on ego-centered self-interest, and the satisfaction of one's own interests and desires is constantly given priority, all people, fellow beings and things that do not serve these desires, or stand in the way of them, become obstacles that are sometimes radically eliminated, if worst comes to worst.

Beeches do not think and plan in the way we humans do. We therefore do not expect them to be aware of their actions and the consequences that follow, and so we do not get the idea of wanting to reward or punish them for anything.

In dealing with people, we do have the expectation that they know what they are doing and that they try to be aware, as far as possible, of the consequences of their actions. That is why rewards and punishments are included in the various educational systems of this world that are devised to regulate human behavior in a way that is desirable in each case. However, one cannot but take note of the fact that all the efforts made so far to educate people have overwhelmingly failed to result in a peacefully cooperating and constructively communicating human community.

At this point, the answer to the question of why Dōgen Zenji felt it necessary to write about the actions of bodhisattvas and to leave us this text arises all by itself: people need to explore to the best of their ability what is eating away at them, why it is eating away at them, who is actually being eaten away at, what the consequences are, and how to get out of this messy situation. This is because most people have lost the experience of their connection with completely normal reality, which holds equally valid for all beings, and so is "nothing special."

Greed, envy, hatred, delusion and ideas of success and failure that have been conditioned into us are deep-seated. They are anchored in our physicality as motivators of human spiritual life and physical behavior, and they do damage. The list of damages, which can be expanded at will, is extensive: stress, delusions of grandeur, inferiority complexes, depression, violent fantasies, suicidal thoughts, eating disorders, psychosomatic complaints of all kinds, and drug/alcohol/medication abuse. Beeches are free from harm of this kind.

However, as humans we can't, of course, become like beeches by giving up our brains. There is nothing left for us to do but to find out how to live with our brain and its ways of functioning, and how to approach again a truly social, real reality: that of neither beech nor eaten-away, suffering human being.

That is why Dōgen Zenji and the ancestors and descendants of our tradition teach us *shikantaza,* just sitting: we settle on the sitting cushion, adopting a physiologically correct, upright zazen posture, and open the hands of thought. We let all fabricated fantasies fall away. We manifest what remains on the sitting cushion when all narrow-minded, greedy, envious, comparative, desirous, and rejecting thoughts, along with all thinking that actively engages with sensory stimuli, are no longer grasped and nurtured. Then something beyond "beech" and "eaten-away, suffering human being" happens in a vastness unlimited by anything. Then, without any narrowing and ego-centered twisting, a resonance and compassion with all existences can emerge unconsciously and naturally: the bodhisattva-mind. It is only through this mind that the way of approaching the world wherein all sentient and nonsentient beings are functioning in an unintentional and mutually supportive way, opens up to us. This is nothing special, but rather the fully normal reality of this universe. Only this can expose the deep source from which GIVING gushes forth in its purest form: without ulterior motives, expectations or calculation.

This *shikantaza* (just sitting), letting body and mind drop away, is something we must do for as long as we are able, until the end of our lives, sparing no effort: *ganbarimasho!* (in Japanese),

"Let us do our best!" Our human brains will not stop producing new wild notions as long as we live. Neither can we, because of our human nature, simply stop clinging to these figments of our imagination. They are simply part and parcel of our human existence. Neither excellent education nor good intentions help. The only thing that helps is to let go persistently again and again. This letting go leads into an expanse beyond "beech" and "eaten-away, suffering human being." Thus, paradoxically, it is the human brain that not only produces fantasies, but also opens the way for dealing with them.

I consider one of the most disastrous brain fabrications to be the endeavor of many people to want to show off something special and stand out. There are those who, with tunnel vision, seek out closeness to supposedly special people and strive for the possession of seemingly special things, which are to highlight a specialness of their own that they are longing for. Beeches can't even dream of considering such mischief.

"Nothing special" is the true treasure. To value "nothing special" is to recognize that the presence and energy of countless bodhisattvas support and accompany us at all times. We humans can only exist as part of the interactively supportive functioning of all sentient and non-sentient beings. We do not exist by ourselves, but because this universal functioning makes possible the existence of the earth together with water, air, light, food, and innumerable small and large creatures—all without any discernible calculation. The human being is inseparable from this community.

The practice of GIVING (oneself), living by giving and receiving, does not need to be striven for by effort. It is basically a very quiet and peaceful acceptance of the fact that one is, quite naturally, "nothing special." It means merging—without any ifs, ands or buts—into the community of the infinitely innumerable bodhisattvas and making oneself useful like all of them, without any ulterior motives, according to one's own modest powers. This "nothing special" does not result from any distinction between "special" and "not special." It is simply suchness.

One may well imagine a world that knows how to counter greed, envy, hatred and delusion as a more livable place. Unchecked human mental turmoil is like bird poop landing on the birthday cake at an outdoor birthday party. Bird poop is an inevitable and natural part of outdoor scenery, and yet no one wants to come into contact with it, let alone eat it.

Humans being what we are, and often "missing the forest for the trees,"[2] we need guidance and many kinds of assistance in the very long run to stop being consumed by our mental turmoil, from which no one without exception is immune. We are at a loss if we think we can do this alone. All the more should we value our authentic ancestors and teachers who keep the Buddha Way open without deviation, patiently teaching us *shikantaza* and guiding us in studying authentic texts on *shikantaza,* the unity of practice and awakening.

And just as all trees naturally form a mutually nourishing forest community that excludes no form of life, all serious practitioners naturally come together in mutually supportive communities. From these communities and their centers grows a spiritual root system nourished by the generous, warm, and joyful bodhi-mind that cannot be stopped. As a root system naturally does, it sprouts out from the centers in the form of generous, joyful, and compassionate behavior on the part of practitioners. It connects with family members and friends, neighbors, the wider social environment, along with caring for all non-human life forms. Then *dana,*

GIVING, manifests without a lot of hoopla in all of our daily activities. So much for the theory, anyway!

So what now? *Just sit.* Study and learn. Appreciate everyday life.

Ganbarimasho! Let's do our best!

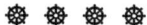

Rev. Kyoku Barbara Lutz was born in 1957. Married and the mother of two children, she is a Dharma successor of Hoko Karnegis and has practiced in Germany as well as the USA and Japan. She now directs the Spring Moon Zendo Hannover practice center in northern Germany. She holds a doctorate in education and has other accredited training in physiotherapy, Bobath Therapy, Systemic Therapy and Counseling, companionship of the critically ill and dying, Vinyasa Yoga, etc.

Takuhatsu in Daily Life

EIDO REINHART

WHEN SOMETHING IS OFFERED there is the possibility that it will be received. However, does offering depend on being received? Can our offering be unconditional and free of expectations? Can our receiving also be unconditional and free of expectations or obligation? Can it be pure? Whenever we are not greedy or covetous we are offering/giving.

Can our giving and receiving be free of greed and covetousness? If it cannot be pure, is its value negated? Although we may intend our actions to be pure, is it actually possible? Should we not even bother if our intentions cannot be pure? I value self reflection and discernment, but there is a temptation even with our best intentions for our actions to be tainted by some ego-centered desire. It can be as simple as wanting to be a good person with pure intentions. When we see we have failed at this, how does it affect our generosity? I propose that we generously accept our own limitations, not expect our intentions to be pure and perfect. We can act generously anyway without giving ourselves much thought or weight, as all that personal discernment is often ego-based and does not help us very much. It keeps the focus on "me" and "my inten-tions" instead of moving it outward to the other who is in need. The need may be material, emotional, or spiritual; it may be a need for dharma. Can we offer the dharma without holding back and being limited by our own awareness of how imperfect we are, without asking, "Who am I to be offering the dharma if I cannot do it with pure, unselfish intention?" What is the alternative—to withhold what the other needs from us because what we have to offer is not pure enough or may be tainted by our hypocrisy?

Have you ever kept yourself from acting because of your awareness of the impurity of your motives? Our awareness of our flaws can be immobilizing, if we let it be. We will find, if we look closely, that it is not possible to be pure in our motives. We need to learn to be more focused on offering and receiving than on our own motives. Some of us can always find something to feel guilty about. One might think this is only a Catholic tendency, but it is really everywhere, including in Zen practice.

I can offer an example from my own life and practice as a Catholic in the seventies and eighties. I became a Roman Cath-olic as an adult, following the spiritual path of Thomas Merton, from whom I gained great wisdom, and I learned to pray, or so I thought. My prayer was not for anything except union with God. This sounds fairly pure, but my intention was still to get some-thing for me. I became rather scrupulous about finding fault in myself and going to confession. I was always looking for impu-rity in my intentions so I could confess them. Thus my prayer and spiritual life was very self (ego) centered, more than it was God (other) centered. I entered a Christian monastery, where I lived for a year, and I noticed this tendency of mine became even more pronounced and more apparent, at least to me. I thought my motivation for going to the monastery was to live for God and others, but there was so much "me" in my continual discernment that there was not much room for God. I became more and more aware of my preoccupation with myself, and saw that while intending to live a life for God and others, I couldn't seem to escape this tendency while living in the monastic container. This was one of the insights motivating me to leave that community. My introspection had almost become pathological. This decision was very difficult and even quite traumatic for me. I had been visiting this monastery for years before I entered and had given up many things of the world, including relationships, in order to be there. This community was my family and I felt very bereft and lost after I left it.

I didn't know the answer, but I was very aware of experiencing longing and held out hope that I would one day find the way and the place for me. At this time, I still expected it to be in a religious community. In the meantime, before I even went to the monastery I had started practicing Zen; at least, I used the Zen posture for my private prayer. I think what I was doing was zazen or zazen-like in that it was primarily with the intention of opening up and surrendering. At that time I thought of it as surrendering to God's will, or becoming one with God. This eventually evolved into a wordless, receptive existential posture of just being present. I was influenced by several important texts, including *The Cloud of Unknowing*, written in the 14th century, and *Practicing the Presence of God*, written in the 17th century. Eventually I realized that what I was seeking was already there, that God was not separate from me, that I did not need to strive for this unity because it was already there. God included me and I included God. There was no place I needed to go with my body, mind or heart. I could just sit and enjoy, savor, cherish, be aware of that oneness that was. This also led to experiencing and practicing gratitude.

You may ask or wonder what all this personal history has to do with offering/giving. Well, this gradual spiritual awakening also led to an evolving understanding of giving and receiving. We also have many Buddhist teachings about this, including our meal chant, which says that "giver, receiver and gift" are empty (one). Can this be so, and can we actually experience and actualize this, not just believe it? Can we know it?

We also say in the meal chant,

> We reflect on the effort that brought us this food and consider how it comes to us.
> We reflect on our virtue and practice, and whether we are worthy of this offering.
> We regard greed as the obstacle to freedom of mind.
> We regard this meal as medicine to sustain our life.
> For the sake of enlightenment we now receive this food.

In this same way, every encounter is one of giving and receiving, and there is no difference between giver, receiver and gift.

No doubt we do get a good feeling from giving, but this is a by-product and cannot be our motivation; if that is why we give, then it is not a genuine and generous offering. It is a means to get a good feeling for "me." Even though we may experience that good feeling, is it possible to give without that expectation? Can that feeling just be a by-product, and can we manage not to give it much weight? After all, such good feelings are very transient and fleeting, not really very life sustaining. So, let's not value that too much. Maybe we do not need to value it at all. Maybe we can give (and receive?) without any expectation, without greed and without covetousness.

Receiving is also an offering if we can do it without expectation and without selfishness—for example, the expectation that I must reciprocate, that the giving and receiving need to be equal. If you give me something, perhaps my first response is something like "Oh, you shouldn't have!" (very American) or "I must reciprocate as soon as possible!" If so, I cannot just be graciously grateful; I cannot accept your gift without feeling like I owe you one also. This kind of thinking is really not being willing to accept the gift without conditions. This is even more difficult for us than it is to give without expectation.

I think giving and receiving are virtuous practices to be done just for their sake and not for any secondary benefit (or guilt). I call this *Takuhatsu* in Daily Life. I don't need to be good at it to advocate it; I need this admonition as much as anyone else. It is so difficult for us to receive without feeling the need to even the score. We cannot allow other people to give more to us than we have given to them. When written down in black and white, I think that sounds a little silly, but that is what we tend to do and feel.

In order to explain what I mean by *Takuhatsu* in Daily Life, it may help if I share my understanding of *takuhatsu*. When I was practicing in a temple in Japan, we did this practice several times in the old traditional and formal way. This meant dressing in a particular way to beg, as monks have done for centuries in Japan. We wear robes in a particular way, hand covers, leg covers and straw hats that cover our eyes. We carry bowls and handbells. We stop at various homes or businesses, ring our bells and chant. Someone may or may not come to put something in our bowls. In any case, we chant and move on. This is an ancient practice which can still be carried out in some places in Japan because people still understand it and they are often honored to give an offering. When I did this in 2012 we carried a sign saying that we were collecting for the tsunami victims, but it does not matter if we are begging for ourselves or others. One of the primary benefits of this practice is that it gives others the opportunity to practice generosity, and it actualizes and manifests our interdependence in a way that allows us to actually experience it. At the time of this ango, or three-month practice period, Hoitsu Suzuki was the leader and visited frequently. Before we went on *takuhatsu,* he gave a talk about why we do this and what its value is. His primary point was the need to practice interdependence so we experience and internalize this reality, not just think about it as a concept. He went so far as to say that we need to practice receiving in order to live a pure life. This is not a common admonition, but one we should take to heart. We say we believe it, but do we really? If we believe this, why is it so difficult to receive from others? We need to not only believe this but know this from experience.

This *takuhatsu* experience led me to value and more deeply ponder this teaching and particularly how one might translate this teaching to our lives in the West. We don't go out begging here, since no one would understand this practice. It would just seem odd, eccentric and maybe offensive. We do see a lot of begging these days, and how to express compassion and generosity to the beggars on the street is another area of conflict for us (which I am not going to address here).

What I would like you to consider is how you can practice *takuhatsu* in your daily life. What that means to me is being willing to receive (and give) without expectations or conditions. Receiving is also offering. In response to receiving, we express our gratitude and our hearts. We may also feel some accountability for using the gifts wisely and responsibly. When doing *takuhatsu* in Japan there is an implicit response or promise by the receiver to continue our practice so as to be worthy of the offering. That promise also includes using the gift wisely and being grateful.

Besides the difficulty we have in receiving, we have even more difficulty asking for help, and we must cultivate this as a practice so we continue to deeply realize that we are interdependent. We are not independent as we would like to think we are. Not only are we not independent, but it is arrogant of us to insist on that under-standing and not recognize and practice receiving from others. I suggest not only being willing to receive graciously but also increasing these practice opportunities by asking others for what we need. This could be anything: help in the yard, help with a project, emotional or spiritual help. It can be as simple as deciding that when someone offers to pay for your cup of coffee, you accept it gratefully and do not refuse it. In some cultures it is very offensive to refuse an offering. We in the West, however, are very accustomed to refusing offerings.

In our current culture, we value being independent and self sufficient. We like to claim when at all possible that "I can do it by myself" and we usually do not ask for help unless there actually is something we cannot do alone.

Many of us have jobs and income so that we can buy what we need. "I" buy things with "my" money and then "I" own them so "I" can use them as "I" please. Because I have worked for what I have, there is no need for gratitude or accountability.

Even in Zen centers, we buy services. We pay for retreats and classes and therefore sometimes we think we have a right to complain about what is offered, including the food as if it was a restaurant, and we question whether we are getting our money's worth. We have expectations about the accommodations, food and content and we do not realize deeply that the retreat is an offering to us. Yes, we pay something because offering this retreat has expenses associated with it. However, it is an offering, not a commodity that we have purchased. It is not just money offered for a service. Our part is to be grateful for what is given and to understand that whatever we paid for it is also an offering of gratitude for what is given.

It is so much easier for us to give than receive, and we are reluctant to accept, receive or ask for support. Receiving can make us feel dependent, vulnerable, obligated, powerless and even ashamed if we are in need of help. We don't like to need or be dependent and we don't realize we already are dependent and therefore have reason to be constantly grateful. We actually need to learn to feel dependent and vulnerable—and to learn this we need to practice.

I worked in home care for a long time as a physical therapist, and often my clients were angry and resentful about getting older and more dependent on others. I would sometimes try to convince them of the positive side of this: that their need was providing an opportunity for others to practice generosity and for the client to offer gratitude. Let us remember that we will all grow old and become frail, gradually becoming more dependent on others. Can we see this as an opportunity to offer gratitude instead of resenting our dependence?

I have a friend who wisely decided some years ago that we should not exchange gifts so we could lift ourselves out of this obligation to find a gift for someone who does not need anything. At this point in our lives, we are downsizing, not collecting. I thought this was a wise proposal and I agreed. However, every once in awhile I find something I want to give her, and it became a little difficult and awkward because from her point of view it was one sided; she wasn't giving anything to me and we had agreed not to do this. Therefore, she had difficulty receiving anything from me because it felt unbalanced to her, and she felt guilty instead of grateful. This of course was not the outcome I wanted, but I also did not want to be constrained by our mutually agreed upon rule of not exchanging gifts. I did agree not to exchange gifts as a routine practice, but I guess I did not actually agree to never giving anything. She became accustomed to this and to her credit she did learn to receive without needing to reciprocate. However, there is a little joke between us about that and it is that I have to kind of camouflage the gift so she does not need to acknowledge it as a gift. It's a bit of a funny game between us, but it is done with mutual affection. This required that I not feel constrained and obligated to follow this rule about not exchanging gifts, and it required her to learn to accept a gift without guilt or need to reciprocate. I really enjoy it when a person can just accept a gift or offering without the need to feel guilty for not reciprocating. It is a skill and I think one worth practicing.

My experience in the Catholic monastery taught me a lot about giving and receiving. This community lived on alms and was therefore dependent upon benefactors for its existence. What this meant in daily life was that we would receive donations of food and we felt a responsibility to use them and not waste them. That could mean dropping everything right now to process bushels of beans and preserve them. It also meant making meals from what was available rather than going shopping for whatever was wanted. It also meant feeling some responsibility for living a life worthy of the support. Concretely, this included praying for others, answering letters, not wasting, being grateful. The nuns did not work for a living and the community did not save money. Even medical needs were dependent on charity. There was no private ownership. It was quite a freeing experience in ways not easy to explain.

I think we can incorporate these practices or virtues in our daily lives and here are some of the ways to do that:

- accepting graciously what is offered to us
- not saying "no" when offered something
- remembering and practicing that there is no difference between giver, receiver and gift
- feeling some accountability for how we use resources including those we have purchased
- being grateful that we have the resources to buy what we need
- being grateful for all that is given, reflecting on the effort that has provided these resources, and considering how they have come to us, even if they are things we purchase

Be grateful to the store clerk who is helping you; it is not just a job. This person is serving you and it's an offering to be grateful for. Our gratitude is also an offering. Let us make it explicit so the person actually experiences our gratitude. It could change that person's day or even the person's life.

Remember that every encounter is an opportunity to practice offering and gratitude. Therefore. we need to provide opportunities for others to give by asking for help even if we don't need help. Just do it to practice interdependence.

We can take advantage of our frailties and limitations, especially as we age, as these are opportunities for others to practice generosity.

Let us not miss the opportunity to give someone else a chance to practice generosity and for us to practice gratitude. Let us consider even making the effort to create these opportunities by asking others to help us. It is all right to need and depend on others. It is not only all right, but it is virtuous and it is reality manifesting. Whether we know it or not, we are interdependent.

Eido Reinhart was brought up as a Presbyterian and as an adult was drawn to the contemplative monastic tradition of the Roman Catholic church. She became a Catholic in 1973 and her prayer practice brought her to the practice of zazen, which she practiced for many years alone. Her first sesshin was at Minnesota Zen Meditation Center in 1978. In 1979 she entered a Catholic monastery intending to become a nun and lived there for one year. Following that, she participated in a practice period at Mount Baldy in California with the abbot Joshu Sasaki Roshi, a Rinzai teacher. She continued to practice zazen and Catholicism for many years. She lived in Juneau, AK for seven years and after returning to Minnesota she practiced primarily at MZMC in Minneapolis where Shohaku Okumura was the interim teacher starting in 1993. She became his student, was ordained in 2006 and received dharma transmission in 2015. She has participated in two angos in Japan and was accepted by Sotoshu as *kokusai fukyoshi* in 2018. She belongs to the Association of Soto Zen Buddhists and the Soto Zen Buddhist Association. She lives in Minneapolis, has two adult sons, two daughters-in-law and two granddaughters, ages 4 and 2. She retired in 2023 after working for 50 years as a physical therapist.

The Generosity of the Dead Little Mouse

DORYU CAPPELLI

IT IS A MORNING IN LATE JULY in the Eternal City, and I am taking my dogs out for their usual walk along the banks of the Tiber River, through rows of trees and the ruins of the ancient Roman port— one of the many oases that this amazing city offers, just a stone's throw away from its hustle and bustle. It's hot, very hot. It hasn't rained in several weeks. Italy and much of Europe are plagued by an unprecedented drought, a symptom of the undeniable global climate change. The river level has dropped significantly, but there is still enough water to provide refreshment and nourishment for the multitude of birds, fish and animals that live there.

Despite the mugginess, the shade of the trees makes the walk quite enjoyable. My gaze is caught by something on the ground, on a spot bathed in the light and warmth of the sun. It's a little mouse, the kind that inhabits the old city and its green areas. Lying on its side, it is close to death, probably injured by a cat or seagull. It's breathing feebly, just waiting to die, panting from the great heat.

I take the bottle of water I use to cool my dogs and let them drink, and bring its rim close to the little creature's open mouth. At first it gives a weak nibble, maybe fearing a threat, but then eagerly drinks a few drops of water. There is nothing I can do for it but recite the "Taking of Refuge" as a viaticum for a good transformation. I leave with a feeling of sadness, but also with a sense of relief mixed with a fair dose of self-satisfaction: how generous I have been! I have given relief to a dying animal, one that most people loathe or find repulsive. A true bodhisattva action. As Dōgen says: "Whether our gifts are Dharma or material objects, each gift is truly endowed with the virtue of offering or *dana*." I bask for a while in this state, but then feel a little ashamed of this boasting of mine and try to think of something else.

On my way back, the mouse is still there, now dead. Its little body has already turned into a home and food for tiny worms, and ants are about to take its various parts to their underground dwellings to feed themselves and their larvae.

I stand looking at it and realize that it has become brighter than any living thing. It is the essence of love and of pure generosity: abandoned on the riverbank, it generously leaves its body to animals and insects. It will be exposed uncomplainingly to the sun, the hot wind, and the rain, donating to the earth its bones, its skin, and its fluids: nothing will remain that is not a gift.

This is *dana paramita* in its pure essence. "It is like offering treasures we are about to discard to those we do not know," as Dōgen says.

I understand how much ego, discrimination, judgment, and prejudice there are in our actions of generosity, even those we regard as the purest and most selfless. "No gift is too small, but our effort should be genuine." How can we be genuine in our giving?

The purest generosity, the kind that plants, trees, animals, mountains, and rivers have in their unconditional giving of them-selves – "Trusting flowers to the wind, and trusting birds to the season" – does not belong to us. The perpetual gift that the sky, the sun, the fog, the mountains offer, is beyond our reach. It is some-thing we have lost forever in exchange for discrimination, judg-ment, and even wisdom. And it is something we will never get back – at least, as long as we are alive. We will never attain that kind of love or generosity, the total and undiscriminating compassion of Kannon Bosatsu, and yet we keep seeking it. As long as we have a mind and an ego, we will persist in discriminating; even with our effort to practice generosity, this will never be as genuine as the generosity of the dead little mouse.

I believe, however, that the meaning of our life, and the meaning of our practice, is just to keep searching: an everlasting search, yet without solution. "The vastness or narrowness of mind cannot be measured, and the greatness or smallness of material things cannot be weighed." To keep striving for this absolute love, despite knowing that it is bound to fail. In this striving, in this endless pursuit, the possibility of living as much as we can in harmony with this abso-lute love, with the eternal gift of life and death, is realized.

Guglielmo Doryu Cappelli is the abbot and resident teacher at Anshin Zen Center in Rome, Italy. He received ordination according to the Soto Zen School in 1999 at the Zen Temple La Gendronniere, France, from Master Roland Yuno Rech, a disciple of Master Taisen Deshimaru Roshi.

In 2006, together with Annamaria Gyoetsu Epifanìa, he estab-lished Anshin Zen Centre and beginning 2010, he became a disciple of Shohaku Okumura and completed his training. In March 2015, he received Dharma transmission from Okumura Roshi and since 2016 he has had the rank of *kokusai fukyoshi,* i.e. a teacher devoting himself to spreading the teachings of Soto Zen Buddhism outside Japan.

Especially interested in interreligious dialogue, he co-operates with the National Office for Ecumenism and Interreligious Dialogue of the Italian Episcopal Conference in connection with the Christian-Buddhist dialogue; with DIM/MID (Monastic Interreligious Dialogue), and with the Fondazione Astalli in education for diversity and inter-religious dialogue in schools. He is regularly invited as guest speaker by the departments of Saint John's University and University of California in Rome. He lectured at the Lateranense, Gregoriana and Urbaniana Pontifical Universities and La Sapienza University of Rome.

La Generosità
del Topolino Morto

Doryu Cappelli

E' una mattina di luglio inoltrato nella Città Eterna e sto portando i miei cani a fare la consueta passeggiata mattutina lungo il greto del fiume Tevere, fra filari di alberi e rovine dell'antico porto romano. Una delle tante oasi che questa incredibile città offre, a un soffio dal trambusto e dal caos della Capitale. Fa caldo, molto caldo. Non piove da parecchie settimane. L'Italia e gran parte dell'Europa è attanagliata da una siccità senza precedenti, sintomo dell'evidente cambiamento climatico mondiale. Il livello fiume si è notevolmente abbassato, ma c'è ancora abbastanza acqua da offrire refrigerio e nutrimento alla moltitudine di uccelli, pesci e animali che vi abitano. L'ombra degli alberi rende la camminata abbastanza piacevole nonostante l'afa. Il mio sguardo viene attratto da qualcosa sul terreno, in un punto inondato dalla luce e dal calore del sole. E' un piccolo topolino, di quelli che popolano la vecchia città e i suoi spazi verdi. E' agonizzante, sdraiato su un lato. Probabilmente ferito da un gatto o da un gabbiano. Respira flebilmente, aspettando di morire, ansimando dal gran caldo. Prendo la bottiglia dell'acqua che uso per rinfrescare e dare da bere ai miei cani e ne avvicino l'orlo alla bocca aperta del piccolo animale. Dapprima le da un debole morso, forse temendo una minaccia, ma poi beve avidamente qualche goccia d'acqua. Non posso fare altro per lui tranne che recitare la Presa di Rifugio come viatico per una buona trasformazione. Me ne vado con un sentimento di tristezza ma anche con un senso di sollievo misto a una buona dose di autocompiacimento: Come sono stato generoso! Ho dato sollievo a un animale morente, uno di quelli, per giunta, che la maggior parte della gente detesta o trova repellenti. Una vera Azione da Bodhisattva. Come dice Dōgen: *"Sia che i nostri doni siano Dharma o oggetti materiali, ogni dono è veramente dotato della virtù dell'offerta o dana."* Mi crogiolo un po,' ma poi provo un minimo di vergogna di questo mio vantarmi e cerco di pensare ad altro.

Sulla via del ritorno il topolino è ancora là, ormai morto. Il suo piccolo corpicino è già diventato casa e nutrimento per minuscoli vermetti e le formiche si apprestano a pendere le varie parti del suo corpo da portare nelle loro sotterranee case come cibo per loro e le loro larve.

Resto a guardarlo e realizzo che è diventato più splendente di qualsiasi cosa vivente. E' l'essenza dell'amore e della Generosità pura: abbandonato lì, sul greto del fiume, lascia generosamente il suo corpo agli animali e agli insetti. Resterà esposto al sole, al vento caldo e alla pioggia, senza lamentarsi, donando alla terra le sue ossa, la sua pelle, i suoi liquidi: niente resterà che non sia dono.

È *Dana Paramita* nella sua pura essenza: *"È come offrire delle cose preziose che stiamo per buttare via a persone che non conosciamo,"* dice Dōgen.

Capisco quanto, anche nelle nostre azioni di generosità, anche quelle che riteniamo più pure e disinteressate, c'è di ego, di discriminazione, di giudizio e pregiudizio. *"Nessun regalo è troppo piccolo, ma il nostro sforzo dovrebbe essere genuino."* Come possiamo essere genuini nel nostro donare?

La generosità più pura, quella che hanno le piante, gli alberi, gli animali, i monti e i fiumi nel loro donarsi incondizionato," *Affidare i fiori al vento e gli uccelli alla stagione,"* non ci appartiene. Il dono perenne che offrono il cielo, il sole, il vento, la nebbia, le montagne è fuori della nostra portata. E' qualcosa che abbiamo perso per sempre in cambio della discriminazione, del giudizio, anche della saggezza. Ed è qualcosa che non riavremo mai, almeno finché saremo vivi. Non raggiungeremo mai quel tipo di amore, di generosità, la totale equanime compassione di Kannon Bosatsu, eppure continuiamo a cercarla. Finché avremo una mente, un ego, continueremo a discriminare; anche facendo i nostri sforzi di praticare la generosità, questa non sarà mai così genuina come quella del topolino morto.

Ma credo che il senso della nostra vita, e il senso della nostra pratica, sia quello di continuare a cercare: una ricerca eterna e senza soluzione. *"La vastità o la ristrettezza della mente non può essere misurata, e la grandezza o la piccolezza delle cose materiali non può essere soppesata."* Continuare a tendere verso questo amore assoluto, pur sapendo che è destinato a fallire. In questa tensione, in questa ricerca senza fine si realizza la possibilità di vivere quanto più possibile in armonia con questo amore assoluto, con il dono eterno della vita e della morte.

Guglielmo Doryu Cappelli è abate e insegnante residente presso il Centro Zen Anshin di Roma, Italia.

Ha ricevuto l'ordinazione secondo la Scuola Zen Soto nel 1999 presso il Tempio Zen La Gendronniere, Francia, dal Maestro Roland Yuno Rech, discepolo del Maestro Taisen Deshimaru Roshi.

Nel 2006, insieme ad Annamaria Gyoetsu Epifanìa, fonda il Centro Zen Anshin e dal 2010 diventa discepolo di Shohaku Okumura con cui completa la sua formazione.

Nel marzo 2015 ha ricevuto la trasmissione del Dharma da Okumura Roshi e dal 2016 ha il grado di kokusai fukyoshi, cioè un insegnante che si dedica alla diffusione degli insegnamenti del Buddismo Soto Zen fuori dal Giappone.

Particolarmente interessato al dialogo interreligioso, collabora con l'Ufficio Nazionale per l'Ecumenismo e il Dialogo Interreligioso della Conferenza Episcopale Italiana nell'ambito del dialogo cristiano-buddhista; con DIM/MID (Dialogo Interreligioso Monastico), e con la Fondazione Astalli nell'educazione alla diversità e nel dialogo interreligioso nelle scuole. È regolarmente invitato come relatore ospite dai dipartimenti della Saint John's University e dell'Università della California a Roma. Ha insegnato alle Pontificie Università Lateranense, Gregoriana e Urbaniana e all'Università La Sapienza di Roma.

Dana (Offering)

SHOJU MAHLER

When I began to practice, I sat in a small zendo in the middle of the woods of New Hampshire, by a brook. To me, it was heaven on earth. Hogetsu, the monk who opened the zendo, always said, "I am not a teacher," and if we seemed interested in continuing to practice, he encouraged us to find one. So, after a couple of years, I went to several Zen centers and temples looking for a teacher with whom I felt an affinity and could practice and study.

In one temple in California, a monk taught me the practice of *gyohatsu,* the formal way of eating meals with several bowls that we wrap in a cloth tied by a large knot. At the end of the meal, when it was time to rewrap the bowls in the cloth, this monk said, folding the edge of the fabric away from him over the bowls, "We give," and folding the other edge toward himself, "and we receive." I don't remember the name of the monk, but those words pierced my whole being, even though I did not perceive their profound meaning.

This teaching of thirty years ago was a pure offering from a monk who did not know me. Today, I continue to deepen its significance in my life and those words keep on supporting my practice.

Sometimes we give with a calculating mind, selfishly, expecting to receive something in exchange, if only an expression of gratitude. We might give solely depending on our affinities. We choose who we give to. This is called "giving with intention." Maybe we mention the point of view of a person we think is powerful, in hopes of obtaining what we want.

When we "have to" give someone a present, do we look around in our belongings to find an object we no longer need and can dispense with?

None of these are offerings of course, only self-centered actions that do not help anyone, and certainly not us. They do not help the Dharma flow.

DANA

The Sanskrit word *dana,* offering, does not mean a one way gift, nor is it "give and take." In English, the words "to donate" and "donation" come directly from *dana* and mean to abandon something voluntarily, neither expecting something in exchange nor knowing who receives it.

In early Buddhism, since the days of Shakyamuni Buddha, *bhikkhus* and *bhikkhunis,* monks and nuns, offered Dharma teachings to lay people who in turn offered them clothing, food and medicine. In Thailand, a country of the Theravada tradition, I saw in the streets of Bangkok very early in the morning, monks carrying their large metal bowls hanging from their necks and receiving cooked food from lay practitioners.

Our sangha recently invited Ajahn Medhino, a Theravada bhikkhu who lives in Sri Lanka and practices in the tradition of the Forest Monks of Ajahn Chah, to visit us. He lives on alms and eats only the food he receives. If he is not offered food, he does not eat.

His brother Charles practices in our sangha, and so Ajanh Medhino came to our temple, Hosuiji, and offered the teaching of his traditional way of meditation. In turn, our sangha had the opportunity to practice the offering of food as *dana* to a renunciant, each one of us in turn placing some in his large bowl before he retired to eat by himself.

In our tradition, when we eat formally with the bowls we chant:

Now we set out Buddha's bowls;
may we, with all living beings,
realize the emptiness of the three wheels:
giver, receiver and gift.

Here, "Buddha" means awakening. The practice of *gyohatsu* helps us to awaken to the reality that everything is interconnected. When we realize how many causes and conditions are present in order for this food to be in our bowl or on our plate, we begin to perceive that we are a knot in Indra's net. How many people have worked for us, not knowing who would eat the food we now receive?

When we eat, we receive much more than just food. We receive everything that contributed to its being in our bowl: gifts from the earth, the sun, the rain, the farmers, the workers in the store, the tenzo—what *dana!* We realize that we receive from all directions and that this food is not only ours, but everyone's nourishment.

When we comprehend, when we take in, with more than only the intellect the fact that we cannot and do not exist alone, we are less attached to our thoughts being always the only valid way to see things.

This approach becomes part of our daily life and we therefore create fewer problems and live in harmony with other people and nature.

DANA AS PARAMITA

In our tradition, when we receive the bodhisattva precepts we vow to help all beings to attain liberation from the three poisonous minds: greed, anger and delusion. Before making this vow we are pulled by our karma, but as bodhisattvas there has to be a change in the way we live. When we see that we are going in the wrong direction, we observe our actions and again take up the correct path.

In order to cross over we have to make an effort, and this effort is the practice of the *paramitas,* which is a very down-to-earth practice of our daily lives on the path. It is the practice of *dana,* offering, in helping all beings cross over before us to the shore of peace, no fear and understanding.

Paramita means "perfection" or "perfect realization," and in Chinese, the character means "crossing to the other shore," the shore of liberation. When we act selflessly by including everyone, we all cross at the same time. To truly practice the six *paramitas* is to be free from self-clinging and from holding on to any idea for the good of all beings, and this is expressing compassion through our actions.

The six *paramitas* are guides for our lives, not rules to judge ourselves or others. *Dana,* translated as generosity, giving or offering, is the first of the six *paramitas.* It is giving, caring with no conditions, giving with no grasping, hands, mind and heart open. It is not being attached to the offering, the giver or the receiver. The five other *paramitas* are:

Sila: proper conduct, morality, honesty, uprightness, ethics, precepts.
It is leading a correct way of life.

Ksanti: patience, tolerance, acceptation, inclusivity.
It is embracing all beings.

Virya: energy, diligence, effort, courage, resolve.
It is continuous practice.

Dhyana: meditation, concentration, vigilance, zazen.
It is the manifestation of zazen in our lives, through action.

Prajna: Wisdom, understanding through right view and right intent.
It is the perfection of understanding.

The image of water and waves is sometimes used to help us understand that nothing exists by itself. The ocean is made up of all kinds of waves: small waves, beautiful waves, foamy waves, huge waves, calm waves. All waves are waves, and they are the ocean as well. They have no separate existence from the ocean's existence. Water is the ground of being of each wave.

It is important that the waves know that they are the ocean, and it is essential that we understand that we are part of the interdependence of all beings. We need to make an effort and practice the paramitas to actualize this understanding.

PRAJNA

Prajna, the sixth *paramita,* is the perfection of understanding, the highest kind of perception, free from all concepts, ideas and points of view. This kind of perception has the power to carry us to the shore of peace and freedom.

The five first *paramitas,* in order to be *paramitas,* contain the sixth, *prajna,* this deep wisdom. Without it being present, they are ordinary activities but not *paramitas.* "In Mahayana Buddhism, *prajna paramita* is described as the mother of all buddhas. Everything that is good, beautiful and true is born from *prajna paramita.* She is in us, we only need to touch her to help her manifest herself," says Venerable Thich Nhat Hanh. This wisdom is something very basic, not something grand or lofty. It is something down-to-earth, grounded, something we can all manifest in everyday life. With its support, we are able to go forward with compassion and understanding.

Manjushri, one of the great bodhisattvas, represents wisdom. He usually sits on a lion on the altar in the zendo or the monks hall in a temple. This image is of the lion's roar, expounding the Dharma. In some traditions, Manjushri holds the sword that cuts through ignorance and duality.

Because the *paramitas* contain *prajna,* each one of the six includes the other five. When we practice one, we practice them all.

Yuko Okumura, Sanshin's sewing teacher, told me that during her training it was the students' practice to be given measurements for an okesa to be sewn and not know who it was for. This is *dana paramita,* giving with no attachment— a beneficial action carried out simply for its own sake, for the sake of the Dharma. In *dana* there is no expectation, and it has the meaning that the giver and the receivers always go together. Along with the gift, they are one.

In many Japanese Buddhist traditions, including Zen, practitioners carry out *takuhatsu,* the practice of walking through the streets stopping in front of each house and chanting the Heart Sutra. Sometimes donors put coins into their bowls, which are held high in both hands. When I practiced at the Aichi Senmon Nisodo, the Soto Zen women's training temple in Nagoya, Japan, we went out on the alms rounds as a group of six or seven nuns a few times a month. At first I did not understand the teachings of *takuhatsu* practice and did not like it at all. I felt it was phony. I was closed and almost angry.

All I saw was that we were asking for donations when we already had enough to eat at the temple.

Today, it is clearer to me. *Takuhatsu* is a very important practice, teaching us the deep meaning of offering as *dana,* for the sake of all beings. Each time we went out, we would go to a different neighborhood as Shakyamuni Buddha instructed, walking in a line, halting at every door, be it a house, a shop or an office. We chanted "Ho-o-o-o-o" everywhere we stopped, giving all people, rich or poor, old or young, the opportunity to offer alms and for us to receive or not, with no expectation. Whether we received a coin, were ignored or chased away, we bowed including everyone. We wore large bamboo hats hiding our faces so we could not see who gave, and in turn the donors could not see to whom they made an offering or who they ignored.

We walked in a line, sometimes really feeling the heat, sometimes really feeling the cold, just walking, just chanting, just bowing, in the present moment, simply being. Once when we were practicing *takuhatsu* in a large and very busy market, a young woman ran up to us. She was very excited that we were women, and joining the end of the line of nuns, she followed us back to the nisodo. Through that encounter she became a zazen practitioner.

Today, I perceive better that *takuhatsu* is *dana paramita* embracing all beings, pervading everywhere, a practice for the sake of the Dharma, not for us personally.

Wade Hogetsu Hancock, the priest who opened the zendo where I started practicing zazen and met the Dharma, always said, "Zazen and the teachings are free," meaning that they are offerings from the monks or priests who teach and guide the practitioners. Nobody "owns" the Dharma, and Shakyamuni's teachings are always an offering.

Once, when I thanked Hogetsu for making a zendo available for anyone to come and practice, he answered, "It's not me." I was surprised at his answer, but deep down I understood. Of course it was him, but at the same time, not him. What is it that makes us practice and give?

Daily and weekly practice is open and free of charge to all at Sanshin. Okumura Roshi wanted everyone to be able to come, do zazen and listen to the teachings. It is the same at my temple here in France. The practice of *dana* from the teacher is showing the way, and the practitioners who come and receive the teachings give from the heart to support the temple.

OFFERING EMBRACEMENT

The English expression "to embrace" comes to us from Greek, through Latin and more recently the French *embrasser*. *En* means in and *bras* means arms, so altogether the meaning is to clasp in the arms. It signifies, among other meanings, to contain, accepting eagerly, to include as part of something broader, to encompass.

Of course when we embrace somebody, our arms are part of it. It is not a one way action; we also are included in the embrace. *Dana* is a beneficial action and encompasses us as well as all beings. *Dana* is also the underpinning of the four embracing actions; they do not exist without it. When we act with loving speech, act in a beneficial way or identify with someone and act accordingly, they are all *dana* embracement. Everything is touched and embraced by *dana,* is *dana,* when the action is genuine and everything is already in the realm of peace, of no fear and steadfastness.

Our teacher, Okumura Roshi, says; "The practice of awakening to the reality of interdependent origination and expressing it is the reality of the four embracing actions." Today in the West, we cannot practice *takuhatsu*. How can we as bodhisattvas express the reality of life day to day and embody the four embracing actions? What can we offer with equanimity?

- *Material things.* Giving to all beings in need, with no choosing.
- *Dharma teachings.* Sometimes a single sentence or action brings understanding and relief to everyone who hears it.
- *Caring words.* Opening our hearts and speaking truly, with no false words or intention.
- *Our attention.* Being present, body and mind, solid.
- *Receiving.* As Westerners, we can learn to work with others, not saying "No thanks, I want to do it alone."
- *Our freedom.* The truth expands endlessly when we are free from greed, anger and wrong perceptions.
- *Space.* Letting others just be, not trying to control them in order to fulfill our own desires.
- *Understanding.* Living the fact that there are many ways to see things and being in harmony with others and with everything.
- *The example of a Dharma-centered life,* whether we live with a sangha, our family or alone.

Some years ago when I was traveling and going through a very large American airport. I found a spot where I was alone, very happy to be by myself and waiting peacefully, reading and drinking a cup of coffee. Suddenly I perceived the presence of someone arriving noiselessly, and raising my head I saw a *bhikkhu* wearing the ochre robes, who had also found a quiet spot! With no thought, I stood up and offered him the cookies I had just bought. He looked up surprised, accepted them and without a word, simply put them in his bag before going to sit by himself.

In the city where I live, on my way to the grocery store I walk by a few young homeless men sitting beside the movie theater. Smoking and drinking beer, a hat in front of them, they hope to receive a few coins. I rarely give them money, and why don't I? In my mind I criticize, I prefer one way of life over another, and I choose who to give to.

When we look deeply at these two situations, we see that the *bhikkhu* and the beggar are both homeless, simply human beings. So is each one of us. All human beings are homeless; nothing belongs to any particular person. There is nothing superior, nothing inferior. Life itself is impartial; it does not choose. We all have the same needs in order to live and we all receive from the universe. We are all embraced by the Buddhadharma.

We study the teaching that each being exists because everything else exists, and that we live and awaken together with everyone. As bodhisattvas, we walk on the Buddha way, the path of awakening, of realization, in order to help all beings. How can we embrace and embody this practice in our daily lives, each one of us with our own different capabilities?

In the nisodo, all the nuns would walk to the close-by Toganji temple and chant the Hannya Shingyo in front of the huge Buddha statue on the temple grounds. I noticed that there was an opened bronze hand on a low pillar close to the statue, and I was curious. "Why does Buddha have three hands?" I wondered. Then a mother and her young son walked up and the little boy sat in the palm of the third hand, its fingers curled up around him. It took me a long time to understand what this represents: we all are in the hand of the Buddha. It is not a choice—we always are.

We cannot fathom the source of what we receive and the reach of what is given. We always live in the hand of the Buddha, and our practice as bodhisattvas is to give and receive with an open mind, with no attachment. This giving and receiving is *dana* embracement.

Dana contains *prajna,* the Great Wisdom which sees emptiness and see things as they are. When we offer something, if we are attached to anything, it is not *dana* free of grasping and it is not *Dana* Embracement. Therefore, nothing in the net of interdependent origination is liberated.

Dana as embracing action is the practice of working with whatever we encounter in our lives, without trying to control others, without stubbornly striving to obtain whatever we imagine we must have, whether objects, fame, contentment, a certain person or even "understanding." Each one of us is part of this great whole and we each have a place, so why insist on controlling everything? Why close ourselves to life as it is and not walk on the path where everyone has his or her own space? Why not just be?

In the Diamond Sutra, named for the diamond that cuts through illusion, Subhuti asks Shakyamuni how a bodhisattva should practice. Shakyamuni Buddha answers, "When bodhisattvas give a gift, they should not be attached to a thing... They should not be attached to a sight when they give a gift. Nor should they be attached to a sound, a smell, a taste, a touch, or a dharma [an existing thing]... Subhuti, the body of merit of those bodhisattvas who give a gift without being attached is not easy to measure."[1]

Merit is not beneficial to one person, the giver, alone. When a bodhisattva gives without being attached to anything, everything receives endlessly. However difficult to fathom it might be, like an endless echo we can no longer hear, it pervades everywhere. This in and of itself is *dana* embracement.

A long time ago, my friend Yuko Yamada Wakayama, also a nun, and I were in a restaurant in Japan. As we were leaving, the cook stepped out of the kitchen and prostrated himself in front of us. I was extremely embarrassed, froze, and could not respond in any way. At that moment I did not understand the cook's gesture and intention. I took it personally and could not simply forget myself and receive his prostration as *dana* to the two nuns in front of him. Neither did I perceive the reach of his gesture far beyond the person bowing and the visible receivers of the prostration at that moment in time.

When we bow wholeheartedly to show our gratitude, who bows? Who gives and who receives? Where is the bow?

Everything gives through unreserved actions. *Dana* as gratitude is *dana* embracement, and all four embracing actions are actualized. It permeates all and resonates through everything.

When giving or receiving, can we just be? Are we able to simply let go of our ideas about ourselves and be one with what is happening in the moment? If so, whether we give or we receive, the offering, *dana,* is free from the three poisons of greed, anger and illusion and is *dana* embracement. This practice liberates us from our attachments. It is an offering touching all beings in the universe and for everyone's benefit as well as our own.

"*Dana* is an offering done and received without envy," says Okumura Roshi.

"What is a teacher?" I asked him many years ago. He answered: "Someone who opens the door."

The longer we practice, the clearer it becomes how much our teachers and Dharma ancestors offer freely and how much we receive from them. The vast *dana* embracement of their practice and teachings exists endlessly and reaches us all. Deep gratitude to them.

Shoju Mahler received priest precepts from Dai-en Bennage Roshi in 1999 and lived and practiced under her guidance at Mt. Equity Zendo in Pennsdale Pennsylvania, from 1998 to 2003. She practiced for two angos at the Aichi Senmon Nisodo in Nagoya Japan, in 2000 and 2002 under the guidance of the abbess, Shundo Aoyama Roshi. She began practicing at Sanshin in 2004, became Okumura Roshi's disciple in 2005, received transmission from him in 2009 and completed zuisse in 2011. She is recognized as *kokusai fukyoshi* by Sotoshu. She is the guiding teacher of Zendo l'Eau Vive, Hosuiji, in Alès, France and is the translator of several of Okumura Roshi's books into French.

Loving Speech

Morada de Amor Benevolente

Jakushō Pignatiello

En reverencia y humildad asumí el reto de escribir acerca de la palabra amorosa porque diversas actividades y experiencias de vida me acercan a ella. Quizás también porque en mi historia individual he aspirado a salir de silencios impuestos, tener acceso a la palabra y cultivar vínculos basados en ella. En ese recorrido veo ahora en el trasfondo mi voto personal dando energía a una búsqueda, pero también reconozco que en muchas ocasiones mi ejercicio de la palabra fue ansioso por avidez, rudo, cargado de rabia y hasta violento en ocasiones. Diez años abandonando cuerpo y mente en zazen me han abierto a percibir cargas aflictivas que interfieren mi habla y mi escucha, a practicar el arrepentimiento y encontrar nuevos campos en los que florecen pensamientos, palabras y acciones orientados a la liberación del sufrimiento, a eliminar el mal y cultivar el bien.

Veo la palabra amorosa en el contexto de la práctica continua desde zazen a la vida diaria y de vuelta a zazen. Vida diaria que discurre por donde este humilde monje novicio en Caracas aspira a hacer de cada lugar y cada momento un templo en el que el buddha dharma se manifieste. Las notas que siguen en este texto fueron surgiendo desde que asumí la tarea de escribir acerca de la palabra amorosa, tomando como punto de partida la enseñanza de Okumura roshi acerca de *Shobogenzo Shishobo* de Dōgen Zenji. Día a día, observando, dándome cuenta, practicando arrepentimiento y volviendo al voto fueron surgiendo anotaciones en las que dialogaron la experiencia vivida y las enseñanzas de los maestros. Las experiencias cotidianas me fueron mostrando que la palabra amorosa "es nutrida poco a poco" (Dōgen Zenji). En las relaciones interpersonales de la vida cotidiana, las actividades en la sangha, en mi trabajo como psicoterapeuta y como docente, la práctica continua me fue abriendo a ver, comprender, atesorar y proteger la palabra amorosa, algo "que usualmente no es conocido o visto" (Dōgen Zenji). ¿Está presente en mi vida diaria la palabra amorosa? ¿En qué consiste? ¿Qué hace posible que ella surja? ¿En qué momentos eso ocurre? Son preguntas que me acompañaron en la elaboración de las anotaciones que aquí comparto y que me seguirán acompañando en lo sucesivo.

En este momento me atrevo a afirmar que la palabra amorosa no es algo extraordinario, anormal, de otro mundo. En la comprensión que alcanzo a tener, la palabra amorosa no es más que la manifestación de la naturaleza profunda de la palabra, la expresión pura de sus funciones fundamentales. Palabra es vínculo e integración, es medio para dar y recibir, es reconocimiento, cuidado, presencia. Es intercambio que nos hace humanos; las primeras palabras que recibimos de nuestras madres y padres al nacer son amorosas respuestas que unen lo que necesitamos para vivir (alimento, aseo, cuidado, afecto) con aquello que puede satisfacer esa necesidad, y así entramos a la vida. En ese intercambio, si solo recibimos objetos o acciones vacías de comunicación amorosa la vida languidece. Practicar la palabra amorosa es cuidar a todos los seres así como fuimos, somos y seremos cuidados en nuestra vida.

Nos dice Okumura roshi que "no somos más que colecciones de vínculos." La palabra es intrínseca al vínculo; la palabra hace vínculo, para producir sufrimiento, cuando es utilizada con fines egoístas, o para cultivar el bien y liberar a los seres que sufren. Con la palabra amorosa producimos vínculos que nos constituyen junto con otros actualizando nirvana en todo lugar y circunstancia. Así, por ejemplo, en los espacios institucionales en los que realizamos nuestras actividades profesionales o en aquellos donde se resuelven asuntos de la comunidad en que vivimos, promovemos cálida acogida, receptividad y apertura a colaborar que emergen de algo que trasciende las cualidades o limitaciones individuales. La práctica de la palabra amorosa puede ser un perfume que propicia condiciones personales y grupales de confianza para percibir, tomar en consideración, compartir y analizar experiencias ligadas al bienestar común. La palabra amorosa puede manifestarse como apertura al diálogo sobre asuntos usualmente silenciados, temidos o descartados. También es una palabra que puede sensibilizar a cada integrante de una comunidad de trabajo o de vida hacia el cuidado de los otros.

Vivimos en entornos culturales que promueven el uso de palabras de amor para seducir, obtener algo, ejercer el poder, incitar a consumir o poseer al otro como objeto. La palabra amorosa es entrega generosa que no trata de obtener algo, que se dirige al bien y el alivio de quien la recibe. Viendo la realidad de cada ser con corazón compasivo, se acerca a esa realidad y procura ubicarse en el centro desde el que la palabra puede ayudar al alivio del sufrimiento.

Okumura roshi nos dice que "cuando hablamos con un corazón amable y compasivo, incluso un saludo diario se convierte en palabra amorosa." Este saludo es mucho más que un evento puntual, puede ser expresión de la práctica continua. Sostener día a día, persona a persona, de un lugar a otro el saludo cordial a todo ser sin distinción y con atención a lo que el otro siente es cultivo de compasión, no solo en el propio corazón sino en toda la red de relaciones que nos constituyen. Despierta alegría, sosiego y hasta esperanza en quien recibe el saludo y, debemos repetir, alegría, sosiego y esperanza en toda la red de relaciones que conforman a esa persona. Completamos un círculo cuando al amoroso cuidado de las palabras que ofrendamos se une en simultáneo la atenta y jubilosa escucha de la respuesta al saludo. Decimos y escuchamos con una apertura sincera que sostiene al vínculo que en ese instante se ilumina.

En italiano una manera de decir hola es "*salve*" que viene de "*salvezza*" (salvación). El círculo de la práctica continua en la palabra amorosa, al saludar "salva" al interlocutor, lo rescata, lo acoge amablemente y así alivia, cultiva bienestar. Avanzamos en esta práctica, igual que en zazen, por la asiduidad. Saludo sincero y compasivo con constancia, no a veces, no el día en que amanecimos de buen humor, sino siempre que podamos, siempre que tengamos la oportunidad. Se trata de estar atentos y abiertos. Veo esta práctica en innumerables lugares y circunstancias. Al salir de casa, al subir al ascensor o el transporte público, al entrar a una tienda. Quisiera resaltar como un ejemplo especial el saludo a las personas que prestan un servicio en actividades de limpieza del entorno donde vivimos, circulamos o trabajamos. Estas personas usualmente ni siquiera son percibidas y muchas veces lo son para denigrar de su trabajo. En cambio, si esa persona recibe un saludo cálido, "su cara brilla y su mente se alegra" tal como nos dice Dōgen Zenji. Nos responde desde ese brillo y alegría con un saludo agradecido que purifica y siembra armonía en todo el espacio y para todas las personas a las que sirve su labor.

La palabra amorosa es lugar seguro. ¿Qué significa lugar seguro? Es espacio de bienestar para quien la recibe, para un ser que gracias a ella puede decir y ser escuchado en un modo que alivia el sufrimiento (sin juicio, sin reproche, sin imperativos de silencio, sin imponer un voluntarismo salvador), que abre puertas a los procesos que traen alivio, que genera condiciones de confianza en el espacio interpersonal. Lugar seguro pueden ser también todas nuestras relaciones en la sangha, la familia, la pareja, los amigos, el contexto de trabajo profesional. En el contexto de la psicoterapia crear un lugar seguro desde la palabra es condición necesaria para que pueda realizarse un proceso de cura. La palabra amorosa es espacio de bienestar que reúne a quien la recibe y quien la da. Es espacio intermedio que no pertenece a uno u otro individuo, es una misma realidad que a ambos contiene, actualizando sabiduría y compasión intrínsecas en la realidad transcendente del ser interdependiente.

La palabra amorosa no procede de habilidades, técnica o voluntad. No surge de un querer ser amoroso o ser querido. No es resultado de un entrenamiento luego del cual se repiten mecánicamente fórmulas memorizadas. No es algo que posee una u otra persona para darla o negarla a otros. La palabra amorosa se manifiesta por sí misma en ciertas condiciones derivadas de una práctica sostenida.

La palabra amorosa no tiene prisa, no busca obtener algo. Es palabra tranquila, nace de tranquilidad en la enunciación. En situaciones donde hay tensión, posible disputa o conflicto, la palabra amorosa es comunicar desde la tranquilidad, centro, ecuanimidad y apertura compasiva. En presencia compasiva y magnánima, mueve condiciones para el despertar de los interlocutores en apertura, flexibilidad, sosiego, compromiso y atención al otro.

Amorosa no por un sentimiento o emoción que la acompaña, es amorosa por sus consecuencias en quienes la reciben y se abren a la conexión interdependiente, a la amabilidad en la convivencia. Amorosa también porque se enuncia desde la interdependencia. No es un ego que habla para validar sus significados; la palabra amable surge de la red interdependiente que obra a través de nosotros, y somos medio para su obrar en cada momento. Surge de un despertar a la red de origen interdependiente actualizado en el momento en el que hablar, escuchar, escribir, cantar o recitar se asumen como servicio para el alivio del sufrimiento de los seres sin distingos. La palabra se manifiesta por sí misma desde una práctica de entrega confiada a la red de origen interdependiente. En este sentido la palabra amorosa es confianza; ella confía y despierta confianza.

La palabra amorosa nace de un lugar más allá de nosotros, más allá de un yo que reúne habilidades o herramientas adquiridas. Tiene una intención que se manifiesta al soltar la identidad con motivaciones egoístas basadas en fantasías (conscientes o inconscientes) de heroísmo y sacrificio. Ayudamos más cuando menos nos identificamos a un personaje que quiere salvar a los demás con lo que les dice; liberamos a otros cuando nos liberamos de personajes que pretenden saber y decidir acerca del bien de los demás. La palabra amorosa se vale de medios hábiles, pero no se reduce a un uso de esos medios como si de una técnica se tratase. Surge del estar presente, confiado, vacío de expectativas, abierto a la palabra o el silencio que viene en el momento preciso, necesario y benéfico.

Confiando en que no deriva de habilidades propias, sino que viene de más allá de los límites de la individualidad, simplemente me presto como medio para que ella surja. La palabra que sana y alivia viene de una realidad interdependiente que me trasciende a mí y al interlocutor, haciéndonos parte de un todo. Este no es un estado, es círculo ininterrumpido de práctica con esta visión e intención, algo ilimitado a lo que se dirige un voto. Esta práctica me acompaña en situaciones cotidianas dentro de mi comunidad, en la actividad docente y en el trabajo con pacientes. Es una práctica en la que se cultiva humildad.

En su enseñanza, Okumura roshi nos invita a buscar intencionalmente los rasgos virtuosos y dignos de elogio en los demás como algo intrínseco a la práctica de la palabra amorosa. Afirma que esto puede moldear nuestra personalidad, haciéndola más solidaria con los otros. Nos rodean hábitos y prácticas culturales que asumen que se aprende corrigiendo errores y que se resuelven problemas eliminando cosas que fallan. Es habitual hablar de los defectos de los otros y autocastigarse por las propias debilidades. Todo eso contribuye a producir entornos regidos por la hostilidad y la violencia.

Ver a la persona en sus cualidades y virtudes corta con los hábitos establecidos que tienden a resaltar las fallas, errores y debilidades del otro. Todas las actividades de docencia que realizamos son espacios para la práctica de esta perspectiva de la palabra amorosa. Sea dando una clase en la universidad o una charla de introducción al zazen, la palabra amorosa es práctica que ayuda a ver la luz en cada ser, y a esa luz se dirige. Desde esta perspectiva, enseñar es colocarse junto al otro en la tarea de aprender, es hacerse uno con sus condiciones y su percepción de la realidad. La palabra amorosa en la docencia no apunta a carencias que se tienen que llenar, sino a capacidades y recursos que los alumnos pueden activar para producir por sí mismos aprendizajes significativos y abrir nuevas perspectivas. En lugar de señalar y penalizar errores por medio de diversas formas de evaluar, quien instruye a otro puede hacerlo desde un corazón compasivo que se ubica en la realidad particular de la persona y en lo que la mueve a aprender. En lugar de resaltar el error, mostramos opciones que abren caminos de aprendizaje, liberación y transformación.

Ver la virtud, recursos y potencialidades de la persona es práctica fundamental en la labor psicoterapéutica. En mi experiencia actual no hay dualidad entre el monje que practica la Vía y el terapeuta dedicado a ayudar a personas que sufren. Las profesiones de la salud mental pueden ser disciplinas crueles cuando en ellas se enfatiza la falla, la debilidad, la carencia o la disfunción de un paciente tomado como objeto de examen, sin saber muchas veces qué hacer con eso que se ha diagnosticado o ni siquiera plantearse qué se puede hacer con eso. En la práctica terapéutica el camino de ayuda sincera y real a quienes sufren me llevó al encuentro con la necesidad de ver la luz en medio de realidades aparentemente imposibles de superar o transformar. La acción terapéutica que involucra al ser sufriente como protagonista de una transformación se basa en estar siempre abiertos y atentos para ver la virtud, la energía, los recursos y el movimiento interior de una psique transindividual que lleva a la persona a resolver causas y condiciones de sufrimiento. La academia, las escuelas terapéuticas no enseñan esto; me tocó aprenderlo para poder ayudar a personas en las situaciones más difíciles de trauma, duelo, depresión, ansiedad o psicosis, por mencionar algunas. Estas son situaciones complejas, dolorosas y aparentemente sin salida. No se trata solo de verlas, se trata de confiar en esas virtudes y recursos que quizás la misma persona no ve y no cree tener. La palabra amorosa renueva en cada encuentro este mensaje compasivo: "confío en ti, confío en que puedes cambiar las condiciones y superar lo que te aflige. Confío a pesar de que ahora no confíes en ti ni en tu capacidad para salir adelante." Entrego mi confianza en que los procesos sanadores vienen de más allá de las individualidades involucradas en una relación de ayuda. Son como la energía de la ola que rompe llegando a la orilla produciendo sonido y burbujas. Escuchamos el sonido, vemos burbujas en la orilla, pero la energía que las produce viene de lugares y causas infinitas que se esconden tras el horizonte al que llega nuestra limitada mirada.

Llegados a este punto, cabe preguntar: ¿la palabra amorosa es solo palabra? Hay tanto que sé que se comunica y transmite más allá de las palabras. Como lugar seguro y refugio dhármico, la palabra amorosa es también silencio, espacio para hacer pausa y solo respirar en plena presencia de quien nos acompaña. Atención, quietud y entrega al presente son también el centro de la escucha, y la palabra amorosa es necesariamente escucha. No es solo mensaje que se emite; tal mensaje no sería posible sin una entrega amorosa a lo que el otro nos comunica, desprendiéndose de esquemas mentales que filtran y dejan pasar solo aquello afín a lo habitual y gratificante. Escuchar es apertura a lo que es, presencia sostenida, serena, compasiva que ayuda a que otro se valga de la palabra para expresar su realidad, comprenderla y elaborar soluciones al sufrimiento de cuerpo y mente. Volviendo al contexto de la psicoterapia, la práctica de la palabra amorosa es cultivo de la capacidad de escucha compasiva en el terapeuta. Esto es algo que no está escrito en un libro, ni lo explican las teorías psicológicas, ni se entrena como una técnica impersonal. La escucha no es técnica, no es pose, es práctica compasiva; es camino que requiere momento a momento desprenderse de la ignorancia que separa, emite juicios o rechaza la realidad de los otros.

Pasando a otro ámbito de la práctica en la vida diaria, me refiero ahora a lo que podemos aportar desde los votos del bodhisattva a la comunidad en la que vivimos. En nuestra sociedad, la vida en comunidad puede estar llena de dificultades, problemas con servicios públicos, hostilidad entre vecinos y deterioro del ambiente. Gran parte de esos problemas requieren cooperación y compromiso de todos los integrantes de la comunidad. En ese contexto, cuando nuestra presencia aporta la tranquilidad de una palabra amorosa, estamos aportando pequeños granos de arena que contribuyen a tender puentes y cultivar vínculos. En nuestra sociedad atravesada por la violencia naturalizada en lo cotidiano y la polarización, los conflictos entre miembros de una comunidad se exacerban. En tales situaciones podemos aportar paz por medio de una palabra amorosa que abandona el objetivo de convencer o cambiar la mente del otro, para dirigirse al alivio del sufrimiento presente en todos los actores de un conflicto. Se trata de dejar de ver el conflicto como enfrentamiento de enemigos para abordarlo como confluencia de seres en sufrimiento entre quienes pueden surgir las vías para el bienestar común. No hay alguien a quien vencer ni alguien que deba vencer. La palabra amorosa es aquella que, en lugar de crear separaciones como es frecuente en contextos de conflicto, crea modos de incluir e involucrar al diferente, al que piensa distinto, al que no actúa como creemos que se debe, en la búsqueda de soluciones para el bienestar común.

En todos los ámbitos de la sociedad, la palabra amorosa se desprende de creencias y hábitos condicionados por circunstancias personales y culturales que imponen como norma la palabra ruda, la crítica descalificadora y la hostilidad verbal. Necesitamos transformaciones profundas para que la palabra deje de ser usada en el ejercicio del poder para someter, dañar o abusar. Recientemente, en una clase en la universidad veíamos la importancia de ejercer la palabra para nombrar la violencia, hacer visible su manifestación en la vida diaria, identificar sus consecuencias y encontrar en colectivo caminos de cambio orientados a extinguirla. En esto la palabra surgida desde un corazón compasivo tiene un papel importante. Pero surgió también otro punto esclarecedor. En la promoción de condiciones que hagan viable la paz, es necesario también cortar el silencio que la cultura de competencia, hostilidad y destrucción ha impuesto al amor, la gratitud, el cuidado, la ternura, la solidaridad y la benevolencia en las relaciones con todos los seres.

Una cultura que naturaliza la violencia impone silencio a la profunda naturaleza compasiva del ser, fomenta la ilusoria separación entre individuos para ponerlos a luchar entre sí. La palabra amorosa es entrega sincera que confía en la infinita red interdependiente que contiene a todos los seres. Con esa confianza jubilosa, nuestra comunicación cotidiana se convierte en medio para que se exprese la benevolencia, el cuidado amoroso y la solidaridad en todas las relaciones humanas sin distingos. Despertamos junto a todos los seres en nuestro mundo solo con una sonrisa o una palabra amable que ayudan a ver el día de otra manera. La palabra que florece de un corazón compasivo abre los ojos a todo lo que está más allá de las circunstancias que pueden ser tensas, dolorosas o desesperadas. Emisor y receptor son uno en la práctica compasiva; la palabra amorosa es despertar simultáneo que los reúne, expresando la naturaleza de Buddha que abarca a todos los seres.

Somos red de ofrendas en la que circula energía de vida, y momento a momento creamos lugares seguros en los que entra, circula y queda impregnado el amor benevolente. Un círculo de la Vía sin interrupción.

Jakushō Pignatiello. Monje novicio discípulo del maestro Densho Quintero. En 2013 se inició en la práctica Zen Soto y desde 2014 estuvo bajo la guía espiritual de la maestra Kaikyo Roby. Con ella compartió práctica, realizó estudio e inició la preparación para recibir la ordenación monástica. Bajo sus directrices participó junto con otros practicantes en la fundación de Dokan Grupo de práctica Zen Soto en 2017. Al fallecer la maestra Kaikyo en 2018 inició vínculo con el maestro Densho con el cual estableció profundo vínculo espiritual y bajo su guía recibió en 2019 la ordenación monástica. Fiel a la guía espiritual de Densho sensei sigue el voto de mantener viva la práctica del buddha dharma y continúa el camino de entrenamiento. Actualmente es responsable de la Sangha Dokan, que es ahora integrante de la Comunidad Soto Zen de Colombia. Es psicólogo y psicoanalista que ejerce la labor terapéutica con clientes en consulta privada. Es profesor de la Escuela de Psicología de la Universidad Central de Venezuela. Su labor terapéutica y docente la realiza actualmente con el Dharma como fuente de comprensión del sufrimiento humano y de prácticas compasivas que abren caminos liberadores.

Abode of Benevolent Love

Jakushō Pignatello
TRANSLATED BY Seigen Hartkemeyer

IN REVERENCE AND HUMILITY I have taken on the challenge of writing about loving speech, because various activities and life experiences have brought me closer to it, and also perhaps because in my individual history I have aspired to emerge out of imposed silences, have access to speech, and cultivate bonds based on it. In that journey I now see in the background my personal vow that was activating a search, but I also recognize that on many occasions my exercise of speech was anguished because of greed, harsh, full of rage, and even at times violent.

Ten years of abandoning body and mind in zazen have opened me up to perceiving distressing burdens that interfere with my speaking and listening, and to practicing repentance and finding new fields in which thoughts, words and actions oriented toward liberation from suffering and eliminating evil and cultivating good, may flourish.

I see loving speech in the context of continuous practice—from zazen to daily life and back to zazen. This is a daily life that takes place where this humble novice monk in Caracas aspires to make every place and every moment a temple in which the Buddha-dharma manifests. The notes that follow in this text have been arising since I took on the task of writing about loving speech, taking as starting point Okumura Roshi's teaching about Dōgen Zenji's *Shobogenzo Shishobo*. Day by day, while observing, becoming aware, practicing repentance and returning to vow, annotations came up for me in which lived experience and the teachings of the masters were in dialogue. Everyday experiences showed me that loving speech "is nurtured little by little" (Dōgen Zenji). In the interpersonal relationships of daily life, activities in the sangha, and my work as a psychotherapist and as a teacher, ongoing practice opened me up to seeing, understanding, treasuring, and protecting loving speech, something "that is not usually known or seen" (Dōgen Zenji). Is loving speech present in my daily life? What does it consist of? What makes it possible for it to arise, and at what moments does that occur? These are questions that accompanied me in the elaboration of the notes that I am sharing here and that will continue to stay with me in the future.

At this moment I dare to affirm that loving speech is nothing extraordinary, abnormal, or otherworldly. As far as I understand it, loving speech is nothing more than the manifestation of the profound nature of speech, the pure expression of its fundamental functions. Speech is bond and integration, a means of giving and receiving; it is recognition, care, and presence. It is an exchange that makes us human; the first words we receive from our parents at birth are loving responses that link what we need to survive (food, cleanliness, care, and affection) with what can satisfy that need, and in this way we enter life. In that interaction, if we receive only objects or actions devoid of loving communication, life languishes.

To practice loving speech is to care for all beings, just as we were, are, and will be cared for in our life.

Okumura Roshi tells us that "we are nothing but collections of bonds." Speech is intrinsic to the bond; words make a link in such a way as to produce suffering, when it is used for selfish purposes, or to cultivate good and liberate suffering beings. With loving speech we produce bonds that constitute us along with others, actualizing nirvana in every place and circumstance. And so, for example, in the institutional spaces in which we carry out our professional activities or in those where the issues of the community in which we live are resolved, we promote warm welcome, receptivity, and openness to collaboration that emerge from something that transcends individual qualities or limitations. The practice of loving speech can be a perfume that fosters personal and group conditions of trust toward perceiving, taking into consideration, sharing, and analyzing experiences linked to the common welfare. Loving speech can manifest as openness to dialogue on issues that are usually silenced, feared, or discarded. It is also speech that can sensitize each member of a work or life community to care for others.

We live in cultural environments that promote the use of loving words to seduce, obtain something, exercise power, incite us to consume, or possess the other as an object. Loving speech is a generous surrender that does not try to obtain something, but is directed to the good and the relief of the one who receives it. Seeing the reality of each being with a compassionate heart, it approaches that reality and tries to situate itself in the center from where speech can help to alleviate suffering.

Okumura Roshi tells us that "when we speak with a kind and compassionate heart, even a daily greeting becomes loving speech." This greeting is much more than a one-time event; it can be an expression of continuous practice. To sustain a cordial greeting—day by day, person by person, from one place to another—to every being without distinction and with attention to what the other is feeling is a cultivation of compassion, not only in one's own heart, but in the whole network of relationships that constitute us. It awakens joy, calm, and even hope in the one who receives the greeting and, we must repeat, joy, calm and hope in the whole network of relationships that make up that person. We complete a circle when, along with the loving care of the words we offer, there is simultaneously an attentive and joyful listening to the response to the greeting. We speak and listen with a sincere openness that sustains the bond that is illuminated at that instant.

In Italian one way of saying hello is *salve,* which comes from *salvezza* (salvation). The circle of continuous practice in loving speech, when offering a greeting, "saves" the interlocutor, rescues him/her, and welcomes him/her kindly, thus soothing and cultivating well-being. We advance in this practice, as in zazen, through assiduousness. This is sincere and compassionate greeting with constancy—not just sometimes, not just the day we wake up in a good mood, but whenever we can, whenever we have the opportunity. It's about being attentive and open. I see this practice in countless places and circumstances: when leaving the house, when getting on the elevator or public transportation, when entering a store. I would like to highlight, as a special example, greeting people who provide sanitation services in the environment where we live, circulate, or work. These people are usually not even noticed, and when they are, often only in order to denigrate their work. On the other hand, if such a person receives a warm greeting, "his face shines and his mind is happy," as Dōgen Zenji tells us. Such a person responds from that brightness and joy with a grateful greeting that purifies and sows harmony in the whole space, and for all the people that his work serves.

Loving speech is a safe place. What does "safe place" mean? It is a space of well-being for the one who receives the speech, for a being who, thanks to it, can speak and be heard in a way that alleviates suffering (without judgment, without reproach, without enforced silence, without imposing some saving will-power), that opens doors to processes that bring relief, and that generate conditions of trust within the interpersonal space. All of our relationships within the sangha, the family, the married couple, among friends, and within the context of professional work can also be a safe place. In the context of psychotherapy, creating a safe place through speech is the necessary condition for a healing process to take place. Loving speech is a space of well-being that brings together the one receiving it and the one giving it. It is an intermediate space not belonging to one or the other individual; it is the selfsame reality that contains both of them, actualizing wisdom and compassion intrinsic to the transcendental reality of interdependent being.

Loving speech does not stem from skills, technique, or will. It does not arise from a desire to be loving or to be loved. It is not the result of training after which memorized formulas are mechanically repeated. It is not something possessed by one or another person to be given or denied to others. Loving speech manifests under certain conditions that derive from a sustained practice.

Loving speech is not in a hurry; it does not seek to obtain anything. It is calm speech, born from tranquility in the process of enunciating. In situations where there is tension, or possible dispute or conflict, loving speech means communicating from tranquility, a center, equanimity, and compassionate openness. In compassionate and magnanimous presence, it activates conditions for the awakening of the interlocutors in openness, flexibility, calmness, commitment, and attention to the other.

It is "loving" not because of a feeling or emotion accompanying it; it is loving because of its consequences in those who receive it and open themselves to interdependent connection, to kindness in coexistence. It is "loving" also because it is enunciated from interdependence. It is not an ego that speaks to validate its meanings; rather, kind speech arises from the interdependent network that works through us, and we are the means for its working in every moment. It arises from an awakening to the network of interdependent origination actualized in the moment in which speaking, listening, writing, singing or reciting are taken on as service for the relief of the suffering of all beings without distinction. Speech arises from a practice of trusting surrender to the network of interdependent origination. In this sense, loving speech is trust; it trusts and awakens trust.

Loving speech is born from a place beyond ourselves, beyond a self that collects acquired skills or tools. It has an intention that arises by letting go of identification with selfish motivations based on fantasies, whether conscious or unconscious, of heroism and sacrifice. We help more when we see ourselves less as characters who want to save others by what we tell them; we free others when we free ourselves from characters who claim to know and decide about the welfare of others. Loving speech makes use of skillful means, but it cannot be reduced to the use of those means as if it were a technique. It arises from being present, trusting, devoid of expectations, open to the speech or the silence that comes at the precise, necessary, or beneficial moment.

Trusting that it does not derive from my own abilities, but comes from beyond the limits of individuality, I simply lend myself as a means for it to arise. Speech that heals and soothes comes from an interdependent reality that transcends me and the interlocutor, making us part of a whole. This is not a state; it is an uninterrupted circle of practice with this vision and intention, something boundless toward which we direct a vow. This practice accompanies me in everyday situations within my community, in my teaching activity, and in my work with patients. It is a practice in which humility is cultivated.

In his teaching, Okumura Roshi invites us to look intentionally for virtuous and praiseworthy traits in others as intrinsic to the practice of loving speech. He asserts that this can shape our personality by making it more supportive of others. We are surrounded by cultural habits and practices that assume that we learn by correcting mistakes and that we solve problems by eliminating things that go wrong. It is common to talk about the shortcomings of others and to punish oneself for one's own weaknesses. All this contributes to producing environments governed by hostility and violence.

Seeing the person in his/her qualities and virtues cuts through the established habits that tend to highlight the faults, mistakes, and weaknesses of the other. All the teaching activities we carry out are spaces for the practice of this perspective of loving speech. Whether giving a class at the university or an introductory talk on zazen, loving speech is a practice that helps in seeing the light in each being, and is directed toward that light. From this perspective, to teach is to place oneself alongside the other in the task of learning; it is to become one with his/her conditions and perception of reality. Loving speech in teaching does not point out deficiencies that need to be filled, but rather to capacities and resources that students can activate to produce meaningful learning and open up new perspectives. Instead of pointing out and penalizing errors through various forms of evaluation, the one who instructs another can do so from a compassionate heart that is located in the particular reality of the person and in what moves him/her to learn. Instead of highlighting the error, we show options that open paths of learning, liberation, and transformation.

Seeing the virtue, resources, and potential of the person is a fundamental practice in psychotherapeutic work. In my current experience, there is no duality between the monk practicing the Way and the therapist dedicated to helping suffering people. The mental health professions can be cruel disciplines when they emphasize the failure, weakness, lack, or dysfunction of a patient taken as an object of examination, often without knowing what to do with what has been diagnosed or even considering what might be done about it. In my therapeutic practice, the path of sincere and real help toward those who suffer led me to the encounter with the need to see light amidst realities seemingly impossible to overcome or transform. Therapeutic action that involves the suffering being as the protagonist of a transformation is based on always being open and attentive to seeing the virtue, energy, resources, and inner movement of a trans-individual psyche that leads the person to resolve the causes and conditions of suffering. Academia and the therapeutic schools do not teach this; I had to learn it so as to be able to help people in the most difficult situations of trauma, grief, depression, anxiety or psychosis, to mention just a few. These are complex, painful, and seemingly hopeless situations. It is not just about seeing them; it is a matter of trusting in those virtues and resources that perhaps the person him/herself does not see and does not believe that he/she has. In each encounter loving speech renews this compassionate message: "I trust you, I trust that you can change the conditions and overcome what is distressing you. I trust, even though you do not now trust yourself or your ability to move forward." I offer my confidence that healing processes come from beyond the individuals involved in a helping relationship. They are like the energy of a breaking wave coming ashore, producing sound and bubbles. We hear the roar, we see the foam on the shore, but the energy that produces them comes from infinite places and causes that are hidden well beyond the horizon to which our limited gaze can reach.

At this point it is worth asking: is loving speech just words? There is so much that I know is communicated and transmitted beyond words. As a safe place and dharmic refuge, loving speech is also silence, a space for just pausing and breathing in the full presence of the one accompanying us. Attention, stillness, and surrender to the present are also the center point of listening, and loving speech is necessarily listening. It is not only a message that is emitted, for such a message would not be possible without a loving surrender to what another is communicating to us, bypassing the mental frameworks that filter and let through only that which relates to what is habitual and gratifying. Listening is openness to what is—a sustained, serene, compassionate presence that helps others use words to express their reality, to understand it, and to elaborate solutions to the suffering of body and mind. Returning to the context of psychotherapy, the practice of loving speech is the cultivation of the psychotherapist's capacity for compassionate listening—something that is not written in a book, is not explained by psychological theories, and is not drilled as some impersonal technique. Listening is not a technique, nor is it a pose; it is a compassionate practice, a path requiring moment-to-moment detachment from the ignorance that separates from, makes judgments about, or rejects the reality of others.

Moving on to another area of practice in daily life, I am referring now to what we can contribute on the basis of the bodhisattva vows to the community we live in. In our society, community life can be full of difficulties, problems with public services, hostility among neighbors, and deterioration of the environment. Many of these problems require the cooperation and commitment of everyone in the community. In this context, when our presence brings the reassurance of some loving words, we are contributing small grains of sand that help to build bridges and cultivate bonds. In our society, where violence and polarization are normalized on a daily basis, conflicts between members of a community are exacerbated. In such situations, we can bring peace by means of loving speech that abandons the aim of convincing or changing the other's mind, so as to alleviate the suffering present in all the actors of a conflict. This is a matter of ceasing to see the conflict as a confrontation of adversaries and approaching it as a confluence of suffering beings, among whom avenues for common well-being can emerge. There is no one to be defeated, and no one who should defeat. Loving speech is speech that, instead of creating separations as is frequent in conflict contexts, creates ways to include and involve one who is different, one who thinks differently, one who does not act as we believe he/she should, in seeking solutions for the common welfare.

In all spheres of society, loving speech does away with beliefs and habits conditioned by personal and cultural circumstances that impose harsh words, disqualifying criticism, and verbal hostility as the norm. We need profound transformations so that speech is no longer used in the exercise of the power to subdue, harm or abuse. Recently, in a class at the university, we saw the importance of using words to name violence, to make visible its manifestation in daily life, to identify its consequences, and collectively to find avenues of change oriented toward extinguishing it. In this, speech that comes from a compassionate heart has an important role to play. But another enlightening point also emerged. In promoting conditions that make peace viable, it is also necessary to cut through the silence that the culture of competition, hostility and destruction has imposed upon love, gratitude, care, tenderness, solidarity, and benevolence in relationships with all beings.

A culture that normalizes violence imposes silence on the deep, compassionate nature of being, fosters an illusory separation among individuals, and sets them at each other other's throats. Loving speech is sincere surrender that trusts in the infinite, interdependent network that contains all beings. With that joyful trust, our daily communication becomes a means for benevolence, loving care, and solidarity to be expressed in all human relationships without distinction. We wake up along with all beings in our world with just a smile or a kind word that helps us to look at the day differently. Speech that blossoms from a compassionate heart opens our eyes to everything that is beyond circumstances that may be tense, painful, or desperate. Sender and receiver are one in compassionate practice; loving speech is a simultaneous awakening that brings them together, expressing the Buddha-nature that embraces all beings.

We are a network of offerings in which life's energy circulates, and moment by moment we are creating safe places where benevolent love enters, circulates, and remains imbued—an uninterrupted circle of the Way.

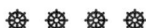

Jakushō Pignatiello is a disciple of master Densho Quintero. In 2013 he began to practice Soto Zen and from 2014 to 2018 he was under the spiritual guidance of Kaikyo Roby. With her he shared practice, studied and began the preparation to receive novice ordination. He participated with other practitioners in the formation of the Dokan Soto Zen Practice Group in 2017. On Kaikyo's death in 2018, he connected with Densho, established a deep spiritual bond, and under his guidance received ordination in 2019. True to Densho's spiritual guidance, he follows the vow to keep alive the practice of the buddhadharma and continues the path of training. He is responsible for the Dokan Sangha, which is now a member of the Soto Zen Community of Colombia. A psychologist and psychoanalyst who performs therapeutic work with clients in private practice, he is also a professor at the School of Psychology of the Central University of Venezuela. His therapeutic and teaching work is carried out with the Dharma as a source of understanding human suffering and compassionate practices that open liberating paths.

Árboles que Cantan

Reigen Sanjuán

En nuestra práctica en Daishinji, Densho Sensei insiste en cuatro enseñanzas de formulación sencilla que repite una y otra vez para ayudarnos a despertar. La formulación puede ser sencilla, pero su comprensión y puesta en práctica no lo es. Las veo como cuatro píldoras medicinales que hay que tomar con regularidad para aliviar el sufrimiento: (1) nuestra práctica consiste en no reaccionar, (2) nuestra práctica es una práctica corporal, (3) en nuestra práctica debemos tener en cuenta a los otros y (4) en nuestra práctica soltamos la identidad con los procesos mentales o, como diría Uchiyama Roshi, abrimos la mano del pensamiento.

Aquí trataré de exponer y ejemplificar mi comprensión de estas enseñanzas aterrizadas en la práctica de despertar una mente compasiva que nos permita ofrecer palabras amorosas y evitar palabras hirientes.

No reaccionar

Las palabras se propagan a través del aire y son procesadas en el cerebro a gran velocidad. Esto hace que la brecha entre el estímulo que creo que me invita a hablar y la palabra ofrecida sea muy breve. Es así como la mayoría de las cosas que digo pueden no ser más que reacciones inconscientes surgidas de mis tendencias kármicas. Para poder aliviar el sufrimiento con la palabra amorosa, procuro practicar en observar y dilatar esa brevísima brecha entre todas las cosas que me estimulan a hablar y las palabras que salen de mi boca.

Detenerme entre el estímulo y la respuesta me parece a ratos imposible, sobre todo cuando lo intento con la fuerza de voluntad de mi ego diciendo: "debo estar atento, no voy a reaccionar." Si bien es un ejercicio que consume energía, porque hay que involucrar la voluntad y las funciones del lóbulo frontal del cerebro, no es algo que pueda practicar sólo con buenas intenciones. Tal vez hay otro camino. Esa brecha se ha venido ampliando naturalmente, por sí sola y con el tiempo, gracias a mi práctica de zazen. Cuando no está mi ego interviniendo, las brechas entre estímulos y reacciones son como las junturas entre los ladrillos de una pared abandonada: la vida misma se abre paso en esos intervalos. El silencio del zazen en medio del ruido se me parece mucho a este breve silencio entre estímulo y reacción. Cuando puedo tomar conciencia de ese instante, noto que a veces la mejor respuesta es no decir nada, guardar silencio y no fabricar más paredes con los ladrillos de mis palabras necias.

En mis viejas tendencias reactivas, para los demás siempre tenía un chiste, un comentario sarcástico o ingenioso, una anécdota, una opinión política o técnica, una explicación, un consejo, una palabrota, una queja o una crítica. No me podía quedar callado y llamaba la atención de manera continua. Incluso llevé estas tendencias a un blog y a las redes sociales donde alcancé a tener un número de seguidores por encima del promedio. Cuando inicié mi práctica, mis amigos me reclamaban por guardar mucho silencio en las reuniones y por haber cerrado mis redes sociales. Gracias a la práctica pude empezar a detenerme antes de hablar y a ser consciente de que la mayoría de cosas que decía (o escribía) eran básicamente ruido en medio del ruido. A veces gracioso, a veces sin sentido y a veces causando sufrimiento en los demás. Pero no sólo en los demás, también en mí, porque el personaje que había creado con mis palabras se había vuelto insostenible. Todavía hago chistes bobos y continúo llamando la atención con las cosas que digo, pero con la práctica en comunidad he podido descansar bastante de ese personaje que tiene que reaccionar a todo con un comentario. Antes de poder ofrecer palabras amorosas tuve que aprender a guardar silencio al compartir con los demás. Sólo de esta forma pude empezar a tener conciencia de algunas de mis tendencias reactivas en relación con la palabra.

Para mí es de vital importancia (en el sentido estricto de la palabra vital) evitar decir cualquier cosa cuando estoy experimentando sentimientos negativos muy intensos. Ese esfuerzo puede llegar a demandar toda mi energía vital. Ahora, cuando reacciono mal, me doy cuenta que ayuda mucho pedir disculpas sinceras lo antes posible para procurar enmendar el error. A pesar de eso, muchas veces las palabras generan un daño irreparable.

Espero no estar apuntando al karma de los demás con el siguiente ejemplo. Lo menciono porque me ayuda a tener presente la importancia de lo que estoy tratando de exponer. En mis veintes, cuando mi mejor amigo de aquel entonces salió del armario con su señora madre, ella le contestó que prefería un hijo muerto antes que homosexual. Mi amigo entró en una depresión profunda y a los tres meses murió de una neumonía. No es la primera vez en la historia que una madre y su hijo gay pasan por algo tan doloroso. Incluso hay una película, *Prayers for Bobby,* sobre este tema recurrente.

Una sola palabra lanzada con mala intención puede llegar a causar un gran sufrimiento en innumerables seres y en uno mismo.

PRÁCTICA CORPORAL

Que nuestra práctica, más que una práctica espiritual, fuese una práctica corporal, es una de las cosas que más me llamó la atención del zen. De qué otra forma podríamos practicar la vía si no es con el propio cuerpo. Incluso hay expresiones como quemar el cuerpo o que el cuerpo arda con la práctica. En el zazen la descripción de la postura corporal es detallada. En las ceremonias son muy exigentes las maneras como se tocan los instrumentos y se usan los hábitos. Es necesario prestar atención a los detalles de los movimientos y mantener una conciencia del cuerpo. Tengo entendido que para los monjes en entrenamiento esta práctica es continua y regula hasta las formas de dormir y usar el servicio sanitario. No he tenido la oportunidad de practicar en un monasterio de entrenamiento, pero eso no significa que no pueda practicar con el cuerpo en mi vida como laico que involucra lazos familiares y responsabilidades laborales.

Antes de llegar al zen, tenía la idea de que los seres humanos oíamos por los oídos y hablábamos por la boca. En efecto, desde cierta perspectiva es así. Pero cuando aprendí a estar más presente gracias a la práctica, empecé a notar que en verdad oímos y hablamos con todo el cuerpo y que en ese proceso de comunicación nuestro cuerpo se proyecta en todo el espacio-tiempo.

Cuando mis familiares le preguntaron a mi segundo esposo que si el zen me estaba sirviendo para algo, él contestó que antes yo me quejaba continuamente de las actitudes de los demás y que, afortunadamente, eso ya no era así. Hablar mal de los demás (una persona cercana, conocida, un enemigo o un personaje público) me hacía sentir superior. Claro está que hablar mal de los demás genera malestar, sufrimiento y división entre la gente, y es una falta a los preceptos. Pero hay más implicaciones. Cuando lograba estar atento en ese tipo de conversaciones, hablando sin consideración de los demás, me podía dar cuenta de mis sensaciones corporales. Es como si envenenara mi propio cuerpo de una manera tan nociva como cuando fumaba cigarrillo. Esa sensación de toxicidad es muy clara en el uso de las redes sociales.

He tenido tres nacimientos y tres muertes en Twitter. La primera vez que lo dejé estaba intoxicado por todo lo que yo decía. Ya no podía seguir sosteniendo el personaje que había creado. La segunda vez terminé armando un personaje aún más molesto. La tercera vez que abrí mi cuenta de Twitter ya había empezado a practicar, pero sin importar cuán buenas fueran mis intenciones, cualquier cosa que decía ahí me hacía sentir mal (con el agravante de que todo queda registrado). Luego decidí que era mejor guardar silencio y sólo observar, pero así yo no aportara a la discusión pública, sólo presenciar la agresividad verbal y los dramas ajenos era tan adictivo como intoxicante. Llegaba siempre a un punto en el que terminaba en unas posiciones corporales deformes con toda mi energía vital absorbida por la aplicación del celular. El caso es que en Twitter no encontré forma de silenciar, filtrar o bloquear cuentas para tener un *timeline* virtuoso. Ni siquiera siguiendo cuentas budistas. El sistema de recomendación de inteligencia artificial de Twitter parece estar diseñado para la confrontación y la toxicidad. Caigo a veces en la ilusión de que tengo el control en determinados ambientes si entro con buenas intenciones, pero la verdad es que para muchos ambientes la única opción virtuosa que tengo es abandonar el viejo nido y migrar a sitios en donde cantan los pájaros de verdad.

Poder ser consciente de ese malestar corporal que en general se produce con ciertas formas de hablar fue importante para poder entender la necesidad de despertar una mente compasiva que me permitiera practicar la palabra amorosa.

Con el cuerpo también se habla y por eso hay que estar muy atento a lo que se transmite con él. Otra cosa que me cautivó de la práctica es todo el lenguaje no verbal y sutil que circula cuando estamos practicando en comunidad. Densho Sensei dice que debemos caminar dentro del zendo como si fuéramos el humo del incienso. Los hábitos exigen un gran cuidado en los movimientos: no es permitida la torpeza al cargar las ollas o al limpiar el incensario, y hay que evitar andar con la cabeza agachada o altiva, o con la espalda encorvada. Los sonidos de los instrumentos y las recitaciones de los sutras son expresiones del corazón, y el corazón está en el cuerpo. En el ritual del *ōryōki* no se habla, porque todo el ritual habla un lenguaje amoroso que se expresa con el cuerpo. En la práctica en comunidad también se experimenta la comunicación sutil entre amigos espirituales, la camaradería, las risas ahogadas porque hay que guardar silencio, las miradas de complicidad y los gestos compasivos. Con la práctica nuestro cuerpo se va transformando por sí solo en un medio de comunicación que transmite amor. Tengo registros fotográficos que acreditan esta transformación.

En particular, tengo una foto de carné (de la universidad para la que trabajo) de hace cinco años (justo antes de empezar mi práctica) y una de ahora. Un antes y un después. Le mostré el contraste a un compañero de la sangha y me dijo que mi mirada se había dulcificado, que antes era muy agresiva. Adoro mi trabajo como profesor universitario, en especial por mi relación con los estudiantes con quienes siempre he tenido una relación de gran aprecio y respeto mutuo. Sin embargo, en la época de la primera foto recuerdo que los estudiantes me habían dejado en los comentarios de la evaluación del semestre cosas como "es muy buen profesor, pero intimida a sus estudiantes." Incluso una estudiante me confesó sentir pánico con mi presencia. Era la primera vez, tras casi dos décadas de docencia, que recibía comentarios de ese estilo. El sufrimiento que tenía acumulado en todo mi cuerpo por ese entonces no sólo salpicaba a los demás con comentarios rudos o necios, también estaba asustando a mis estudiantes con mis expresiones corporales y faciales agresivas o displicentes. La aplicación de fotos de Google a veces me trae recuerdos de esa época y, al compararlas con las de ahora, se pueden ver dos personas que comunican con sus cuerpos cosas totalmente diferentes. Como si fuéramos muñecos de arcilla, la práctica moldea nuestros cuerpos para que aprendan a hablar con amor.

Tener en cuenta a los otros

Si bien la cortesía no es suficiente para practicar la palabra amorosa, sí es necesaria. La cortesía puede llegar a ser una forma vacía e hipócrita de relacionarse con los demás, pero una cortesía sincera puede ser suficiente para practicar la palabra amorosa. El zen trae consigo muchos detalles de cortesía para tener en cuenta a los otros. Es claro que estos detalles vienen de una etiqueta japonesa muy delicada que me generó un choque cultural cuando me encontré con la práctica. Entiendo que no se trata de convertirnos en japoneses, sino de tener presente que los modales y la cortesía sincera son formas de expresión amorosa que nos permite tener en cuenta a los demás. Densho Sensei nos insiste en que en nuestra práctica debemos ser cuidadosos en cómo nos ponemos los zapatos, en cómo entregamos las cosas y en cómo hacemos *gasshō* para saludarnos. Muchos de estos modales permiten reconocer y respetar el espacio de los demás. Claro, en la medida de lo posible, porque de todas maneras somos una sangha latinoamericana y nos abrazamos entre nosotros cada vez que podemos.

Abrazarse como muestra de afecto es parte de las expresiones latinoamericanas innegociables y no le veo nada de malo. Pero también en Colombia tenemos tendencias culturales que no me parecen muy amorosas a la hora de encontrarnos con los demás. Muchas veces nos saludamos (incluso con personas que acabamos de conocer) y automáticamente emitimos opiniones sobre el aspecto físico (gordo, flaco, pálido) o hacemos preguntas atrevidas que agreden la intimidad de la personas (estados de salud, trabajo, situaciones de pareja). Entre el estímulo (encontrarnos con alguien) y la reacción (emitir opiniones o realizar preguntas) hay muy poco tiempo para reaccionar. Estoy seguro de que la mayoría de las veces no son comentarios con mala intención, sino una preocupación sincera por el otro, pero estas pequeñas transgresiones pueden generar sufrimiento en los otros y lo tenemos validado culturalmente. De la misma forma, tenemos normalizado el tener discusiones acaloradas de pareja, de trabajo o de política en frente de terceros. Lo hacemos en un centro comercial, en el carro, en la oficina o en un grupo de chat. El malestar no es solo para los que están participando de la discusión, salpica.

Hablando de discusiones, con la práctica he aprendido la importancia de renunciar a tener siempre la razón, escuchar atentamente (con todo el cuerpo) lo que el otro está diciendo y esperar el momento adecuado para contestar de la manera más hábil posible. Demanda mucha energía vital, pero es liberador. Puede ser desviando la atención, cambiando de tema, guardando silencio o dejando que el detonante se disipe por sí solo ya que, en general, lo que se discute no tiene ninguna importancia. También me ha ayudado hacer un esfuerzo en mantener los buenos modales occidentales cuando se pierden por la confianza y la familiaridad. Es más interesante practicar la cortesía cuando se trata de alguien que no es de mis afectos porque se puede volver un juego si logro mantener la calma. Lo cierto es que tanta informalidad validada por la cultura puede convertirse en agresión. No hay cómo llevar los honoríficos japoneses a la vida cotidiana, pero dirigirme a mis colegas con cortesía sincera usando el prefijo de Profesor, a mis superiores con el de Señor Decano y dirigirme a mi madre y a mi padre con la mayor devoción posible ayudan mucho a no generar un sufrimiento innecesario con la palabra.

Abrir la mano del pensamiento

Ya sea por mis tendencias kármicas culturales o personales, para poder cultivar una mente compasiva y evitar reaccionar con la palabra es crucial la práctica de zazen. El zazen me ayuda a soltar la identidad con los procesos mentales, a abrir la mano del pensamiento. Especialmente a soltar la identidad con los personajes con los que me identifico, porque cada vez que esto sucede, termino inevitablemente generando sufrimiento con mis palabras.

Por ejemplo, es malo identificarse con un personaje bueno. Cuando empecé mi práctica, en la universidad tenía un cargo directivo y, como tenía que ser un buen budista, un bodhisattva compasivo, no me ponía de mal genio con nadie y siempre tenía palabras pacientes sin importar la situación. Eso es muy peligroso, me estaba haciendo daño porque estaba permitiendo que algunas personas se aprovecharan de mí. A veces la palabra más compasiva que puedo dar es una palabra cortante y contundente que establezca límites, así no sea coherente con mis ideas de virtud.

Tampoco ayuda identificarse con personajes importantes o inteligentes. Cuando entré a trabajar en la universidad, me veía envuelto en toda clase de discusiones académicas con mis colegas. Por temporadas, el ambiente laboral se podía tornar infernal. Los académicos somos propensos a renacer en el reino de los asuras y ese reino carece de palabras amorosas. Para mí es difícil salir de esos ciclos de renacimiento por mi tendencia a fabricar ideas sobre mis capacidades.

También identificarse como víctima lo puede convertir a uno en victimario. Caer en una defensa permanente del espacio personal es nocivo. Mi estrategia de adaptación al matoneo que experimenté en mi época escolar por ser gay y algo afeminado fue aprender a ser sarcástico, rápido e hiriente con la palabra. Siendo un adulto joven me identifiqué con la idea que los gays nos tenemos que defender del heteropatriarcado con palabras ponzoñosas. En algunos sectores del mundo gay, esa forma de reaccionar es considerada como una virtud y puede llegar a ser muy entretenida. Incluso hay un show de televisión muy popular y divertido, *RuPaul Drag Race,* en donde de manera continua se hace humor de esa manera. Una vez aprendí esta forma de defensa con la palabra, la gente lo pensaba dos veces antes de intentar lastimarme, pero también me estaba convirtiendo en un personaje antipático, aislado y lleno de un veneno que me tenía que tomar yo también. Afortunadamente ese personaje no duró mucho gracias a mi primer esposo, con el que estuve casado once años. Hicimos activismo y participamos en política por la defensa de los derechos LGBT. Él era considerado el Harvey Milk colombiano por los medios de comunicación. Cuando falleció, a los pocos días, una emisora de difusión nacional empezó a emitir mensajes homofóbicos llenos de odio contra mí y mi difunto marido. En medio del duelo, el ataque había sido devastador y no podía entender el porqué de tanta crueldad. Aparecieron de un momento a otro una gran red de amigos y muchos desconocidos para ayudar a liberar el sufrimiento. Frente a la emisora hicimos una manifestación, llena de amor, canciones, bailes y flores. Los medios de comunicación nos respaldaron y a la emisora le tocó pedir disculpas, realizar campañas de capacitación e invitar a expertos en derechos sexuales y reproductivos al programa radial. Es el poder de la expresión amorosa. Ningún sufrimiento se habría aliviado reaccionado desde el veneno o el rencor.

En resumen

Así entiendo estas cuatro enseñanzas de Densho Sensei aplicadas, en este caso, a la palabra amorosa. Cuando se recibe un estímulo y se está tentado a contestar con palabras, es importante tomar conciencia de la pequeña brecha entre el estímulo y la reacción. Una forma puede ser estando atento con el cuerpo, qué siente y qué se transmite con él. En esa brecha podemos tener en cuenta a los demás y no reaccionar desde tendencias reactivas personales o culturales. Abrir la mano del pensamiento, soltar las ideas fijas que tenemos de nosotros mismos y de los demás, permite que de forma natural se dilate esa brecha, se pueda expresar palabras amorosas y se logre evitar palabras hirientes. No creo que sea una práctica sólo de la voluntad de querer hablar amorosamente, es la expresión del zazen con nuestro cuerpo cuando se sale al encuentro de todos los seres.

En una sesshin estuve encargado del servicio de las comidas. Recuerdo haberlo hecho con todo el corazón al punto que me olvidé por completo de mí mismo. Al terminar el retiro una practicante laica se me acercó y me dijo que estaba conmovida porque me veía como una mariposa dentro del zendo con las mangas como alas. Era la primera vez que alguien usaba la palabra mariposa para decirme algo bello y sin intención de ofenderme. Alcancé a detenerme y a no reaccionar con la palabra para defenderme. Fue una experiencia sanadora. Creo que la práctica transforma nuestros cuerpos para transmitir amor y eso se nota con más claridad en los cuerpos de los maestros que llevan toda una vida de práctica.

Una de las cosas más bonitas que he experimentado con la práctica son esos momentos zen que ocurren de manera espontánea y que muchos practicantes refieren. Uno muy especial me pasa cuando voy caminando por la ciudad y siento que de pronto la presencia de un árbol me atraviesa, que no hay separación, que transmite dicha, que se puede escuchar con el cuerpo, que no se sabe con certeza si está cantando o si está hablando, pero es claro que está vibrando con su cuerpo de árbol. Cuando no hay un yo reaccionando con palabras necias en mi cabeza, en mi cuerpo o en mi boca, siento que puedo percibir el canto de los árboles. Ojalá pudiera aprender a hablar como ellos, con todo el cuerpo, dejando que se manifieste el amor fundamental del que está hecho el universo entero.

Reigen Sanjuán es un monje novicio ordenado el 21 de marzo de 2022 por Densho Quintero Sensei. Es Oriundo de Bogotá, Colombia, donde vive y practica en Daishinji. En su vida laica trabaja como profesor de matemáticas en una pequeña universidad. Le encanta enseñar matemáticas, programar computadores y hacer algo de investigación en matemáticas puras y física matemática cuando las condiciones lo permiten. En los últimos años, la práctica ha ido ganando cada vez más espacio en su vida. Años atras participó activamente en el activismo por los derechos LGBT en Colombia motivado por el amor, la supervivencia y la resistencia.

Singing Trees

REIGEN SANJUÁN

IN OUR PRACTICE AT DAISHINJI, Densho Sensei insists on four simply formulated teachings that he repeats over and over again to help us awaken. The formulation may be simple, but understanding and putting them into practice is not. I see them as four medicinal pills to be taken regularly to relieve suffering: (1) our practice is not to react, (2) our practice is a bodily practice, (3) in our practice we must be mindful of others, and (4) in our practice we let go of our habit of identifying with mental processes or, as Uchiyama Roshi would say, we open the hand of thought.

Here I will try to expound and exemplify my understanding of these teachings grounded in the practice of awakening a compassionate mind that enables us to offer loving speech to all sentient beings and avoid hurtful words.

NOT REACTING

Words travel through the air and are processed in the brain at high speed. This causes the gap between the stimulus that I think invites me to speak and the speech offered in response (to that stimulus) to be very short. This is how most of the things I say may be nothing more than unconscious reactions arising from my karmic tendencies. To alleviate suffering with loving speech, I try to practice observing and dilating that very brief gap between all the things that stimulate me to speak and the words that come out of my mouth.

Stopping between the stimulus and the response seems impossible at times, especially when I attempt this with the willpower of my ego saying, "I must pay attention; I will not react." While this is an energy-consuming exercise, because I have to engage willpower and the frontal lobe functions of my brain, it is not something I can practice with good intentions alone. Perhaps there is another way. That gap has been widening naturally, on its own and over time, thanks to my zazen practice. When my ego is not intervening, the gaps between stimuli and reactions are like the joints between the bricks of an abandoned wall: life itself breaks through in those intervals. The silence of zazen amid the noise is very much like this brief silence between the stimulus and the reaction. When I can become aware of that instant, I notice that sometimes the best response is to say nothing, to keep silent and not to build any more walls with the bricks of my foolish words.

In my old reactive tendencies, for others I always had a joke, a sarcastic or witty remark, an anecdote, a political or technical opinion, an explanation, a piece of advice, a swear word, a complaint, or a criticism. I could not keep quiet and was constantly drawing attention to myself. I even took these tendencies to a blog and to social media where I reached an above-average number of followers. When I started my practice, my friends complained to me that I was too silent in meetings and that I had quit my social media. Thanks to the practice I was able to pause before I spoke and be aware that most of the things I said (or wrote) were just noise in the middle of noise—sometimes funny, sometimes meaningless, and sometimes causing suffering in others. But not only in others, but also in myself, because the character I had created with my words had become untenable. I still make silly jokes and continue to attract attention with the things I say, but with sangha practice, I have been able to rest from that character that has to react to everything with a comment. Before I could offer loving words, I had to learn how to be silent when sharing with others. Only in this way could I begin to become aware of some of my reactive tendencies regarding my speech.

For me, it is of vital importance (in the strict sense of the word vital) to avoid saying anything when I am experiencing very intense negative feelings. That effort can take all my vital energy. Now, when I react badly, I find that it helps a lot to apologize sincerely as soon as possible to try to make amends. Despite that, words often do irreparable damage.

I hope I am not pointing out the karma of others with the following example. I mention it because it helps me to keep in mind the importance of what I am trying to say. In my twenties, when my best friend at the time came out to his mother, she told him that she would rather have a dead son than a homosexual. My friend fell into a deep depression and three months later he died of pneumonia. It is not the first time in history that a mother and her gay son have gone through something so painful. There's even a movie, *Prayers for Bobby,* about this recurring theme. A single word tossed out with bad intentions can cause great suffering in countless beings and oneself.

BODILY PRACTICE

That our practice, more than a spiritual one, is a bodily practice, is one of the things that most caught my attention about Zen. How else could we practice the way but with our bodies? There are even expressions such as burning the body with the practice. In zazen, the description of the body posture is detailed. In ceremonies, how the instruments are played and the robes are used is very demanding. It is necessary to pay attention to the details of movements and to maintain awareness of the body. I understand that for monks in training, this practice is continuous and regulates even the ways of sleeping and using the toilet. I have not had the opportunity to practice in a training monastery, but that does not mean I cannot practice with my body in my lay life which involves family ties and work responsibilities.

Before coming to Zen, I had the idea that human beings heard through their ears and spoke through their mouths. Indeed, from one perspective it is so. But when I learned to be more present through practice, I began to notice that we hear and speak with our whole bodies and that in that process of communication, our bodies are projected into all of space-time.

When my relatives asked my second husband if Zen was helping me at all, he replied that previously I used to complain constantly about the attitudes of others, and that fortunately that was no longer the case. Speaking ill of others (a close person, an acquaintance, an enemy, or a public figure) made me feel superior. Of course, speaking ill of others generates discomfort, suffering, and division among people, and it goes against the precepts. But there are more implications. When I managed to be attentive in these types of conversations, speaking recklessly of others, I could become aware of my bodily sensations. It is as if I were poisoning my own body in as noxious a way as when I used to smoke cigarettes. That feeling of toxicity is very clear in the use of social media.

I have had three births and three deaths on Twitter. The first time I left, I was intoxicated by everything I was saying. I could no longer keep up the character I had created. The second time, I ended up putting together an even more annoying character. The third time I opened my Twitter account, I had already started practicing, but no matter how good my intentions were, anything I said there made me feel bad (worsened by the fact that everything is on record). Then I decided that it was better to remain silent and just watch, but even if I did not contribute to the public discussion, just witnessing other people's verbal aggressions and dramas was as addictive as it was intoxicating. I always reached a point where I ended up in deformed bodily postures with all my vital energy absorbed by the cell phone app. The fact is that on Twitter I could not find a way to silence, filter or block accounts so as to have a virtuous timeline, not even following Buddhist accounts. Twitter's artificial intelligence recommendation system seems to be designed for confrontation and toxicity. I sometimes fall into the illusion that I am in control in certain environments if I enter with good intentions, but the truth is that for many environments the only virtuous option I have is to leave the old nest and migrate to places where real birds sing.

Being able to be aware of that bodily discomfort that generally occurs with certain ways of speaking was important toward understanding the need to awaken a compassionate mind that would allow me to practice loving speech.

The body also speaks and that is why it is important to be attentive to what is transmitted with it. Another thing that captivated me about practice is all the non-verbal and subtle language that flows when we practice with sangha friends. Densho Sensei says that we should walk inside the zendo as if we were incense smoke. Robes demand great care in movement, clumsiness is not allowed when carrying pots or cleaning the censer, and we must avoid walking with the head bowed or haughty, or with the back bent. The instruments' sounds and the sutra recitations are expressions of the heart, and the heart is in the body. In the *ōryōki* ritual, there is no speaking, because the entire ritual speaks a loving language that is expressed with the body. In sangha practice, one also experiences subtle communication between spiritual friends, camaraderie, chuckles because one must remain silent, knowing glances, and compassionate gestures. With practice, our body is transformed into a means of communication that transmits love. I have photographic records that prove this transformation.

In particular, I have an ID photo (from the university I work for) from five years ago (just before I started my practice) and one from now. A before and an after image. I showed the contrast to a sangha friend and he told me that my gaze had softened, that previously it was very aggressive. I love my job as a university professor, especially because of my relationship with the students with whom I have always had a relationship of great appreciation and mutual respect. However, at the time of the first photo, I remember that the students had left me evaluation comments like "he is a very good teacher, but he intimidates his students." Even a student confessed to feeling panic in my presence. It was the first time, after almost two decades of teaching, that I had received comments of this kind. The suffering that I had accumulated in my whole body at that time was not only splashing rude or foolish comments onto others, but I was also scaring my students with my aggressive or dismissive bodily and facial expressions. The Google Photos app sometimes brings me back memories of that time, and when compared to now, you can see two people communicating different things with their bodies. As if we were clay dolls, the practice molds our bodies so that they learn to speak with love.

Taking others into account

Although courtesy is not enough for practicing loving speech, it is necessary. Courtesy can become an empty and hypocritical way of relating to others, but sincere courtesy can be enough for practicing loving speech. Zen brings with it many courtesy details for taking others into account. These details come from a very delicate Japanese etiquette, one which gave me a culture shock when I first came across practice. I understand that it is not about becoming Japanese, but keeping in mind that manners and sincere courtesy are forms of loving expression that allow us to take others into account. Sensei insists that in our practice we must be careful how we put our shoes on the shelf, how we hand things over, and how we do *gasshō* to greet each other. Many of these manners allow you to recognize and respect the personal space of others. Of course, to whatever extent possible, because we are, after all, a Latin American sangha and we hug each other whenever we can.

Showing affection with hugs is part of non-negotiable Latin American expressions and I do not see anything wrong with it. But many of us also have cultural tendencies that do not seem very loving to me when it comes to meeting others. Many times we greet each other (even people we have just met) and we automatically issue opinions about physical appearance (fat, skinny, pale) or ask daring questions that go against people's privacy (states of health, work, relationship situations). There is very little time to react between the stimulus (meeting someone) and the reaction (voicing opinions or asking questions). I am sure that most of the time they are not malicious comments, but sincere concerns. However, these small, culturally validated transgressions can cause suffering in others. In the same way, we have normalized having heated discussions or arguments about work or politics in front of third parties. We do it in a mall, in the car, in the office, or a chat group. The discomfort affects not only those who are participating in the discussion, it also splashes outward.

Speaking of arguments, with practice I have learned the importance of giving up on always being right, listening carefully (with the whole body) to what other people are saying, and waiting for the right moment to answer in the most skillful way possible. It demands a lot of vital energy, but it is liberating. It can be achieved by diverting attention, changing the subject, keeping silent, or letting the trigger dissipate on its own since, in general, the topic of discussion is of no importance. This has also helped me to make an effort to maintain good Western manners when they become lost because of familiarity. It is more interesting to practice courtesy when dealing with someone I do not like, because it can become a game if I manage to stay calm. The truth is that so much informality validated by culture can turn into aggression. There is no way to carry Japanese honorifics into everyday life, but addressing my colleagues with sincere courtesy by calling them Professor, or my superiors by using Mr. Dean, and addressing my mother and father with the greatest possible devotion, go a long way toward not generating unnecessary suffering with my words.

OPENING THE HAND OF THOUGHT

Whether due to my cultural or personal karmic tendencies, the practice of zazen is crucial for cultivating a compassionate mind and avoiding reacting with words. Zazen helps me to release my identifying with mental processes, to open the hand of thought, and especially to let go of my identifying with characters with whom I like to identify, because every time this happens, I inevitably end up generating suffering with my words.

For example, it is sometimes unwholesome to identify with a good character. When I started my practice, I had a leading position at the university, and since I thought that I had to be a good Buddhist, a compassionate bodhisattva, I did not get short-tempered with anyone and always had patient words, no matter what the situation was. That can be very dangerous. I was hurting myself because I was allowing some people to take advantage of me. Sometimes the most compassionate word I can give is a cutting and forceful word that sets boundaries, even if it is not consistent with my ideas of virtue.

It does not help to identify with important or intelligent characters either. When I started working at the university, I was involved in all kinds of academic discussions with my colleagues. Sometimes, the work environment could turn hellish. We scholars are prone to be reborn in the asura realm, and that realm is devoid of loving speech. It is hard for me to get out of those rebirth cycles because I tend to form ideas about my abilities.

Also, identifying as a victim can turn one into a victimizer. A continuous defense of personal space is harmful. My coping mechanism in response to the bullying that I experienced in my school days for being gay and a little effeminate was to learn to be sarcastic, quick, and hurtful with words. As a young adult, I identified with the idea that we gays have to defend ourselves against heteropatriarchy with poisonous words. In some sectors of the gay world, this way of reacting is considered a virtue and can be very entertaining. There is even a very popular and funny TV show, *RuPaul's Drag Race,* where humor is continually done that way. Once I learned this form of defense with words, people thought twice before trying to hurt me, but I was also becoming an unsympathetic character, isolated and full of a poison that I too had to ingest. Fortunately, that character did not last long thanks to my first husband, with whom I was married for eleven years. We did activism and participated in politics for the defense of LGBT rights. He was considered by the media as the Colombian Harvey Milk. A few days after he passed away, a national radio station began broadcasting hate-filled homophobic messages against me and my late husband. While I was mourning, the attack was devastating and I could not understand the reasons for such cruelty. Unexpectedly, an extensive network of friends and many strangers came forward to help ease the suffering. In front of the station, we made a flash mob, full of love, songs, dances, and flowers. The media supported us and the station had to apologize, carry out campaigns and invite experts in sexual and reproductive rights to the radio program. That is the power of loving expression, whereas no suffering would have been alleviated with poison or rancor.

IN SUMMARY

This is how I understand these four teachings of Densho Sensei applied, in this case, to loving speech. When a stimulus is received and there is the temptation to respond with words, it is important to become aware of the small gap between the stimulus and the reaction. One way can be by being attentive to the bodily sensations, what is felt, and what is transmitted with the body. In that gap, we can take others into account and avoid reacting based on automatic personal or cultural tendencies. Opening the hand of thought and letting go of the fixed ideas we have about ourselves and others, allows that gap to widen naturally. Then, loving words can be expressed and hurtful words can be avoided. I do not think it is a practice that relies only on the willpower of wanting to speak with loving words; rather, it is the expression of zazen practice when one goes out to meet all beings.

At one sesshin I was in charge of serving meals. I remember doing it with all my heart to the point that I completely forgot myself. At the end of the retreat, a lay practitioner came up to me and told me she was touched because she saw me as a butterfly inside the zendo with sleeves like wings. It was the first time someone had used the word butterfly to say something beautiful to me and with no offense intended. I managed to stop myself from reacting with a comment to defend myself. It was a healing experience. I believe that practice transforms our bodies to transmit love, and this is most clearly seen in the bodies of teachers who have been practicing for a lifetime.

One of the most beautiful things that I have experienced with the practice are those zen moments that occur spontaneously and that many practitioners refer to. A very special one happens to me when I am walking through the city and I feel that suddenly the presence of a tree breaks through me, that there is no separation, that it transmits joy, that I can hear it with my body, that it is unclear if it is singing or talking, but it is clear that it is vibrating with its tree body. When there is no me reacting with foolish words in my head, in my body, or my mouth, I feel that I can perceive the song of the trees. I wish I could learn to speak like them, with my whole body, letting the fundamental love of which the entire universe is made manifest itself.

Reigen Sanjuán is a novice monk ordained on March 21, 2022, by Densho Quintero Sensei. He is from Bogotá, Colombia where he lives and practices at Daishinji. In his worldly life, he works as a mathematics professor at a small, local university in Bogotá. He loves teaching, mathematics, programming computers, and sometimes doing some academic research in pure mathematics and mathematical physics. In recent years, the practice has been taking up more space in his life. He did some LGBT rights activism in Colombia years ago for love, survival, and resistance.

Silencio amoroso

EISHŌ AMAYA

"Póngase el *okesa* y siéntese en zazen: eso es todo."
— *Kodo Sawaki*

HACE POCO MÁS DE UN AÑO me ordené como monje Zen. Dejé mi trabajo, mi apartamento en renta, mis cosas que fui regalando y arrojando a la basura. Dejé otras de mis pertenencias con algunos amigos, libros, muebles, ropa, y cosas inservibles que acumulé durante mi vida. Dejé mi rango de profesor. Dejé mi rango de magister en antropología un mes después de recibir el cartón de grado. Y simplemente me convertí en el guardián del templo Daishin en Bogotá, lugar de práctica de la Comunidad Soto Zen de Colombia.

Vivir en Daishinji ha sido un proceso de auto descubrimiento, a veces muy directo y confrontador. A pesar de que la vida en templo implica vivir en comunidad, a menudo vivo solo, pues soy el único monje residente. La mayor soledad, evidentemente, se vive en las noches. Sin embargo, durante el día, en cualquier momento llegan personas, abro la puerta, contesto el teléfono. Soy la puerta para muchos que se acercan por primera vez a la práctica del Zen. Mi voz y mi palabra es la entrada a la práctica para algunos. Reconociendo esta responsabilidad, ¿cuál es la importancia de la palabra en nuestra tradición Soto Zen?

Dōgen Zenji escribe sobre la palabra amorosa que hay un vínculo estrecho entre ésta y la compasión.[1] Pienso mucho en la compasión cuando viene a mi mente la imagen de Avalokiteshvara y sus múltiples cabezas y brazos. ¿Cómo es la mirada de este gran bodhisattva? Okumura Roshi, en su libro *Vivir guiados por el voto,* nos dice que Avalokiteshvara tiene dos acepciones. La primera es *Kanjizai,* como lo recitamos en el Sutra del Corazón. Y Okumura traduce *Kanjizai* como "una persona que puede ver libremente sin obstrucciones."[2] Pero agrega que, en el Sutra del Loto, a Alvalokiteshvara se le llama *Kanzeon,* "Aquél que escucha el sonido del mundo."[3] Para efectos de mi relato, siento que es más propicia esta traducción, y mucho más contundentes la raíz de "Avalokita" (ver) y "svara" (sonido), como señala Okumura. Esta contrariedad de sentidos y percepciones que se reúnen en "*Kanzeon,*" me atrae y me cuestiona: ¿qué significa ver el sonido, ver, en específico, los lamentos de todos los seres que sufren?

Ver el sonido, para mí implica un extraordinario campo de visión que solo tiene *Kanzeon.* Por ello es el bodhisattva de la gran compasión, y por ello Dōgen Zenji escribe sobre él, que "es el padre y la madre de todos los budas."[4] Además, es una mirada que abarca no solo el espectro visible del sufrimiento, a veces no bastan las imágenes para despertar la compasión. Estamos acostumbrados a ver imágenes de violencia, de dolor, de guerra, de muerte, en los medios de comunicación, en la calle, en nuestros mismos hogares, con nuestras familias. Quizás no basta solo con ver el sufrimiento, tal vez *Kanzeon* "libera todo el sufrimiento" (como atestigua el

Sutra del Corazón) al dejar que el sonido de todos los seres atraviese todos sus sentidos. Es esa la mirada que escucha el sufrimiento de todos los seres. Si es una mirada que puede percibir tales sonidos (a veces para nosotros muy imperceptibles), entonces es una mirada que alumbra un mundo en su totalidad, un mundo que no tiene nada que esconder. La mirada compasiva entonces está ligada al habla amorosa, según Dōgen Zenji.

Cuando comencé a vivir en el templo Daishin experimenté esa claridad, esa mirada de los budas que recuerda la cualidad de Avalokiteshvara. No tenía nada que esconder, porque materialmente no tenía dónde esconder algo. Por ejemplo, compartir el cuarto de ropa con los demás monjes, es no tener nada que esconder. Dormir en el zendo con la estatua de Manjusri, es no tener nada que esconder. Cocinar en la cocina del templo y usar todos los espacios comunales, es no tener nada que esconder. Estaba muy al descubierto, y esta situación me hizo ver mi tendencia a ocultarme de los demás, bajo alguna máscara o bajo mi guarida austera, o bajo la música en mis oídos, o una caminata de escapatoria, o una pedaleada en la bicicleta. Siempre estaba escapando y ocultándome.

En el templo no tenía opción. Y además no quería ocultarme más. Entonces, con el tiempo fui pensando menos en ese ocultamiento, y simplemente estaba con lo que se presentara. Si llegaba a dormir alguien que roncara mucho al templo, no escapaba al segundo piso (excepto un par de veces) del ruido. Simplemente compartía los ronquidos con mi difícil sueño y el león apacible de Manjusri que nunca duerme (creo). Acepté la claridad o el desvelamiento, y recordé nuevamente las palabras de Dōgen en el *Zuimonki,* donde exhorta a sus discípulos a comportarse en soledad como si estuvieran acompañados, y a mantener la actitud en compañía cuando estuvieran solos. Este fue el primer paso, de aceptación. Luego de ello, vino el sonido. Si la mirada de la compasión revela los sonidos ocultos, del sufrimiento de todos los seres, entonces esa mirada de des-ocultamiento, no solo reveló mi afán de escapatoria (*escapachitta*[5], contrario a *bodhichitta*), sino que también reveló los sonidos que yo no estaba atendiendo. Reveló mi voz y mi palabra. Comencé a tomar conciencia de mi voz y mi palabra. Todo empezó con las recitaciones. Me di cuenta de que mi voz era muy leve, que casi no se escuchaba. Y no quería sobresalir. Pero cuando se vive solo en un templo, hasta la más tenue voz se escucha. En el silencio de la noche, los budas también guardan silencio, por eso comencé a escuchar más mi voz y lo que no podía callar en mis pensamientos. Y resolví que a veces no era la voz que esperaba. Que no sonaba como yo siempre había esperado, e incluso incomodaba y podía llegar a herir a alguien si hacía alguna broma que se malinterpretara (me pasa a menudo). Entendí de manera cruda que no quería esa voz, que mis palabras a veces eran duras, no compasivas. Entonces me preguntaba cómo poder reconocer nuestro sonido propio, y qué podemos hacer para mantener y cultivar la palabra amorosa. Aún me cuestiono. Pero en mi caso, el silencio es algo que puede ayudar.

SILENCIO

Es algo contradictorio escribir sobre el silencio, y mucho más escribir sobre el silencio desde la práctica del Zen. Creo que hay muchos tipos de silencios, y esa variopinta diversidad la he vivido también en la Sangha. Hay un silencio de zazen, del cual no es necesario decir mucho. Cuando en mi tesis de maestría intentaba describir un ritual de zazen, me enfrentaba en algún punto con el silencio. ¿Cómo representarlo? No es ausencia de sonido. No hay un vacío sonoro, decía yo, lo que hay en el silencio compartido es una modulación de ruidos. Cuando silenciamos el habla, pueden pasar muchas cosas. Puede que la voz que ya no emite sonidos ahora comience a resonar en nuestras cabezas. ¿Cómo callamos esa voz? Son los pensamientos que soltamos. No se puede silenciar a voluntad, pero se puede abrir la mano del pensamiento y liberar esas voces, momento a momento. Entonces no hay un silencio total en zazen. A veces nos sorprende un ruido estridente de la calle, o la vecina saludando a los vecinos. Y todos esos sonidos, en mi caso, estando sentado en silencio en el zendo, es como si surgieran de mi cabeza. En mi monografía, así describía el silencio de la práctica en comunidad:

[…] por un tiempo exacto las personas allí reunidas en esta sala comparten el silencio y la quietud. Comparten los sonidos de la calle, de los carros, de los perros, de la vecina. Comparten los sonidos de las respiraciones de los otros. La tos. El estornudo que asusta. El tambaleo del que se duerme. El dolor. La calma. La agitación mental […][6]

[…] después viene la campana final. Se hace *gasshō*, saco mi *rakusu* del sobre de tela, no tengo mis gafas, así que la borrosidad del ambiente me sorprende al abrir de nuevo mis ojos completamente y salir del zazen. Creo que esa es mi forma de terminar con la campana: abrir los ojos completamente, ver mi sobre borroso al frente, sacar mi *rakusu* borroso y ponerlo en la cabeza. La recitación comienza suave, pero mientras va avanzando el verso se va haciendo más fuerte. En la resonancia de la sala se pierden todas las voces. Luego el silencio. En el silencio se viste el Gran Hábito. En el silencio de las voces, porque al mismo tiempo es el sonido silencioso de las telas abriéndose y creando aire y haciendo ese sonido que corta el viento del incienso. Ese es el sonido del momento de vestir el *rakusu* o el *okesa,* todavía sentados en postura de zazen.[7]

[...] Si me aventuro a describir el silencio de la costura, debo advertir en seguida que no existe tal cosa. Si digo que la costura es silenciosa, por momentos, es como si dijera que todos los silencios son iguales. Y eso tampoco es así. El silencio que presenciamos los tres, en aquel momento, fue producto de un mudo acuerdo. Pero no solo callaron las palabras en ese espacio de seis manos y tres agujas. Dejé de pensar en "lo que pasa cuando uno deja de coser por un tiempo," ya no importaba. Arturo dejó de pensar en lo que estaba diciendo Hosen sobre la enseñanza en los monasterios de Japón. Ya no importaba la enseñanza, ni los monasterios, ni Hosen, ni Arturo, ni yo, ni la costura. Tiene que ver con el volumen. Todo lo que había en las mentes de esos tres budistas bajó de volumen, y el sonido de la aguja al entrar en la tela y salir suavemente, el sonido del hilo que atraviesa la tela, una y otra vez, fue mucho más alto que todo lo demás. No hay silencios en la costura, hay modulaciones, de lo físico, de lo material y de lo que hay en la mente y en el cuerpo.[8]

También hay otros tipos de silencios, cuando no estamos en zazen, en el samu, por ejemplo. Se mantiene la actitud de *shikan* (comprometerse solamente con la acción de ese momento) y el silencio son palabras mudas (aunque a veces no se puede evitar pensar algo mientras barremos o limpiamos el polvo), pero son los sonidos de los trapos húmedos sobre el piso. Es el sonido de nuestros samues que se mueven al unísono con nuestros brazos y piernas. Es el sonido del agua que corre mientras lavamos los baños. Es también el sonido de las ollas que dejamos caer por accidente, y que nos dice, oiga, tenga más cuidado.

También hay silencios incómodos. Hay silencios necesarios. Silencios inesperados. Silencios forzados. Silencios abruptos. Hay silencios que producen risa. Hay silencios que producen palabras. Y, también, hay silencios que hacen herir, que producen dolor. No todos los silencios son amorosos. ¿Cómo reconocer o producir esos silencios que conlleven bienestar a los demás, cómo saber cuándo es el momento necesario para callar?

Cuando se vive solo uno nunca está del todo seguro de callar completamente. Los pensamientos no dejan de revolotear en el silencio. Callar para mí, viviendo en el templo, era más que no emitir sonidos con mi boca. Era iluminar todos los rincones y permitirme descubrir los sonidos, ruidos o señales, sean las que sean. Esos rincones oscurecidos en el templo eran los rincones que yo estaba ocultando en mí. Los budas en los altares ciertamente son muy silenciosos. Y aunque haya aprendido a escuchar a las flores de los altares, a veces tampoco dicen mucho. Entonces escuchaba a las personas que asistían al templo. Escuché más que nunca a las personas y, extrañamente, me sentía mejor etnógrafo a pesar de que justo allí ya había renunciado a la antropología (al menos formalmente).

Escuchar a los demás también puede ser parte del habla amorosa. Aunque a veces yo no tenía nada que decir, ni un buen consejo, ni una buena recomendación. Con el tiempo comprendí que las personas muchas veces no buscan buenos consejos. Solo un silencio amoroso que les permita desahogarse en un lugar tranquilo y seguro como lo es el templo.

El silencio amoroso, en mi experiencia, parte de una escucha amorosa. Escuchar revela los lugares ocultos si estamos atentos. A veces revela cosas muy ocultas que no queríamos ver en nosotros mismos, como me pasó a mí. En mi caso reveló la voz que no era la voz del monje más amoroso. Descubrí que soy duro a veces con la palabra. Y no me daba cuenta, o más bien, ocultaba más de la cuenta mis palabras, las revestía y me olvidaba de sus efectos una vez llegaran a oídos de otros.

Y si el silencio revelaba mi voz con sinceridad, y las voces de los demás que la advertían, sin máscaras de sonidos que la alteraran, si las palabras salen desnudas en el silencio de los budas que me acompañan, en el altar del frente de la biblioteca donde ahora escribo, o el de la cocina donde paso la mayor parte del tiempo; entonces no hay nada que esconder.

Si "el habla amable surge de una mente amorosa, y la semilla de una mente amorosa es la compasión," según Dōgen en el *Shishobo,* entonces ahí estaba la ruptura. Considero que la mente amorosa es aquella que sabe callar, que sabe convivir en el silencio, para luego producir el habla, el gesto o el silencio amable. La mente amorosa es la que discierne. Pero a veces no es tan fácil. Toda esta reflexión se da en un periodo de tiempo muy corto, no hay espacio para detenerse, escuchar a la persona que nos comparte su dolor, evaluar toda la situación, determinar las posibles respuestas y sus posibles efectos, y luego actuar, o hablar de manera amorosa. Cuando examinamos todo ello, la persona ya se ha ido del templo y solo quedamos con esa sensación de no saber si lo que se dijo era lo acertado. Por eso es cuestión de práctica. Los medios hábiles también desarrollan la manera de responder a estas situaciones, en el momento que se requiere. De manera instantánea. No hay mucho tiempo para pensar.

Retomando, si la compasión es un des-ocultamiento, el resultado es una mirada más amplia, que incluye todos los sonidos, incluso los que no emitimos. Nuestras palabras son como son. Y las percibimos con dureza o con amor, según sea el caso. La compasión nos permite verlo. Pero si hay ocultamiento, si nos escondemos a nosotros mismos y ocultamos los matices y tonos de nuestras palabras, entonces no podemos darnos cuenta de lo graves e hirientes que pueden llegar a ser para los demás. La compasión entonces es también olvidarnos de nosotros mismos, como dice Dōgen en el Genjo kōan, y en ese olvido escuchamos más atentamente.

Normalmente soy muy callado. Entonces pienso si puede existir algo así como un "silencio amoroso," y creo que es lo que practicamos. En zazen, por ejemplo, practicamos un silencio amoroso. El silencio permite iluminar también esos rincones ocultos de la indiferencia y la ignorancia, o del ritmo cotidiano que llevamos. Quizás también abrir la *mano del pensamiento* pueda entenderse como un silencio amoroso, porque es lo que hacemos al soltar y estar más atentos a la realidad en la que estamos sentados con las piernas cruzadas.

LAS PUNTADAS Y EL SILENCIO

Pensar en el silencio para mí es remontarme también a la costura de nuestra tradición Soto Zen, esa que heredamos rescatada por Kodo Sawaki Roshi. A menudo se nos dice que la palabra *sutra* viene de "hilo conductor." En mi tesis de maestría en antropología sobre la costura en Daishinji, relaciono ese sentido con los significados implícitos que existen al coser el rakusu o el okesa. Y materialmente en la costura vemos ese hilo conductor que es el que permite fijar los fragmentos de tela y crear el patrón de puntadas que asemeja el campo de arroz, que es finalmente el que vestimos. Vestimos un hilo conductor hecho okesa o rakusu, vestimos también un silencio amoroso, porque ese hilo que sostiene nuestra "túnica de parches" está enredado en el refugio que tomamos en los tres tesoros. Las palabras: *"namu kie butsu, namu kie so, namu kie ho,"* (tomo refugio en el Buda, tomo refugio en el Dharma, tomo refugio en la Sangha), son palabras amorosas. Es lo que recitamos al coser nuestros hábitos, puntada a puntada, así tomamos refugio en los Tres Tesoros. Esas palabras abrazan, material y metafóricamente, al okesa que llevamos. Y nos abrazan a nosotros mismos. Todo monje o monja que haya dado abrazos con su okesa puesto sabe bien a lo que me refiero con abrazar de esta manera. Este es también entonces un silencio amoroso, porque llevamos esa palabra (el triple refugio) grabada en nuestras túnicas y al cobijarnos con ella, cobijamos o abrazamos a los demás.

¿Por qué entonces el silencio en la costura puede ser también un silencio amoroso? Sucede casi igual que en zazen. Al coser ritualizamos nuestra actividad. Nuestro cuerpo toma una disposición especial. Una postura que nos permita coser durante horas, si es posible. Tratamos los objetos, la aguja, el hilo, la tela, con delicadeza, en lo posible. Mantenemos el espacio de costura ordenado. A veces ponemos un incienso. Todo está en su sitio. De repente, cosemos con más personas. Y quizás no haya silencio. Quizás la misma costura desencadene una hilera de diálogo incesante entre los costurantes[9] que, lejos de hacer silencio, se enredan en el hilo de su pensamiento y en el de los demás. Entonces el silencio en la costura es diferente. No es el silencio de zazen. Vemos la manera que toman los puntos en la tela negra. Pero vemos también la voz de quien nos habla. La música del vecino la vemos en la puntada. Vemos también nuestros pensamientos enredándose en la puntada, enredo tras enredo nos devolvemos y descosemos. La costura es el silencio que vivimos. Porque esa es la representación más concreta e inmediata de lo que está sucediendo alrededor y en nosotros mismos. Y es una forma también de traducir, en términos de líneas y puntos de hilo sobre tela (materialmente), la habilidad metafórica de Avalokiteshvara: *ver el sonido del mundo*.

Por otro lado, si llevamos la enseñanza de zazen a la costura[10], esa expresión que tanto conocemos de *shikantaza* (只管打坐), simplemente estar sentados, se traduce, en la costura, en algo que he llamado *shikantanuu* (只管打渫う) simplemente coser. Lo bonito de la costura es que el reflejo de lo que experimentamos, de nuestros estados mentales, de nuestra actitud, de nuestro afán, de nuestros deseos e ilusiones, incluso del clima que estamos viviendo: es el reflejo de nuestra puntada. A veces darnos cuenta de que los puntos en el rakusu o en el okesa son terriblemente chuecos, es algo frustrante. Como cuando sentimos frustración en zazen. Es decepcionante. Pero en la costura podemos descoser y volver a tomar hilo y aguja, y volver a comenzar. Este para mí es una especie de arrepentimiento, es la expresión más tangible del voto y arrepentimiento que nos ha transmitido Uchiyama Roshi. Descoser es arrepentirse. En zazen, arrepentirse es volver a la postura luego de una insensata somnolencia. Esta es la manera (un poco acrobática, lo sé) en la que se pueden relacionar la palabra o el silencio amoroso de nuestra práctica, con la práctica de coser nuestros hábitos, y por supuesto, con la práctica de zazen.

Figura 1. "Zazen Virtual." Lemoine, Camila. 2022.

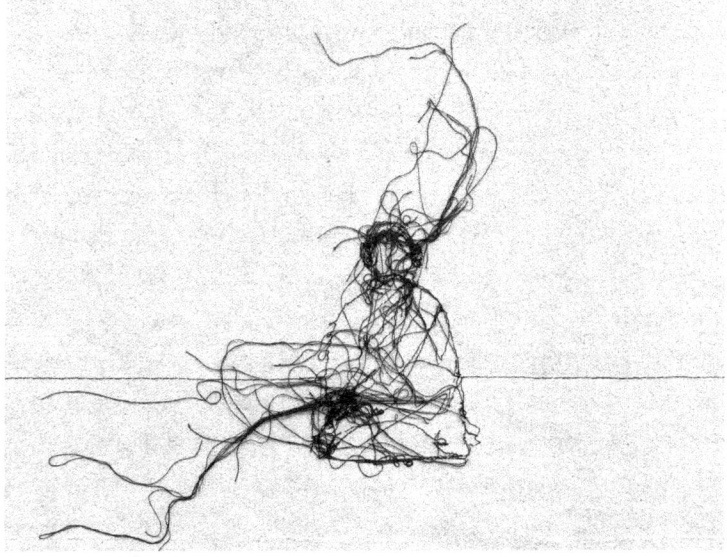

*Figura 2. "Virtual Zazen" (Es el reverso del dibujo
con hilo anterior). Lemoine, Camila, 2022.*

234

Camila Lemoine, la artista que compuso estos cuadros, es practicante de zazen y también practica la costura. No soy experto en arte, pero puedo interpretar esta obra desde mi práctica de monje y asiduo costurante. Los hilos que vemos enredados en el lienzo son los sonidos de la experiencia de zazen de la artista. Es su manera de traducir sus sensaciones, percepciones y emociones, en hilo y aguja.

Es también lo que hace un escritor al componer un poema: hay una codificación de la experiencia en una estructura de símbolos: en blanco y negro, tinta sobre papel, o, para nuestro ejemplo: en hilo sobre lienzo. Ahora bien, si recordamos la habilidad de Avalokiteshvara, es la misma actitud que nos mueve a crear, ya sean obras de arte, o en la escritura, o también, y justamente, en las palabras que pronunciamos. El silencio amoroso permite una especie de introspección, un diálogo del interior con el exterior. Permite un escuchar más atento, una mirada más cercana a la de Avalokiteshvara, despierta la compasión, y esta despierta la mente amorosa que es la que produce el habla amable, como dice Dōgen Zenji. Por ello, hacer estas equiparaciones no es otra cosa que buscar otros medios en los que se manifieste la palabra amable en nuestra práctica. Y, siendo arriesgado, propongo que la médula de la palabra amable, de este dharma acogedor que nos enseña Dōgen, se puede replicar en otras formas expresivas que toma el lenguaje. Los cuadros de Camila fueron compartidos en la Sangha Virtual de la Comunidad Soto Zen de Colombia. La cantidad de corazones que reaccionaron a la imagen fue desbordante. Quizás sea una forma extraña de medir el impacto de un dharma acogedor (insisto, que sigue siendo arriesgado), pero es la manera en que nos relacionamos hoy por hoy. Y yo quiero confiar en los practicantes "virtuales" y en el latir de sus "corazones virtuales" al ver la "palabra amorosa" de Camila: un monje cosido en lienzo. Sentado en zazen.

A MANERA DE CONCLUSIÓN

Hasta aquí, lo que he presentado no son más que palabras, signos organizados o desorganizados, que de alguna manera dan sentido a mi experiencia. No es quizás la mejor manera de expresarlo o de interpretarlo, como no es posible expresar el silencio de zazen o el silencio que todos experimentamos. Pero al callar, no solo las palabras caen al suelo y se desmoronan, si abrimos la mano del pensamiento, todo cae. Incluso este ensayo se desmorona. Silencio. Abrimos un poco más los ojos, y ya no son palabras, ni ruidos, ni murmullos, ni sonidos atravesados. A veces son líneas. Imágenes, Colores. Puntadas de hilo gris sobre tela negra. La realidad a la que despertamos es impredecible. Y muy sutil.

Lo impactante de todo esto, no es la belleza de las palabras, ni la profundidad de nuestras voces. Es la manera cómo surge la palabra o el silencio amoroso. Okumura Roshi describe esto de manera contundente en su escrito que prologa este libro: Dōgen Zenji estaba realmente en una situación amenazante y difícil al escribir el *Shishobo*. No estaba preocupado por las sutilezas del lenguaje para que se proyectara "amoroso." Los cuatro dharmas acogedores eran la respuesta budista a un mundo que necesitaba compasión y amor. ¡Era un asunto vital!

En Colombia, todos los días es un asunto vital. En un país donde cargamos la violencia como semillas kármicas de los antiguos (y violentos, de todos los colores y banderas), es vital detenerse y volver a las enseñanzas de Dōgen Zenji y de Okumura Roshi. Preguntarse todos los días cuál es la mirada que escucha todos los sonidos del sufrimiento. Detenerse un momento. Permitir el silencio. ¿Qué sonidos inundan nuestros ojos ahora mismo, en este instante? ¿Cómo manifestamos la palabra amorosa después de ver con los ojos de *Kanzeon?*

Eishō Amaya is a Zen monk from Bogota, Colombia, ordained in 2021 by Master Densho Quintero. At this moment he is preparing to do ango in Japan. For more than a year, he has been living in the Daishin Temple in Bogota, headquarters of the Soto Zen Community of Colombia. He is an anthropologist by profession and is interested in ritual sewing in Zen and the study of materiality in Buddhism. He also works as a tailor and cook at the temple.

Loving Silence

Eishō Amaya

"Put on the okesa and sit zazen: that's it."

– *Kodo Sawaki*

A LITTLE OVER A YEAR AGO I ordained as a Zen monk. I left my job, my rented apartment and my belongings, all of which I gave and threw away. I left some of my other things with a few friends: books, furniture, clothes, and useless things that I had accumulated during my life. I gave up my rank of professor. I left my rank of master in anthropology a month after receiving the degree. And I simply became the keeper of the Daishin Temple in Bogotá, the practice place of the Soto Zen Community of Colombia.

Living in Daishinji has been a process of self-discovery, sometimes very direct and confronting. Although the temple lifestyle involves living in community, I often live alone, as I am the only resident monk. The biggest loneliness, obviously, is experienced in the evenings. However, during the day, people arrive at any time: I open the door or answer the phone. This way, I am the doorway for many persons who are approaching Zen practice for the first time. My voice and speech are the entrance to the practice for some. Recognizing this responsibility, what is the importance of the spoken word in our Soto Zen tradition?

Dōgen Zenji writes that there is a close link between loving words and compassion.[1] I think about compassion when I happen to think of Avalokiteshvara, and then his multiple heads and arms come to mind. What could the gaze of this great bodhisattva be like? In his book Living by Vow, Okumura Roshi tells us that Avalokiteshvara has two meanings. The first is Kanjizai, as we recite it in the Heart Sutra; Okumura translates it as "a person who can see freely without obstruction."[2] But he adds further that in the Lotus Sutra, Avalokiteshvara is also named Kanzeon, "One who hears the sound of the world."[3] For the purpose of my story, I feel that this translation is the more accurate one, because the roots of avalokita (to see) and svara (sound), as Okumura points out, are much more compelling. This contrast of senses and perceptions that come together in Kanzeon attracts and challenges me at the same time: What does it mean to see sound? Actually, what does it mean to see, specifically, the wailing of all suffering beings?

Seeing sound, to me, implies an extraordinary field of vision that only Kanzeon holds. That is indeed the reason why Kanzeon is the bodhisattva of great compassion, and why Dōgen Zenji writes: "He is the father and mother of all buddhas."[4] Moreover, it is a gaze that embraces not only the visible spectrum of suffering, because sometimes images are not enough to arouse compassion. We are used to staring at images of violence, pain, war and death, in the media, in the streets, even in our own homes within our families. Perhaps it is not enough to see suffering; perhaps Kanzeon "liberates all suffering" (as the Heart Sutra attests) by letting the sound of all beings pierce all of his/her senses.

This is the gaze that listens to the suffering of all beings. If this could be a gaze capable of perceiving such sounds (sometimes imperceptible for us), then it is a gaze that sheds light on a world in its totality, on a world that has nothing to hide. According to Dōgen Zenji, the compassionate gaze is linked to loving speech.

When I began to live in the Daishin temple, I experienced that clarity, the glance of the buddhas that recalls the quality of Avalokiteshvara. I had nothing to hide, because materially I had nowhere to keep anything hidden. For example, to share the dressing room with the other monks is to have nothing to cover up with. To sleep in the zendo with the statue of Manjushri is to have nothing to hide. To cook in the temple kitchen, using the communal spaces, is to have nothing to hide. I was uncovered, and this situation made me realize my routine tendency to hide from others, under some mask or under my austere lair, under the music in my ears, through an escape hike, or even through my bike rides. I was always running away and concealing.

In the temple I had no choice. And besides, I didn't want to hide anymore. As time went on, I thought less about hiding and would simply harmonize with whatever came along. If a heavy snorer came to sleep in the temple, I wouldn't run off to the second floor (except for a couple of times, I must admit). I simply shared the snoring with my troubled sleep and the gentle lion of Manjushri who never sleeps (as I believe). I accepted the clarity or sleeplessness and remembered again Dōgen's words in the Zuimonki, where he exhorts his disciples to behave in solitude as if in the company of others, and likewise to maintain the attitude of being alone while in the company of others.

So, this was the first step: acceptance. After that came sound. If the gaze of compassion reveals the hidden sounds of suffering, then the gaze of un-hiding not only revealed my eagerness to escape (escapachitta[5] as opposed to bodhichitta), but also revealed to me the sounds that I was not attending to. It disclosed my voice and words.

Therefore, I started to be aware of my voice and my speech. It all begins with recitations. I realized that my voice was faint, that it was hardly audible. And I didn't want to stand out, but when you live alone in a temple, even the slightest voice is audible. In the silence of the night, the buddhas also keep silent, so I began to listen more to my voice and to what I could not keep quiet in my thoughts. I found that often it was not the voice I had expected. It didn't sound as I intended and even made me uncomfortable, because I had the capacity to hurt someone if a joke was misunderstood (which often happens to me). I understood in a rough way that I didn't want that voice, and that my speech was sometimes harsh, and not very compassionate. Thus, I wondered how to recognize our own sound, and how to maintain and cultivate loving words. Even today I still wonder. But in my case, silence is something that can definitely help.

Silence

It is something of a contradiction to write about silence, and even more so, to write about silence from the practice of Zen. I think there are several kinds of silence, insofar as I have experienced this variegated diversity within the sangha. There is a zazen silence of which it is not necessary to say much. In my Master's dissertation, when I tried to describe a zazen ritual, I was confronted at some point with silence. How can it be represented? It is not an absence of sound. There is no sound void, I said; what we find in the shared silence is a modulation of noises. When we silence speaking, many

things can happen. The voice that no longer makes sounds may now
start to resonate in our heads. How do we mute that voice? It is the
thoughts that we release. You cannot accomplish the silencing at
will, but you can open the hand of thought and free those voices,
step by step. So, there is no total silence in zazen. Sometimes we are
surprised by a raucous noise coming from the street, or the neighbor
greeting other neighbors. And all these sounds, in my case, while
sitting in silence inside the zendo, arise as if they were coming from
my head. In my dissertation, this is how I described the silence of
our community practice:

> [...] for a specific period of time, the people gathered
> in this room share the same silence and stillness. They
> share the sounds of the street, of the cars, of the dogs,
> of the neighbors. They share the sounds of each other's
> breathing. The cough, the sneeze that startles, the wobbling
> of the one who falls asleep, the pain, the calm, the mental
> agitation [...].[6]
> [...] then comes the final bell. We do gassho, and
> I take my rakusu out of the pouch, and since I don't have
> my glasses, the blurriness of the environment surprises
> me as I open my eyes fully again and come out of zazen.
> I think that is my way of finishing with the bell chime:
> I open my eyes fully, see my blurry pouch in front of me,
> take out my blurred rakusu and put it on my head. The
> recitation starts softly, but as the verses advance, it gets
> louder and louder. In the echoing of the hall, all the voices
> are lost. Then silence. The Great Robe is put on during
> the silence. When the voices fade away, the silent sound
> of the cloths opening, creating air and making a sound

that breaks the wafting of the incense. That is the sound of putting on the rakusu or the okesa, while still seated in zazen posture.[7]

[...] If I venture to describe the silence of sewing, I must warn at once that there is no such thing. If I dare to say that sewing is at times silent, it would be as if I were to say that all silences are the same. And that is not the case either. The silence that the three of us witnessed was the product of an unspoken agreement. Nevertheless, it was not only words that were halted in that space of six hands and three needles. I stopped thinking about "what happens when you stop sewing for a while;" that didn't matter anymore. Arturo stopped thinking about what Hosen was saying about the teaching in the monasteries in Japan. It was no longer about the teaching, or the monasteries, or Hosen, or Arturo, or me, or the sewing. It had to do with volume. Everything in the minds of those three Buddhists decreased in volume; and the sound of the needle going smoothly into and out of the cloth, the sound of the thread going through, over and over again, was much louder than everything else. There are no silences in sewing; what there is are modulations of the physical, of the material, of what is in the mind and body.[8]

There are also other types of silence when we are not in zazen, for example, in the middle of *samu*. The attitude of *shikan* (engaging only in the action of that moment) is maintained while the silence consists of silent words (sometimes you can't help but think of something else while sweeping the floor or dusting), but they are the sounds of wet rags on the floor. It is the sound of our *samues* moving in unison. There is the sound of running water as we clean the bathrooms. It is also the sound of the pots and pans we accidentally drop, telling us, "Hey! Be more careful, please."

Also, we encounter uncomfortable silences. There are necessary silences, unexpected silences, forced silences, abrupt silences. There are silences that produce laughter. There are silences that produce words. And likewise, there are silences that hurt, producing pain. Not all silences are loving. Now, how do we recognize (or produce) those kinds of silence that bring well-being to others? How do we know when to shut up?

When living alone, you are never sure that you are entirely silent. Thoughts never stop swirling. To stay silent, during my temple life, was more than not uttering sounds with my mouth. It was illuminating every corner and allowing myself to discover sounds, noises or signs, whatever they might be. Those darkened nooks in the temple were the corners that I was hiding in myself. The buddhas on the altars certainly remain very silent. And even if I have learned to listen to the flowers on the altars, they don't say much either. So, I listened to the people frequenting the temple. I listened more than ever to people and, strangely, I felt like a better ethnographer, even though I had resigned as an anthropologist just at the gates of the temple (at least, formally).

Listening to others can also be part of loving speech. On occasions I had nothing to say, no good advice, no good recommendations. Over time I came to understand, in fact, that people are often not looking for good advice, but just a loving silence that allows them to vent in a quiet and safe place like Daishinji.

Loving silence, from my experience, starts from loving listening. Listening reveals hidden places if we stay attentive. Sometimes it reveals very hidden things that we did not want to see in ourselves, as happened to me. It revealed the voice that was not the voice of the most loving monk; I even discovered that I am harsh with words. And I didn't realize it, or rather, I hid my words more than I should have. I dressed them up and forgot about their effects once they'd reached others' ears.

If silence revealed my voice with sincerity, without sound masks altering it (even if the voices of others noticed it), and if the words come out naked in the silence of the buddhas that accompany me (on the altar at the front of the library where I am writing this, or even the one in the kitchen where I spend most of my time), then there is nothing to hide.

If "loving words arise from a loving mind, and the seed of a loving mind is compassion," according to Dōgen in the *Shishobo,* then there was a rupture there. I consider the loving mind to be the one that knows how to be silent, knows how to coexist in silence, so as to then produce kind speech, gesture, or silence. The loving mind is the one that discerns… but sometimes, it is not so simple. All this reflection takes place in a very short span of time, without any space to stop, carefully listen to the person who shares his/her pain, evaluate the whole situation, determine possible responses and their possible effects, and then, finally, act or speak in a loving way. By the time we examine all this, the person has already left the temple, and we are left with that feeling of not knowing If what was said was the right thing to say. Therefore, it is a matter of practice. *Skillful means* also develop ways of responding to these situations, when required, in an instantaneous way, without any time to think.

Coming back to an earlier point, if compassion is an un-hiding, the result is a broader gaze that includes all sounds, even those we don't emit. Our words are what they are. And we perceive them with harshness or with love. Compassion allows us to see this clearly. But if there is concealment, if we hide ourselves and mask the nuances and tones of our words, then we cannot realize how serious and hurtful they can be to others. Compassion then is also forgetting ourselves, as Dōgen says in the *Genjokoan;* and in that forgetfulness, we listen more attentively.

Normally I am very quiet, and so I have wondered if there can be such a thing as a "loving silence." I soon came to the realization that this is what we practice. In zazen, for example, we practice a loving silence. Silence also allows us to enlighten those hidden corners of indifference and ignorance, or of the daily rhythm that we follow. Perhaps, opening the hand of thought can be understood as a loving silence, what we do when staying attentive, in cross-legged sitting, to this reality in which we find ourselves.

STITCHES AND SILENCE

Thinking about silence for me also means going back to stitching in our Soto Zen tradition, the one we inherited from Kodo Sawaki Roshi, and which he rescued. We are often told that the word 'sutra' comes from "leading or guiding thread." In my MA dissertation where I reflect on the sewing activity at Daishinji, I relate that sense to the implicit meanings that exist in sewing the rakusu or okesa. In the sewing we see materially how this leading thread allows the fastening of fragments of fabric to create a new pattern of stitches, resembling a rice field, the one we end up wearing. We wear a leading thread that becomes an okesa or a rakusu, just as we also wear a loving silence, because that thread, the one that sustains our "patchwork robe," is entwined in the refuge we take in the Three Treasures. The words *namu kie butsu, namu kie ho, namu kie so* (I take refuge in the Buddha, I take refuge in the Dharma, I take refuge in the sangha) are loving words. This is what we recite while sewing our robes, stitch by stich, thus taking refuge in the Three Treasures. Such words embrace, materially and metaphorically, the okesa we wear. At the same time, they embrace or envelop us. Any monk or nun who has given hugs while wearing their okesa knows exactly what I meant by hugging this way. This is a loving silence, because we carry these words (the Triple Refuge) engraved in our robes. When we shelter ourselves within the okesa, we shelter others.

Why can silence during sewing be a loving silence as well? It works almost the same as in zazen. When we sew, we ritualize our activity. Our body takes on a special disposition, a posture that allows us to sew for hours, if possible. We treat objects such as the needle, the thread, and the fabric, with delicacy, as much as we can. We keep the sewing space tidy. Occasionally we light incense. Everything is arranged in its place. Unexpectedly, we may find ourselves sewing with more people. And maybe there is no silence. Perhaps the sewing itself may trigger a stream of ceaseless conversation among the sewers,[9] who, far from being silent, become embroiled in the thread of everyone's thoughts. Silence during sewing is different; it is not the same as zazen silence. We can see the form that stitches take on the black cloth, just as we also see the voice of someone speaking to us. We see the neighbor's music in the stitch. We see our thoughts, tangle after tangle, and we return and unravel the entire afternoon's work. Sewing is the silence we experience, because that is the most concrete representation of what is happening around and within us. And it is also a way of materially translating, in terms of stitches, Avalokiteshvara's metaphorical skill: *seeing the sounds of the world.*

On the other hand, if we apply the teaching of zazen to sewing,[10] that well-known expression *shikantaza* (只管打坐), or simply sitting, translates into what I have called *shikantanuu* (只管

打渫う): simply sewing. The beautiful thing about sewing is that the reflection of everything we experience—our mental states, our attitude, our eagerness, our desires and illusions, even the weather we are living under—is automatically expressed in our sewing. Sometimes realizing that the stitches in a rakusu or an okesa are terribly crooked is frustrating, the same as when we feel frustration in zazen. This is disappointing. But in sewing, we can undo stitches and pick up thread and needle again and start over. To me, this is a kind of repentance, the most tangible expression of the vow and repentance that Uchiyama Roshi has conveyed to us. Unstitching is repenting. In zazen, to repent is to return to the posture after a foolish drowsiness. This is the way (with a bit of a stretch, I admit) in which loving silence can be related to our practice of stitching a monk's robe, and, of course, to our practice of zazen.

Figure 1. "Virtual Zazen." Lemoine, Camila, 2022.

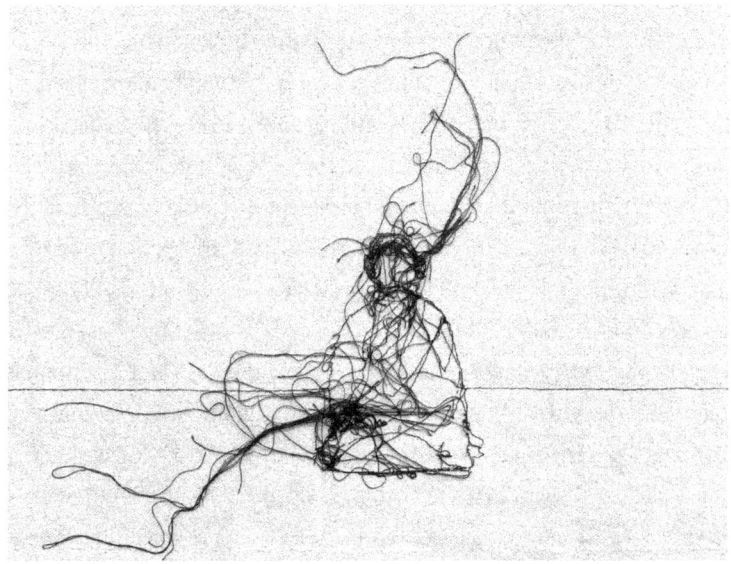

Figure 2. "Zazen Virtual." (The back side of the thread drawing above). Lemoine, Camila, 2022.

Camila Lemoine, the artist who composed these pieces, is also a practitioner and sewer. I am not an art expert, but I can interpret this work from my practice as a monk and assiduous sewer. The threads that we see tangled on the canvas are the sounds of the artist's zazen experience. It is her manner of translating her sensations, perceptions and emotions into a work of thread and needle. It is also what a writer does when composing a poem: there is a codification of the experience in a structure of symbols: in black and white, ink on paper, thread on canvas. Now, if we remember the hearing capacity of Avalokiteshvara, it is the same attitude that moves us to create—whether artworks or choosing the words we utter. Loving silence allows a sort of introspection, a dialogue of the inner with the outer. It allows a more attentive listening, an Avalokiteshvara-like gaze that awakens compassion, and compassion awakens the loving mind which produces kind speech, as Dōgen Zenji says. Drawing these equivalences is nothing other than seeking unexpected means by which kind speech manifests itself during practice. Taking some risks, I propose that the marrow of kind words, of the embracing Dharma that Dōgen teaches, can be replicated in other expressive forms that language takes.

Camila's pictures were shared on the Virtual Sangha of the Soto Zen Community of Colombia. The number of hearts that reacted to the image was overwhelming. Perhaps it is a strange way of measuring the impact of an embracing dharma (I insist this continues to be risky), but it is the way we relate to each other nowadays. I'd like to trust the "virtual" practitioners and the beating of their "virtual hearts" upon seeing Camila's "loving word": a monk sewn on canvas, sitting in zazen.

BY WAY OF CONCLUSION

Up to this point, what I have presented here are nothing more than words, organized or disorganized signs, that somehow give sense to my experience. This is probably not the best way to express it or to interpret it, just as it is not possible to express the silence of zazen or the silence that we all experience. When we become silent, not only do words tumble to the ground and crumble, but if we open the hand of thought, everything else drops as well. Even this essay falls apart. Silence. We open our eyes a little wider, no longer finding noises, words, murmurs, or hindered sounds. Sometimes it's lines, or images, or colors, or even stitches of gray thread on black fabric. The reality that we awaken to is unpredictable, and very subtle.

What is striking about all this is not the beauty of the words, nor the depth of our voices. It is the way speech or loving silence arises. Okumura Roshi describes this cogently in his foreword to this book: Dōgen Zenji was really in a frightening and difficult situation when he wrote the *Shishobo*. He was not concerned about subtleties of language to make it appear "loving." The four embracing dharmas were the Buddhist response to a world in need of compassion and love. It was a vital matter!

In Colombia, every day is a vital matter. In a country where we are burdened with violence as the karmic seeds of our predecessors (and violent ones, of all colors and flags), it is vital to stop and return to the teachings of Dōgen Zenji and Okumura Roshi, asking ourselves every day: Whose gaze listens to all the sounds of suffering? We need to stop for a second and allow silence. What sounds flood into our eyes right now, at this very instant? How will we manifest loving words after seeing with Kanzeon's eyes?

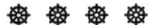

Eishō Amaya is a Zen monk from Bogota, Colombia, ordained in 2021 by Master Densho Quintero. At this moment he is preparing to do ango in Japan. For more than a year, he has been living in the Daishin Temple in Bogota, headquarters of the Soto Zen Community of Colombia. He is an anthropologist by profession and is interested in ritual sewing in Zen and the study of materiality in Buddhism. He also works as a tailor and cook at the temple.

Seeing Buddha,
Speaking Buddha

Esho Morimoto

> These four embracing actions all embrace
> each other; these are not four separate items.
> — *Shohaku Okumura*

THE FOUR EMBRACING ACTIONS ARE CONNECTED AND ONE, so it is not easy to talk about one without relating to the other three actions, but I will try to focus on loving speech here…

In the *Bodaisatta Shishobo,* Dōgen writes, "Loving speech means, first of all, to arouse a compassionate mind when meeting beings, and to offer loving, caring words. In general, we should not use any violent or harmful words when we speak…. We should know that loving speech arises from a loving mind, and that the seed of a loving mind is a compassionate heart. We should study how loving speech has the power to transform the world. It is not merely praising someone's ability."

I recently watched a documentary movie called *Bending the Arc.* The movie tells the story of doctors and health care workers working hard to establish clinics, hospitals, and healthcare systems in underdeveloped countries in the 1980s. In Peru, many tuberculosis patients were dying, even though in most of the world, medicines for tuberculosis were available which could cure the disease. The film introduces a young man in his twenties named Melquiades. He was on the brink of death, having suffered with tuberculosis for several years. He was skin and bone. He had taken medicine for three years without getting better because his tuberculosis was "multi-drug-resistant." When Dr. Kim, one of the doctors, saw him, he thought, "Oh, my goodness... I would not be surprised if he died." When Dr. Kim gave the medicines for multidrug resistant tuberculosis to Melquiades, Melquiades was full of doubt: "Three years I have been on treatment—and nothing. Nothing. Three years. It's worse still." He was exhausted and in despair. He also didn't want to take these medicines—eleven of them—because they had strong side effects and made him feel sick. Dr. Kim told him, "We know it's difficult to take all the medications, but right now we don't have any others. It's difficult now, but please, please continue." Dr. Kim begged and held Melquiades' hand.

Lorena, a community health care worker and nurse, went to Melquiades' home six days a week and made sure he took the medicines. Lorena sat down with him, gave him her hand, listened to his crying and complaints, and encouraged him to take the medicines one by one. Dr. Kim and Lorena aroused compassion, and understood Melquiades' suffering deeply. After a two-year long battle, Melquiades was cured and now lives a healthy life.

I wonder if Melquiades would have survived without Dr. Kim's and Lorena's loving words. If he had just been given the medicines, without any encouraging and compassionate words, would he have taken them and been cured?

I think this is also a good example of how it is not easy to separate the four embracing actions from each other. Dr. Kim and Lorena aroused their compassion, understood Melquiades' pain and suffering, identified with him, offered their time and effort selflessly with nothing in return, spoke with him with loving words—they did everything they could for him. I think they were true bodhisattvas.

The four embracing actions of these doctors, nurses, community health workers, and donors resulted in the development of clinics, hospitals, and healthcare systems in many underdeveloped countries. I think this is proof of "how loving speech has the power to transform the world."

"There are none who fail to change their minds when the Buddhas and ancestors offer a single word," Dōgen wrote in *Gakudo Yojinshu* (Points to Watch in Practicing the Way). It might be easier to say loving words to friends and family than to strangers, but Buddha went above and beyond. He offered loving words to a murderer who was trying to kill him.

The Angulimala Sutta tells the story of Angulimala, who was a murderous bandit. Even after receiving many warnings from villagers not to take the road leading to Angulimala, Buddha proceeded alone in that direction. Angulimala chased Buddha, wanting to kill him. Although Buddha was walking and Angulimala was running, he couldn't catch up, because Buddha had performed a feat of supernatural power:

Angulimala called out to the Blessed One: "Stop, recluse! Stop, recluse!"
Buddha responded, "I have stopped, Angulimala; you stop too."

Then the bandit Angulimala thought: "These recluses, sons of the Sakyans, speak truth, assert truth: but though this recluse is still walking, he says: 'I have stopped, Angulimala; you stop too.' Suppose I question this recluse." Then the bandit Angulimala addressed the Blessed One in stanzas thus:

"While you are walking, recluse, you tell me you have stopped:
But now, when I have stopped, you say I have not stopped.
I ask you now, O recluse, about the meaning:
How is it that you have stopped and I have not?"

"Angulimala, I have stopped forever,
I abstain from violence towards living beings;
But you have no restraint toward things that live:
That is why I have stopped and you have not."

"Oh, at long last this recluse, a venerated sage
Has come to this great forest for my sake.
Having heard your stanza teaching me the Dhamma,
I will indeed renounce evil forever."[1]

Buddha just said a simple word—"Stop"—that changed the murderous Angulimala. It caused him to stop violent actions forever, and so free himself. Buddha did not show any fear or animosity toward Angulimala, but just compassion and peace. Buddha was able to see the true nature of Angulimala. I think that Angulimala felt Buddha's compassion, and it opened his mind. Maybe Buddha knew that Angulimala was ready to change, so he went to see him alone. "Stop" was the most loving word he could offer to Angulimala.

> So saying, the bandit took his sword and weapons
> And flung them in a gaping chasm's pit;
> The bandit worshiped the Sublime One's feet,
> And then and there asked for the going forth.

> The enlightened One, the Sage of Great Compassion,
> The Teacher of the world with [all] its gods,
> Addressed him with these words, "Come, bhikkhu."
> And that was how he came to be a bhikkhu.

Buddha said to Angulimala, "Come, bhikkhu (monk)." Buddha already recognized him as a monk and admitted him to the sangha. He embraced Angulimala as his own. These words—"Come, monk"—are very simple but very loving words. Angulimala must have felt that he was welcomed and loved as he was. When Buddha saw Angulimala, he didn't see a murderer. Buddha saw Anguli-mala's true nature—buddha-nature—and didn't see separation between himself and Angulimala.

Can we see buddha-nature when we see a murderer, a perpetrator of injustice or even the most controversial polit-ical figure? That could be a very challenging practice for us. There is a modern day example: the Dalai Lama calls Chinese people "my Chinese brothers" even though over 1.2 million people have died and many Tibetan temples have been demol-ished as a result of Chinese occupation. The Dalai Lama doesn't see the Chinese as his enemies and lovingly calls them brothers. If we could see the buddha-nature of everyone and see them as our own, I could see the world transforming into a loving and friendly place.

Here is another example of loving words offered by Buddha, in a conversation with Suciloma (a divine spirit) in *Suttanipata, II. Minor Chapter 5 Suciloma.* Suciloma said to Buddha, "I'll ask you a question, ascetic. If you won't answer me, I'll drive you insane, or split your heart, or grab you by the feet and hurl you across the Ganges."

I find Suciloma's threatening attitude toward Buddha kind of comical, and in such contrast to the way in which Buddha replied, "I do not see anyone in this world, friend, who could drive me insane or split my heart or grab me by the feet and hurl me across the Ganges. But ask whatever you want, friend."

Could you be so calm and friendly, like Buddha, if someone was threatening to kill you? I am sure I wouldn't be able to be calm like Buddha. He simply didn't see any evil in Suciloma and didn't believe that Suciloma could do such a harmful action. Hence Buddha was completely calm, called Suciloma "friend," and gave him a teaching.

In a lecture on *Bodhaisatta Shishobo,* Okumura Roshi said, "When we intentionally look for virtuous and praiseworthy traits in others, little by little we will find these traits and our ability to appreciate people's actions will grow... To practice loving speech we need to find a way to recognize the good points of others."

I read a great story on NPR about a man named Daryl Davis, a black blues musician. One night, Davis met a white man after playing music at a bar:

This white gentleman approached me, and he said, "I really enjoy you all's music." Then he says, "You know, this is the first time I ever sat down and had a drink with a black man?"

Soon, the man admitted that he was a member of the Ku Klux Klan. A Klansman and a black person could sit down at the same table and talk about enjoying the same music. The Klansman was surprised to learn from Davis that his favorite style of music, played by Jerry Lee Lewis (a white musician), originated with black musicians. Their conversation about a shared love of music was enough to bring them together.

After that incident, Davis went around the country and sat down with Klan leaders and members to have conversations. He wanted to find out: "How can you hate me when you don't even know me?" Davis explains:

> That began to chip away at their ideology because when two enemies are talking, they're not fighting. It's when the talking ceases that the ground becomes fertile for violence. If you spend five minutes with your worst enemy, you will find that you both have something in common. As you build upon those commonalities, you're forming a relationship and as you build about that relationship, you're forming a friendship. That's what would happen. I didn't convert anybody. They saw the light and converted themselves.[2]

Davis was curious and open enough to actually risk bodily harm in these situations. He was meeting face to face with people who held distorted, hateful views about him. I think, in a way, Davis' ability to use loving speech actually protected him. His openness to understanding allowed the Klansmen to open up to Davis.

Somehow, Davis was able to see each person as a human being like himself—not just as a potentially dangerous member of the KKK. This is like Buddha seeing buddha-nature in Angulimala and Suciloma. Then, he could remain calm, fearless, and friendly. I think that Davis intentionally looked for virtuous and praise-worthy traits in the Klansman and found a way to recognize the good points of those who held an antagonistic view toward him. Somehow, he could find friendliness beneath their hate.

As Davis' story shows, conversations using loving speech are a way to find commonality. If people can create the conditions in which even apparent enemies can share loving speech, they can get to know each other, and find something in common between them. Then, they can form a positive relationship. This is what Davis was able to do with two-hundred members of the KKK.

The four embracing actions are not only for humans. Before I came to Sanshin, I was living with a few monks in a temple in the countryside of New York. On hot summer days, some of us often went to swim in a quarry in the woods near the temple. One day, we were walking in single file on a narrow trail leading to a quarry. The monk who was leading the four of us down the trail stopped suddenly. We all stopped to see why he stopped.

He bent down to the ground and said, "Oh, he is upside down."

The rest of us surrounded him to see what he was looking at. There was a tiny beetle laying upside down, scratching the air. The monk looked around and picked up a twig. He used the twig to gently turn the beetle right side up, moved him to the side of the trail where there was less chance to be stepped on, and said, "There you go, buddy."

His action totally warmed my heart that day, especially his loving words: "There you go, buddy." He spoke with love to a bug as if it were his best friend. There was no separation between monk and beetle. I felt like he was able to hear and understand the monk's loving speech, and the whole world became brighter. I still remember it fondly.

That monk was a good gardener and particularly caring for plants, animals, and insects. The bug could have easily gone unnoticed and been crushed by one of us or someone else, but the monk stopped, like Buddha, and noticed. No life is too small.

To practice the four embracing actions, we have to be deeply rooted in our daily zazen. I believe that the monk's loving speech came from the peace he cultivated in zazen. Through the practice of zazen, we can taste the Dharma: the network of interdependent origination. Somehow we can hold two paradoxical truths: we are everything and all, and at the same time we are a tiny individual being. We sit and open our hands of thought, over and over, moment by moment. If I can ground myself in zazen, I can get up from the cushion carrying the well-being of the network of interdependent origination, and speak lovingly to others from the deepest peace.

Esho Kikuko Morimoto was born in Kobe, Japan. She is an artist and a Japanese language teacher who has been practicing meditation since taking a 10-day silent Vipassana meditation course in 1995. Esho began practicing with the Brooklyn Zen Center sangha in 2011, were she eventually served as co-tenzo (head of kitchen) and as fukuten (assistant to the tenzo), and was lay-ordained by Soshin Teah Strozer in 2017. She also taught meditation classes at Brooklyn Zen Center and was a co-facilitator of the Brooklyn Zen Center BIPOC sangha. From 2019 until Spring of 2022, she lived and practiced at Ancestral Heart Zen Monastery in Millerton,

NY, where she served as shika (guest manager) and tenzo (head of kitchen). She moved to Bloomington in Spring of 2022 to carry out an okesa sewing apprenticeship with Yuko Okumura and to practice with the Sanshin Zen Community. Esho was ordained as a novice by Okumura Roshi in December 2023.

Beneficial Action

How Can We Fulfill Our Bodhisattva Vows?

Shinko Hagn

An attempt to explore what Engaged Buddhism means

My first teacher in our lineage, Kaikyo Roby, wrote in her article "The Bodhisattva-Heart" in *Boundless Vows, Endless Practice* that we are all bodhisattvas. I believe that too, but I believe, as Okumura Roshi likes to say, that we are all baby bodhisattvas at first.

But how do we manage to develop into teenage bodhisattvas, or to grow even more? How can we implement the four embracing bodhisattva actions into our daily lives and fulfil our bodhisattva vows in life? How do we manage to maintain our practice diligently, since our conditioned being always gets in the way and we are constantly telling ourselves our own stories? How do we let go of these stories, of the belief of who we are, and surrender ourselves, to find out who or what we really are?

The basis for our bodhisattva existence is our Buddha nature. In Mahayana Buddhism, we assume that we all have this deep knowledge, this ability to discover our true nature, which we call Buddha nature. However, this true nature is so obscured by our own suffering that we are rarely able to truly perceive it. But how do we penetrate this suffering, in order to awaken our Buddha nature? How do we make it grow and blossom?

The origin of this suffering is that we experience ourselves as separate beings. I am here, and out there, there is the foreign, the other. So, we mostly live in an object-like state of being, in an illusion. But our teaching tells us that this separation is only a fiction about our conditioned self. But how do we experience and recognize this illusion, especially in our everyday, ordinary lives? How do we recognize in every moment that we are all fundamentally connected, without having to enter into social, cultural, family or other relationships? How do we recognize and experience our true nature?

We have many practices within our Zen practice that help us in doing this, especially zazen, but there are also many rituals, and of course conceptual support through our teachings, the sutras and of course our teachers. But besides these monastic practices, how do we manage to keep ourselves sufficiently awake in our modern, busy daily lives to satisfy this deep need, this innate longing, and to embody our true nature?

I have found a home in our Sanshin lineage, but the path that has led me here has not been straight and not necessarily typical for a Zen practitioner ... or perhaps, because of this, it is exactly a typical Zen path. Many coincidences have brought me here. Coincidences? When asked what he thought about coincidence, Shunryu Suzuki once said: "I've heard of that concept before."

Sixteen years ago, my wife's sister got married in a Zen monastery in the Black Forest in Germany, a center of Baker Roshi's sangha. Until then, I did not have the slightest clue about Zen and Buddhism. I only knew that my brother-in-law went there several times a year and then sat in front of a white wall in silence for a week. I found this so incredibly absurd that it didn't even occur to me to find it silly or funny.

About a year before that wedding, at the age of 42, I had to admit to myself that I had a big problem, that I was a severe alcoholic. Thanks to my wife, who gave me a choice – either the booze or her – by the time of this wedding, I had managed to stay sober for more than a year. Of course, I also sought professional help and went to rehab. Until I entered outpatient rehab, I didn't realize what a huge social problem alcohol really was. Unimaginable dramas took place behind the doors of this institution, in the lobby alone. These experiences opened my eyes and showed me the true extent of alcohol addiction in my country.

After the first few months of freedom from my addiction, the desire to give back and support others arose. A friend of mine introduced me to an organization that helped the homeless. We cooked food and served it to hungry people in various locations all over Vienna. This was my first experience of how helping others can make one very happy, through giving without getting any tangible reward in return. The non-tangible showed itself in the joy that we all shared when we went home late in the evening after the meal. We experienced upbeat, pure happiness, despite feeling cold and fatigued from the hard work.

During that time, my wife and I were invited to the wedding in the Black Forest. I, who had no idea about Zen and Buddhism, opened a door in this monastery, entering a room where only people who had spent a week in silence sat together. From today's point of view, I am quite sure that this opening of the door opened a gate inside of me. A gate back into a sense of foreboding, the memory of a kind of connection that was familiar to me from childhood. I used to accompany my grandmother to church, where she prayed the rosary every week with some other old women from the village. It was there that I first experienced this sense of connectedness, this deeply felt trust in the world and everything around me.

This trust, however, was broken by the institution of the Catholic Church and the people acting under its umbrella, and it had been lying dormant until this gate was opened. It had been buried for decades. What I tried instead was to relieve my deep-seated suffering in worldly ways, such as the excessive consumption of alcohol and other drugs, or excessive shopping in general, and of luxurious items in particular. But, of course, these worldly methods only helped in the short run, and the old suffering always wanted to come back to the surface, demanding more and more distraction and covering-up until it was all unsustainable.

All these impressions I took home from the monastery were very confusing. But after a few weeks I asked my brother-in-law to show me how to meditate and he gave me some instructions. Among them was a meditation where I had to lie down. After the first few minutes I jumped up and was really horrified at what I had been observing in my mind. Yes, I had started seeing a therapist in the meantime, but therapy was more about feeling better and challenging certain behaviors. Never before had I observed my awareness as I did in this meditation. It took me a few months to get into it again, and this time I started sitting down. In the meantime, my brother-in-law had referred me to the local Viennese sangha. It wasn't long before I found myself sitting with this group regularly in the morning, several times a week. Soon, I went to my first sesshin at the monastery in the Black Forest, and a few months later, the second.

Those first years of practice were like sweeping my mind, level by level, floor by floor. Memories, ideas, conceptions, everything that wanted to emerge – I allowed it to emerge. It was mostly old wounds from my early childhood that were hidden deep within me. I tore down my inner walls and gave space to these phenomena in my zazen, again and again and again. The many tears I cried in silence could have filled rivers.

Through this giving of space alone, many things dissolved and no longer appeared. During this time, I had my first encounter with Okumura Roshi. I read *Realizing Genjokoan* and heard about repentance in a Zen context for the first time. In Baker Roshi's sangha, there was no emphasis on this concept of repentance, and this distinction between absolute and relative repentance touched me deeply, opened something inside me. The inherent possibility of transformation of all suffering associated with repentance in zazen enabled my original dramas to start disappearing more and more.

In the meantime, my social commitment had also developed further. I had joined a small group who took care of inmates in prison, by visiting them and meditating with them. But soon I realized that there was more to it than that. Going to the prison for the first time was very exciting. My intention was to notice everything with great attention. My teacher advised me to stay with my breath. We were at a special institution for "mentally abnormal" lawbreakers (a highly difficult legal term that comes from very old times). The term refers to inmates with severe mental problems confirmed by a psychiatric report. It was a small institution in the center of Vienna, in a completely normal residential area, in a completely normal house. I was very surprised, because I had once lived right around the corner and had not noticed this institution at all.

I went in with a mentor and after a simple security check (we were patted down) we had to lock up all items. A very friendly security guard who had fun conversations with my mentor the entire time showed us to an elevator. After a short ride, we entered a large room. It was a therapy room, empty except for a few chairs. We placed these against the wall and laid out several thick, old, and rather worn-down blankets that had been provided by the prison. Then, the inmates were brought in. There were five of them. I was again very surprised because they were wearing normal street clothes, and they all looked neat and quite normal. I introduced myself briefly, we all sat down on the blankets in a circle and my mentor began a guided meditation. After about 20 minutes, he concluded, and we began a conversation. The inmates asked me what I did for a living, if I was married, had children. It was a normal conversational situation, as if we were getting together at a seminar or some other occasion. After another 20 minutes, a security guard came and declared our lesson over. We were escorted back to the door and before I knew it, we were outside the door, in the middle of the city bustle. I was very amazed at how smoothly things went, and especially how normal everything was.

The next few days, however, during morning zazen at home, everything was strange. Again, I had to cry constantly, although there was no obvious reason. No old memories or images came up that could have moved me, there was just an incredibly sad, indescribable feeling. This state lasted for days and at some point, I realized it had to do with my visit to the prison. I had taken something home from our prison meditation session that manifested in my tears. Something intangible that was working inside of me and moved me. After a few days, the feeling left, but it kept resurfacing after my prison visits and intensified over time. During my zazen, these experiences merged with my story. Something began to work in me, to take effect, something which I had absorbed without words, taken with me and linked to my life. The reciprocal connection thus became intensely perceptible without words. Of course, I have been functioning like this my whole life, but until then, it had not been clear to me how immediate this connection was. Something inside of me was driving me towards wanting to know more about it, to get to the bottom of it. Thus, my career as chaplain began.

During this process of exploration, I met Kyoku Lutz, who would become my Dharma sister. She was also a prison chaplain at that time. I immediately felt a connection. We were driven by the same longing. During a jukai ceremony at her house, I met her teacher, Kaikyo Roby, who was also working as a chaplain in a hospital in Florida, and to whom I also immediately felt a connection. I realized very quickly that she would become my new teacher. In my first sangha, everyone always said how much they appreciated my chaplaincy work, but honestly speaking, it was not really taken seriously. Being a prison chaplain is always admired in a way. However, it immediately creates a distance for many people. I think that's because most people find it hard to imagine spending time with criminals, or more dramatically speaking, sitting at a table with murderers, robbers, and thieves. Generally speaking, chaplaincy is still in its infancy in European Buddhism, still a tender shoot, especially in Zen.

As luck would have it, Kaikyo was a student of Okumura Roshi, a part of the Sanshin sangha, where repentance, beneficial action, and many other things are emphasized. That had not been the case in my previous sangha. But my practice time with Kaikyo was unfortunately very short. After her unexpected death, only a year after we first met, I was fortunate that Hoko immediately answered "yes" to my question about discipleship. Kaikyo had recorded a video for Hoko during her last days in the intensive care unit and asked her to take over her disciples. Half a year later I was ordained by Hoko and since then she has been a wonderful teacher to me. She has always supported me in all matters and, thanks to her clear view, has brought a lot of order into my practice and into my priestly training as well.

In his commentary on the *Shishobo,* at the beginning of this book, Okumura Roshi explains in great detail what Dōgen might have meant. There is little to add, but I'd like to mention an interesting historical fact. The four embracing actions are not an invention of the Mahayana but were first mentioned in the very early scriptures. They are described in both the fourth and eighth book of the *Anguttara Nikaya,* which are part of the *Suttapitaka* (Buddha's discourses) and are also mentioned in the *Tripitaka* in the Pali canon. In these scriptures, they are still seen as the four teachings of the Buddha, which are about introducing the Buddha's teachings to sentient beings and winning them over.

For me, it is important to emphasize that none of the four embracing actions can exist or be performed separately. All four are mutually dependent. Giving, the action which Okumura Roshi expounds most extensively in his commentary, is probably the most important virtue of these four. *Dana* can show itself in many actions, such as giving time or attention. But what also seems very important to me is that in *Shishobo,* concerning *dana,* the importance of giving material things is also emphasized. Giving is also usually associated with loving speech, and the two together then become a beneficial action that is impossible to perform without identity action.

Beneficial action today often goes hand in hand with the term "Engaged Buddhism," and it has taken many different forms nowadays. Issan Dorsay, Zen priest and drag queen, who opened the first AIDS hospice in San Francisco and whose life is described very impressively in the book *Street Zen,* once said in response to a question about what he had to say about engaged Buddhism: "I don't know anything about it. But when someone is down on the floor, I help them up."

This view has carried me along from the very beginning, it has encouraged me to act from this intention. When we start caring about others, we always must be careful that we don't get stuck in our ideas about the world. We must be careful not to give in to some form of activism that might currently be *en vogue.* Reflecting on this topic and one's own intention seems to be very important in my point of view. Any form of activism shapes our practice into a political action that arises purely out of a discursive attitude of our mind and often only shows our ego-centeredness. Dōgen says in the *Mountains and Waters Sutra* that we must unhook our ideas, that is, take them off the hook of our self. We must always subject these ideas to deep investigation. We must also trace their sources, find out where they come from, and most importantly, whom they benefit in the end. We must not allow ourselves to be taken in by political agendas just because they are fashionable and in line with the spirit of the times. We must never forget our vows. These vows are about helping people to free themselves from suffering, always, without any political agendas or ideologies. In fact, our whole practice is always about realizing the true reality. We can only sense this level of reality in our direct actions. That is, in our direct environment, in our direct relationships with everyone and everything. It is in direct action and not in our ideas about action that this is witnessed. Our ideas about it are all just a fiction, that is, delusion.

The basis of our action as bodhisattvas is the effort to eliminate suffering, or at least to alleviate it. The methods we use as bodhisattvas arise directly in the moment and are based on our own practical experience, and, in the case of chaplains, also on the experience of our training. However, our methods and skills must always be related to the respective moment that we experience right here and now. Of course, we need to train our skills and acquire basic knowledge, but the implementation of this knowledge is only true or real if it is in harmony with the respective moment and whatever it is the moment calls for. However, we can only experience this in the particular moment. The doctrine of cause and condition and mutual interdependence clearly shows that we only know what the situation really requires right in the moment of action.

These days, we express our opinions far too quickly and too often on social media, judging and commenting situations and things with just a few words or simply with emojis. We do this based on our ideas, of which we don't even know how they have been generated over the years, even over generations. We don't know how they came about and where their roots are, who brought them into the world and, above all, whom they benefit in the end. We find things good or bad within a few seconds and spread this opinion on the internet, send it out into the world, instead of witnessing our bodhisattva vows in our real life, in the moment, in face-to-face relationships.

When we learn to step out of our discursive mind during encounters with people and learn to forget our opinions about these people, when we learn to step out of these thoughts about who we are and what is important to us and go beyond all that, namely to what it is that really moves people in their heart, authentic intimacy arises. This intimacy of "not knowing," this space filled with the 10,000 things, emerges from emptiness. When we open this space, true transformation is possible. By truly seeing people as they are, rather than looking at our idea of them, we can authentically get closer to them. "Not knowing is nearest," Dizang tells Faian in koan number 20 in the *Book of Serenity.* This sentence became a guiding principle for the way I conduct my chaplaincy.

Kodo Sawaki once said: "Separated from daily life, Buddhism is a dead thing. All aspects of your life must be the Buddha Way." This phrase has also accompanied me for a very long time. The training of my mind which took place in a social engagement context, outside of monastic practices, has helped me a lot (and still helps me) to put this sentence into practice.

In our daily life we need our ego-centered mind if we want to survive at all. We have to permanently make decisions in order to secure our manifested real existence. We need a job to earn money to be able to feed ourselves and our families. We must make decisions within our families and in our dealings with friends as well. I'm not just talking about the big decisions, like which school to send my kids to, but I'm talking about the small decisions that need be made in practically every second. Do I do this or that, do I need this or that, or maybe not?

It is not easy for me to talk about this field. In my memory, until I was ten or eleven years old, life was quite simple, everything was carefree. Only afterwards did the doubts and begin, and the unease that comes with them. Where do I actually belong, where do I fit in, what is my opinion, which group do I belong to? I felt I belonged everywhere and understood everyone. That's why this process of making these small decisions was a big challenge for me, and it followed me throughout my adolescence. Who am I really, which guidelines do I use when making decisions, what do I identify with, what is the "red herring," the central theme of my life?

During my teenage years, my father's business partners took away everything he had built up after the war. So many beliefs that I had had collapsed for me, too. Of course, being a good son, acting intuitively from my unconscious, I tried to make up for the situation and improve our economic situation again. As life would have it, this happened in the late 1980s, the era of burgeoning neoliberalism. I had ample opportunities to plunge into that ideology. However, the hedonistic lifestyle that comes with it, which was supposed to improve my suffering and that of my family, my father in particular, led to me not being in touch with myself anymore. It got worse and worse, and alcohol helped me disguise my suffering and keep it hidden.

This way, the doubts disappeared, and my identity kept on generating itself. The many small, constant decisions of my life were largely informed by the stories of my father, my mother and the associated stories of their parents, especially their fathers, who, like all grandfathers of that time, were either not present, because they had been killed in the Second World War, or had just come home from the war severely traumatized, which they had lost on top of that.

Our ancestors were and are always present and a big part of our identity. Due to my big crash, when I finally admitted to myself that I was an alcoholic, a large part of my generated identity dissolved. Afterwards, I felt so helpless and lost somehow. At the very beginning of my practice, Baker Roshi once told me: "You don't need an identity; you are just a collection of five skandhas, nothing more. Leave your history behind." A sentence that helped me a lot.

In our modern, incredibly fast-paced lives, we are forced to make decisions in order to sustain our lives and those of our families even more. The space we need to really get to the bottom of things, to deeply explore and surrender to situations and especially encounters, is no longer there. But in social engagement we can open this kind of defined space for ourselves, this kind of awareness space that we cultivate through our zazen. We can step out of our identity, and also out of the decision-making structures associated with it. Then, the only decision left is to remain in direct connection with people and to do everything we can to maintain it.

Opening this defined space of awareness means that we no longer have to act in an ego-centered way but can practice boundless compassion, to practice expanding our compassion while training our mind.

In the first sentence of the *Heart Sutra,* Bodhisattva Avalokiteshvara (and not Buddha!) says that all five skandhas are empty and thus was relieved from suffering. He is the Bodhisattva of unlimited compassion. His name translates to "He who hears the suffering of the world." That is why I have given our sangha the name "Daijihi," which is an ancient Japanese word for "boundless compassion."

The practice in a defined social setting has helped me greatly in making the right decision in the chaos of life. It has enabled me to always keep an open space of awareness, the kind that I got to know from monastic practice, with which I can cover my rational thinking mind. From this more inclusive mind, it is easier to make decisions for the benefit of all.

There was a young man in prison whom I mentored for a few years. When I met him, he was just short over 20 years old. He was serving time for a very serious violent offense, but after his crime he found the Buddhist teachings and practiced very diligently. I cared for him for many years while he was in prison, and when he was released, I did not abandon him, of course. We met regularly. At one of these meetings, we were sitting in a coffee house and once more, he tried to tell me about everything that was bad in his life, again and again, justifying himself and talking, talking, talking. Over and over again, he lamented his suffering to me. I tried to concentrate and to really just listen, but the whole time, all that came up in my mind was advice on how he could immediately improve the situation. As time went on, I became more and more impatient and inwardly resentful because, after all, it seemed like he had possibly understood very little over the years and that perhaps I had wasted my time with him. All this popped up in my mind at the same time, thoughts overlapped one another. But I concentrated on listening, said nothing, just nodded my head in understanding sometimes or said a few loving words. Inwardly, I kept telling myself: "I'm just listening, I'm staying patient, I'm just receiving." But most of all, the phrase "Not knowing is nearest" helped me stay in the moment. That was the antidote that kept me focused and able to follow his narratives. And so, for a very long time, I said nothing, but simply listened.

After what felt like an eternity, he suddenly stopped talking in mid-sentence and there was complete silence. We looked into each other's eyes for a long time. Suddenly he began to grin and said: "Oh, that's what you meant, now I understand." Though I had not said a single word!

This story about listening exemplifies that all four bodhi-sattva actions (embracing actions) are always interrelated. On the one hand, I give my time and attention, which is the first of the four bodhisattva actions. On the other hand, I use the second of the four noble bodhisattva actions, loving speech, which I repeatedly utter in between the narrator's story to support the other person in continuing to tell the story and thus going deeper. Both of these acts taken together make up beneficial action, the third of the bodhisattva actions, because they serve to help the other person open up and help me practice listening. When all of these come together, the fourth bodhisattva action, "identity action," appears, because true, genuine listening only occurs when I give up my identity and fully engage with the other person.

In *Song of the Jewel Mirror Samadhi,* Dongshan Liangjie, the founder of the Caodong lineage, the forerunner of Soto Zen, says: "You are not it, but in truth it is you." We, this collection of five skandhas, are filled with what we think we are and what we are holding onto, with what forms our identity, all the time.

As mentioned above, at the beginning of the *Heart Sutra,* it says, "Avalokiteshvara Bodhisattva, when deeply practicing prajna paramita, clearly saw that all five aggregates are empty and thus relieved all suffering."

Tearing down the walls of our own identity and thus opening ourselves to our compassion is our job as bodhisattvas. For it is only when we give up our identity and leave it behind, take the backwards step, as Dōgen Zenji calls it, that we can truly recognize what that world is actually like, by relating to the world outside. To recognize a person in the specific moment, not as an object, shaped by our ideas about him, but to truly recognize the person who is right there—that is what I believe the fourth bodhisattva action, identity action, is.

In our everyday lives, we often forget that we enter a relationship with the world out there in every moment, whether it's with a person sitting in front of us or whether we're sitting in our office picking up a teacup. In that moment, we enter a relationship with the teacup, but even the word "teacup" generates our world and sticks a label on that object.

The search for truth, for the true reality, is one of the main goals of our practice. But how do we recognize true reality, how can we perceive it? In German, "perception" is *Wahrnehmung,* which means "to take what is true." The word *wahr* has its root, like the English word "truth," in the Indoeuropean *uer,* which means "trustworthy" or "faithful." The English word "perception" has a slightly different meaning; it comes from the Latin word *percipere. Per* means "thoroughly," "exactly," "carefully" or "completely," and *capere* means "to take" or "to take something."

In *Fukanzazengi,* Dōgen speaks of "non-thinking thinking" and the *Heart Sutra* speaks of *prajna paramita,* of the "wisdom from the other shore." We also speak of "wisdom beyond wisdom." This means that it is not about an empirically provable truth, but about a wisdom that I cannot fathom logically, that I cannot reach by thinking, and if I cannot reach it by thinking, how can I put it into words and describe it?

It took me a few years of practice to realize that it is not mainly the empirical that is emphasized, but the intuitive, the tangible, the palpable above all. It is about how things are in relation to each other, in relationship. It is about causes and conditions. In German, "causes and conditions" is often mistakenly translated as *Ursache und Wirkung,* which is actually "cause and effect" in English. Even a very well-known German Buddhist magazine is called *Ursache und Wirkung,* "cause and effect." Seen in this way, it quickly becomes clear why "karma" is often interpreted in such a misleading and one-dimensional way, at least in German-speaking countries.

The question of causes and conditions is one of the most important questions in Buddhism. How are things related to each other? Most koan stories deal almost exclusively with finding out how people relate to each other and to things. Exploring how relationships with everyone and everything arise is, in my view, one of the most important practices. The emergence of our reality is based on our relationships. How do we weave together the many threads of our lives? In the metaphor of Indra's web, which Okumura Roshi so often quotes and draws, we are all connected by invisible threads. Disentangling these intertwined threads is our practice. In the very beginning of the *Path of Purification*, the *Visuddhimagga*, an important part of the *Abhidharma*, we are encouraged to "Disentangle the tangle."

These relationship threads are not visible, but they are tangible. We can sense them and a bodily mechanism tells us intuitively what is true. That's why it's so important to examine our perception closely, to examine how our world arises, how it generates itself within us and how it results in what we believe we are.

Beginning with the *Abhidharma* and continued in the Mahayana school of Yogacara, Buddhism has developed good concepts that explain how our perception arises. Devoting close and intense attention to these teachings, to finding out how our own perception and thus our consciousness arises, can help us to find out from which of these threads the fabric that we call "our being" is woven.

When we have torn down our own walls and our compassion begins to work, we can feel the suffering of others. But we have to be very careful in this process of tearing down, so that we don't get sucked into the suffering of others. I personally interpret Dongshan's phrase as: "It is me now, but I'm not it."

We must be careful to only sympathize and not suffer along. The German language has a clear distinction here between *Mitleid,* "pity" (literally: "to suffer with"), and *Mitgefühl,* "compassion" (lit: "to feel with").

I think this is also the common ground for all of us, the base from which we can feel this suffering of the other, but because we are so distracted all the time, we put up our walls, we separate ourselves. Opening an awareness space in an everyday setting where we can feel these relationship threads in our everyday lives, and in doing so, practicing to notice how our being really emerges, is such an incredible practice opportunity. We can learn and realize who we really are, how we really function. This realization holds great transformational possibilities for expanding our compassion. Chaplaincy (and for me, specifically, prison chaplaincy) provides many of these opportunities for training our minds. We learn to notice how our skandhas are filled and how we can use the teachings, especially those from the Yogacara.

A good example of the emergence of perception, the filling of our skandhas, are the key sounds that one hears during chaplaincy visits in prison. One hears them less and less due to digitalization in institutions, but they are still present in Austrian prisons. Some prison guards are still reminiscent of medieval jailers, with the many keys they carry around, some of which are enormous. Naturally, these keys make a rattling sound when they are carried around, inserted into the lock and turned. The doors, upon opening, creak and squeak, because they are usually made of metal and not always freshly oiled. Immediately after one has passed through, they are locked again. After just a few meters, one comes upon the next door, since there are many security sections in a prison, all of which have to be unlocked and locked again.

These sounds have an effect on us. During such a walk through the prison, we aren't alone, there is usually an inmate and a prison guard with us. Because of the short distances, we often need to stay in very small rooms, usually not even two square meters in size. And then, behind us, the door that was just opened is immediately locked again. The door in front of us, through which one must go on, is not yet open and the guard is looking for the right key on his key ring and does not find it right away. What's more, these passageways are usually very dark, often poorly lit, or altogether dark. Here one can feel what it means to be locked up. To observe one's rising fears in this situation, to recognize that these are all just stories that we are telling ourselves at this moment, is a great practice. Overcoming and penetrating these fears in the very process is a great challenge.

Once, I took a Dharma friend with me as an intern on a prison visit. It was her first visit to an institution. The institution was located in an old monastery, not uncommon in Austria. Having been reconstructed throughout centuries, these old monasteries have many winding corridors. We were standing in one such winding, dark corridor, with many doors at short intervals, when suddenly my friend was about to enter a panic attack. But together we managed to stop it and see her fear only as fear, as a momentary emotion, as momentary energy connected to stories that had nothing to do with reality. After this incident, my Dharma friend worked with me in this prison many times.

Another time, another Dharma friend, who was just visiting Vienna from Germany, wanted to come with me. I was about to plan his first visit to a prison and told him that the admission procedure would take extra-long because it was a high security prison. These words, "maximum security prison," upset him so much that he could not sleep all night. He was tremendously upset when I picked him up the next morning and we drove to the prison two hours by car. We met a group of about ten inmates, meditated with them, and then had a dialogue. The confrontation with reality and the realization that these people are not only felons, but sentient beings, some of whom told touching stories, blew him away and touched him so deeply that after his return to Germany, he too began to go to prisons. He still offers prison chaplaincy with members of his sangha, and we are still in touch, although our practice paths have separated.

Again and again, my protégés, whom I intensively cared for in prison during their sentences and also after they had finished their time, asked me if I knew of a place where they could practice. A place in the outside world where they could find a foothold in life and not fall back into old patterns. I tried to place them in Buddhist monasteries of befriended sanghas. But these attempts failed, because these communities lacked care experience and because everyday monastery life was not suitable. I also could not just take them in at home, my family would have been completely overwhelmed.

The young man, with whom I had had this terrific listening experience, also asked me again and again whether I could look after him more intensively, whether I knew a practice place for him. After his release from prison, he returned to his old circles of friends, and so the drugs came back. Three years later, while he was high on drugs, he choked on a piece of pizza. I have witnessed many biographies of young people over the years, many of whom tragically came to an end at a young age.

For many years it has been my desire to create a place where all these experiences and especially the insights of my practice could find a place. A place where we could care for people on various levels, where we could practice, but also do our jobs to earn our living, where we can simply live our everyday lives. This place should connect all levels of our life. Thanks to the support of Susanne Halbeisen and my wife Sabine, this idea has manifested into an NGO, which we have christened *1000 Hände – gelebte Verbundenheit* (*1000 hands – interconnection in action*). It is like the second side of our practice, like the second side of a medal. On the one side there is our practice with "Daijihi" and on the other side there is "1000 Hands." Taken together, both form a unity in which all levels of the reality of our lives come together. During the pandemic, this idea of connecting all levels has developed into a housing project for "assisted living." For us, however, the term "assisted living" does not only mean that we take care of the elderly or the poor. We interpret the term much more comprehensively and want to take care of, for example, young people who are looking for meaning, spirituality, or answers in life. But it also includes single mothers who need someone to care of their children. In the long term, this and much more should become possible at our place.

We have found people who support this project, also financially, and now, a few years after the first ideas popped up, the project is actually becoming real, and we have bought a large plot of land. Our goal is to really live in connection with everyone and everything and to manifest it in our everyday life on all levels. In doing so, we also try to counteract societal undesirable developments and, above all, to put contemplative community practice in the foreground. Yes, we have set out to do a lot, and what will become of it is another story, which I may be able to tell you more about at some point, perhaps also about the failure of this idea.

Beneficial action has many faces, whether it is taking care of the temple, giving Dharma talks, being involved in the community where one lives, or doing chaplaincy or, as I do in my particular case, prison chaplaincy. The important thing is to take care of our environment according to the talents we have, remembering in every moment that everything is connected to everything else and that we are in the middle of it, a part of it.

Uchiyama Roshi says: "A bodhisattva is a simple person who sets a course in his life that moves toward Buddha. You are a bodhisattva, I am a bodhisattva."

Shinko was born in a small town in the countryside in Austria, was ordained by Hoko Karnegis in 2019 and practices with his sangha in Vienna. He has two grown-up children and is also a grandfather, and lives in Vienna with his wife, with whom he runs a trading company. He volunteers at *1000 Hände,* an NGO which takes care of homeless people and prison inmates. Learn more at www.daijihi.org and www.1000haende.at.

Aliviar el sufrimiento mediante acciones bondadosas

Densho Quintero

> Uno debe asociarse con amigos que sean nobles,
> enérgicos y puros en la vida, que sean cordiales
> y refinados en su conducta. Así, lleno de
> alegría, pondrá fin al sufrimiento.
>
> – *Dhammapada 376*

Una guerra sin sentido

En Colombia llevamos más de **60** años en una guerra continua por diversas circunstancias, guerrilla, narcotráfico, paramilitarismo, terrorismo de estado, etc. Si bien el origen del conflicto se encuentra en la violencia política que se desencadenó tras el asesinato, en 1948, de Jorge Eliecer Gaitán, un líder popular que luchaba por la igualdad social, sin duda, todas las razones que perpetuaron las diversas guerras y las atrocidades que de ahí se derivaron, están

287

originadas en los venenos de la mente, el odio, la codicia, la confusión, la arrogancia, el orgullo, la vanidad, etcétera.

Durante todos estos años se realizaron reuniones entre el gobierno y los grupos disidentes para tratar de llegar a acuerdos y procurar restablecer un país en paz. Muchos de estos diálogos lograron acuerdos parciales, pero los enfrentamientos continuaron y solo en 2016 el gobierno firmó un acuerdo con las FARC, la guerrilla más antigua del país. Esto marcó un paso decisivo para abolir la guerra y por primera vez se estuvo cerca de una paz definitiva. Sin embrago, casi la mitad del país estuvo en contra y hubo muchas manifestaciones para evitar que se firmara el acuerdo. Incluso, el gobierno que reemplazó al que firmó la paz saboteó desde el comienzo el acuerdo, evitando que se cumpliera lo pactado y entre la población se continuó alimentando el odio, los deseos de venganza y promoviendo la prolongación de una guerra absurda.

Después de décadas de una violencia cruda se demostró que nada se logró mediante los combates. Por el contrario, se perdieron cientos de miles de valiosas vidas y el país quedó sumido en una enorme desolación. Por otra parte, los innumerables recursos que se desperdiciaron sosteniendo esta guerra inútil se hubieran podido invertir en educación, salud y empleo, con lo cual se hubiera podido reducir la brecha social causada por la pobreza y construir una sociedad más justa.

Con la firma del acuerdo de paz con las FARC se creó una *Comisión para el esclarecimiento de la verdad* con el objetivo de tratar de entender las atrocidades que se cometieron durante todos estos años. La comisión tenía como propósito esclarecer las razones de cómo pudimos vivir con esta violencia como algo normal y por qué como país no hicimos algo para detenerlo.

A partir de las investigaciones, por primera vez en muchos años, los colombianos empezamos a abrir los ojos ante una dolorosa realidad y el país pudo vislumbrar la barbarie que durante tantos años fue justificada como recurso para acabar con la guerrilla. Pero la violencia no se limitó a ideologías políticas ni a los combates entre la guerrilla, los paramilitares y el ejército. El aferramiento a ideologías radicales llevó a la violencia y a la intolerancia de unos grupos hacia otros. Las ideas desencadenaron emociones como el miedo, el odio y la ira, y la crueldad de unos hacia otros se normalizó. Esto se propagó en diversos niveles de la sociedad y los abusos que se cometieron fueron justificados desde el racismo, la aporofobia, el clasismo, la homofobia y en general, desde el rechazo a todo lo que fuera diferente.

El sacerdote Francisco De Roux S.J., quien dirigió la *Comisión para el esclarecimiento de la verdad,* en su discurso durante la entrega del informe final, dijo que gran parte del horror que se vivió, se debió a la deshumanización del conflicto. El dolor dejó de tener rostro humano y fue así como fueron justificadas las formas inimaginables de horror que se revelaron con las declaraciones de las víctimas y las de algunos de los perpetradores. En la actualidad, el país se plantea la urgencia de sanar las heridas de tantos años de masacres y muchas personas se preguntan cómo vamos a hacer para superarlo. Además, surgió la inminente necesidad de recuperar la memoria de estos años de violencia y divulgar los hechos entre la ciudadanía y, desde edades tempranas, en las aulas escolares. Es de vital importancia no olvidar y al mismo tiempo, encontrar mecanismos para aliviar tanto dolor y resentimiento.

UNA HERRAMIENTA PARA SANAR EL SUFRIMIENTO

Podemos empezar a transformar nuestra sociedad y ayudar a sanar tanto sufrimiento que ha dejado la guerra, mediante acciones bondadosas. Acciones sanas que produzcan resultados benéficos. Cosas simples, empezando con personas cercanas, hacer algo bueno por ellas. Luego podemos extender el acto de bondad a personas extrañas. Y así, poco a poco, emitiendo la luz radiante de un corazón bondadoso, podemos alumbrar algo del camino para otros, para que encuentren su íntima conexión con cada ser vivo y puedan manifestarla en acciones concretas.

En el budismo primitivo, (Sangaha sutta, *Sutra de los vínculos de la solidaridad,* AN 4.32), encontramos una enseñanza del Buda para crear relaciones sanas y vivir en armonía: *"Monjes, he aquí estos cuatro lazos que sostienen las relaciones favorables. Y, ¿cuáles son esos cuatro? El dar, el habla amable, la acción beneficiosa y el trato igualitario. Estos son, monjes, los cuatro lazos que sostienen las relaciones favorables."* Desde la perspectiva de las enseñanzas del budismo theravada, el Buda nos está invitando a considerar a las demás personas en el contexto de Dukkha, la Noble Verdad del Sufrimiento y actuar de modo que nuestras acciones produzcan relaciones saludables y guíen a las personas a entrar en el Noble Sendero que lleva a la liberación del sufrimiento.

El maestro Dōgen, no obstante, lleva esta enseñanza al nivel de la práctica misma como bodhisattvas. Más allá de crear vínculos armoniosos y atraer a las personas a la Vía, nos invita a realizar estas acciones como expresión de nuestro voto de liberar a los seres. En su capítulo *Shishobo del Shobogenzo,* "Los cuatro dharmas acogedores del bodhisattva," nos invita a considerar estas acciones como medios hábiles, como acciones concretas en la vida para tratar a los demás con respeto y compasión, como expresión de nuestros votos mismos de liberar a los seres del sufrimiento. El maestro Okumura dice que, "Dōgen enseña que estas cuatro prácticas permiten que los bodhisattvas se liberen de los tres estados venenosos de la mente:

codicia, ira/odio y confusión. Estas prácticas benefician tanto a la persona que las practica como a los seres vivos al mismo tiempo."

Cuando dirigimos nuestra atención hacia los demás, en lugar de continuar satisfaciendo nuestros propios deseos de gratificación, nos liberamos de nuestras tendencias egoístas y liberamos a los otros mediante acciones conscientes, asumiendo la responsabilidad de las consecuencias de los propios actos.

Desde que iniciamos un centro de práctica en 1989, como Bodhisattvas asumimos el compromiso de aportar herramientas para aliviar el sufrimiento en nuestra sociedad. En 2016, el mismo año de la firma del acuerdo de Paz, realizamos en Bogotá el Tercer Encuentro Zen Latinoamericano. El origen de estos encuentros se remonta a la reunión de maestros realizada durante la celebración en Lima, Perú, de los 110 años de la llegada del Soto Zen a Sudamérica. En esa ocasión se acordó reunir a maestros, practicantes y público en general, interesados en promover la tradición del Zen en América Latina, a través de diferentes disciplinas para brindar alternativas de cambio, aliviar el sufrimiento y ayudar a construir una sociedad en paz. Convencidos de las bondades de las enseñanzas de nuestra tradición fundada por Dōgen Zenji, quisimos ofrecer nuestra práctica en esta tercera versión del Encuentro como alternativa para transformar la manera como nos relacionamos con los demás seres, con la naturaleza y con la vida en general.

Como sustento para nuestro compromiso de aportar herramientas concretas para aliviar el sufrimiento y traer paz a nuestro país, quisiera reflexionar sobre el tercer dharma acogedor del *Shishobo* del maestro Dōgen, la acción bondadosa.

Es claro que los más de 60 años de violencia vividos en Colombia alimentaron el desprecio por la vida. Un desprecio que convirtió a los otros en enemigos sin rostro. Pero ahora que hemos comprendido la inutilidad de la guerra y el desperdicio lamentable de innumerables y preciosas vidas, ha llegado el momento de revisar nuestra conducta. ¿Cómo tratamos a los demás? ¿Qué producimos en los otros mediante nuestras acciones de cuerpo, palabra y pensamiento? ¿Somos conscientes de cómo nuestros actos afectan a los otros? El maestro Dōgen dice en su texto *Shishobo:* "Acción bondadosa significa crear los medios hábiles para ayudar a los seres vivos, ya sean nobles o humildes. Por ejemplo, nos preocupamos por el futuro cercano y distante de los demás, y usamos medios hábiles para beneficiarlos."

Dōgen Zenji dice que debemos beneficiar a amigos y enemigos por igual, y beneficiarnos a nosotros y a los otros de igual forma. Resulta increíble cómo una acción bondadosa puede aliviar el sufrimiento de una persona y transformar a quienes la realizan. Dependiendo del trato que le demos a los demás, vamos a modificar cómo nos relacionamos con la vida y podemos tratar de ayudar a aliviar el sufrimiento de otra persona y así, nos beneficiamos nosotros mismos. La ciencia ha demostrado cómo una acción bondadosa puede producir un estado de bienestar en la persona que la recibe, como se evidencia por el nivel de neurotransmisores que estimulan zonas del cerebro que producen esta gratificación. Pero no solo quien recibe la acción, la persona que realiza un acto bondadoso también experimenta el mismo bienestar que quien la recibe. Sin embargo, lo más increíble es que una persona que observa un acto bondadoso realiza la misma condición que los otros dos. La bondad es de hecho contagiosa.

Se ha llegado incluso a comprobar cómo la compasión no se aprende por explicaciones, sino por imitación. Esto se deduce del estudio de las neuronas espejo, un tipo de neuronas que se activan cuando un animal ejecuta una acción y cuando observa esa misma acción al ser ejecutada por otro individuo. Aprendemos a ser bondadosos reproduciendo las acciones amorosas realizadas por otros. Así, también podemos influir positivamente sobre las personas que nos observan, actuando con amabilidad. Las neuronas espejo sirven para despertar la empatía, ya que, cuando se activan, nos ponemos en el lugar del otro. Los seres humanos aprendemos más por observación e imitación de las conductas de otros, que por lo que se nos enseña con palabras. Esto se evidencia en las niñas y niños pequeños que reproducen los actos de sus padres en lugar de seguir sus recomendaciones.

Si bien cada individuo debe asumir su responsabilidad frente al resultado de sus acciones de manera individual y como Bodhisattva cada uno debe asumir la realización de acciones bondadosas como expresión de su voto de traer alivio al sufrimiento, es claro que una sangha es un entorno perfecto para ponerlo en práctica. Debemos ser cuidadosos en la manera como tratamos a los otros. Por otra parte, la sangha misma puede realizar acciones bondadosas como expresión de su compromiso de aportar herramientas para la construcción de una sociedad solidaria, tolerante, respetuosa y en paz. Desde la expresión de la comprensión de la interdependencia es posible producir eco en la sociedad, mediante actos que beneficien a otros de manera puntual.

ACCIONES CONCRETAS

Es evidente que una Comunidad budista pequeña como la nuestra no puede tener aún mucho impacto en la sociedad. Pero si empezamos con acciones bondadosas pequeñas que produzcan algo de alivio, estaremos cumpliendo nuestro voto. Nuestra pregunta ha sido: ¿Cómo podemos ayudar a los más desprotegidos?

Durante la pandemia viendo el lamentable abandono en que el gobierno tenía a las diversas comunidades indígenas de la Amazonia colombiana, quisimos ayudarlos. Aprovechando las conexiones que una practicante de la sangha tenía con Fany Kuiru, representante de la OPIAC (Organización de los Pueblos Indígenas Amazónicos de Colombia), hicimos una campaña para llevarles tapabocas reutilizables y recogimos algunos donativos para mercados con la esperanza de aliviar en algo los altos riesgos de salud en los que se encontraban.

Pero el maestro Dōgen nos dice que las acciones bondadosas deben extenderse a los demás seres vivos, y no solo a los seres humanos: "Debemos tener compasión de una tortuga acorralada y cuidar a un gorrión enfermo." Esto nos recuerda cómo estamos interconectados con todo. Todo existe en interdependencia y lo que uno hace, afecta no solo a uno mismo y a las personas inmediatamente relacionadas, sino a los demás seres, a la naturaleza y al planeta entero. Debemos comprender que no es posible tener un país en paz, si seguimos destruyendo la naturaleza y acabando con especies de animales y plantas. La vida es un sistema increíble, pero también es un sistema extremadamente frágil.

En nuestra Comunidad hemos hecho el voto de responsabilizarnos por el impacto que nuestras acciones tienen en el mundo. Es así, como hemos incluido en nuestros centros de práctica la Reserva Natural Kasaguadua ubicada en la zona Cafetera, cerca de la población de Salento, Quindío y una montaña cerca de la ciudad de Ibagué en el Departamento de Tolima. En estas dos reservas nos hemos comprometido a cuidar el bosque nativo y el agua, para proteger el entorno natural y las especies que ahí habitan en armonía. Kasaguadua es una reserva natural, con cinco nacimientos de agua y ha sido reconocida como parque natural en Colombia.

Tiene la capacidad de albergar huéspedes en programas de turismo eco-sostenible. Los huéspedes practican zazen en conexión por Zoom, con los otros miembros de la Comunidad. Durante el día se hacen recorridos donde los turistas pueden aprender cómo relacionarse con el bosque produciendo el mínimo impacto posible. Allí tenemos un sistema de manejo de aguas residuales que regresa el agua, que se utiliza en los sanitarios y la cocina, al 100% de pureza al rio Quindío que surte de agua a una extensa población.

En Ibagué, tenemos la Montaña Manantial del Dharma y estamos en la etapa inicial de la construcción de nuestro monasterio rural. Allí tendremos una comunidad permanente para desarrollar una práctica continua y tener un espacio adecuado para la realización de sesshines. El monasterio contará con el mismo sistema de manejo de aguas residuales y como parte de nuestro compromiso con la red de interdependencia vital, esperamos, en un futuro no lejano, registrarlo como reserva natural ante el gobierno colombiano, para proteger la montaña y las especies que en ella habitan.

Por otra parte, la Comunidad está desarrollando "la Sangha Conciencia ecológica" a través del programa Colibrí. Desarrollamos talleres para la concientización del efecto que producimos con nuestros propios hábitos de consumo. En la actualidad estamos trabajando en el diseño de un manual para el manejo responsable de los residuos, con el fin de aliviar la cantidad de basura que llega a los vertederos y el consecuente terrible impacto negativo en la naturaleza. El objetivo de este manual es suministrar información clara sobre el manejo de los residuos. ¿Qué se puede reciclar?, ¿qué se puede reutilizar?, ¿qué se puede aprovechar? El proyecto busca además enseñar la manera correcta de dividir, limpiar y procesar estos residuos para que se pueda hacer una división apropiada para su ideal aprovechamiento. Esperamos en un comienzo publicar el manual de manera digital y distribuirlo ampliamente como un regalo de la Comunidad a la Sociedad.

UNA PRÁCTICA PARA LA VIDA

Es claro que nuestra práctica del zen está fundamentada en la experiencia misma de sentarnos apaciblemente y en silencio, sin buscar ningún objetivo. No obstante, una de las grandes preguntas que como practicantes nos hacemos es, cómo este despertar a la interdependencia y a la impermanencia en zazen se puede manifestar en nuestra vida cotidiana, en la manera como nos relacionamos con los demás seres, con la naturaleza y con la vida en general. Así, el maestro Dōgen nos dice al final de su enseñanza sobre la acción benéfica que, "Debido a que las acciones benéficas nunca prescinden, si logramos una mente así, podremos realizar la acción benéfica incluso para la hierba, los árboles, el viento y el agua. Solo debemos esforzarnos por ayudar a los seres ignorantes." Y, los seres ignorantes somos todos los que habitamos este mundo y que, con nuestras acciones motivadas por los venenos de la mente, deseosos de encontrar auto-gratificación, actuamos sin considerar las consecuencias de nuestros actos, produciendo sufrimiento. Nuestra práctica debe extenderse más allá del zafu, más allá de las paredes de nuestros centros de práctica, y evidenciar nuestro compromiso de transformar nuestra relación con la vida, desde nuestro voto de Bodhisattvas de ayudar a aliviar tanto sufrimiento que hay en el mundo.

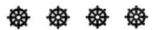

Densho Quintero es maestro misionero de la escuela Soto Zen de Japón desde 2013. Recibió la ordenación de monje en 2001 del abad Shinyu Miyaura Roshi en Antaiji. Tras la muerte de Miyaura

Roshi en 2002, se hizo discípulo de Shohaku Okumura Roshi, de quien recibió la transmisión del Dharma en 2009. En agosto de 2009, completó las ceremonias de Zuise en los templos principales de Sotoshu, Eiheiji y Sojiji. Es el actual abad del templo Zen Mente Magnánima, Daishinji, de la Comunidad Soto Zen de Colombia. Participó en los Angos oficiales de tres meses de la Sotoshu en el templo La Gendroniére en Francia en 2008 y en Yokoji, California, EE. UU. en 2009–2010. En 2011 realizó entrenamiento formal en el Senmon Sodo Myokoji en Fukuoka. También practicó en SFZC, San Francisco, USA y en Shogoji, Kumamoto, Japón, entre otros templos de Europa y USA. Actualmente es miembro activo de la SZBA (Asociación Budista Soto Zen) de Norteamérica.

Es traductor al castellano de *Abrir la mano del pensamiento* de Uchiyama Roshi, (Kairós, 2009), *Corazón del zen, practica sin nada que obtener* de varios autores (CSZC, 2012) y, *Vivir guiados por el voto* de Okumura Roshi (Ed. Nous, 2022). Es autor de los libros: *Conciencia Zen, reflexiones para la vida cotidiana* (Alhue,2006); *El Despertar Zen, el camino de un monje colombiano* (Intermedio Editores, 2012); *Zen, un camino de transformación* (Ed. Kairós, 2016); y *Dudar de la propia comprensión* (Destiempo libros, 2018); También es coautor de Votos ilimitado, práctica sin fin (Dōgen Institute, 2018) y *Budismo y Cristianismo en diálogo* (San Pablo-UPJ, 2018).

Alleviating Suffering through Kind Actions

Densho Quintero

> One should resort to spiritual friends, ener-
> getic and pure in life, who are cordial and
> refined in their conduct. Thus, full of joy,
> he will put an end to suffering.
> – *Dhammapada 376*

A senseless war

In Colombia we have been in a continuous war for more than 60 years due to various circumstances, guerrilla warfare, drug trafficking, paramilitaries, state terrorism, etc. Although the origin of the conflict lies in the political violence that broke out after the assassination in 1948 of Jorge Eliécer Gaitán, a popular leader who fought for social equality, undoubtedly all the reasons that perpetuated the various wars and the atrocities that sprang from there originated in the poisons of the mind: hatred, greed, confusion, arrogance, pride, vanity, etc.

Over all these years, meetings were held between the government and the dissident groups to try to reach agreements and restore the country to peace. Many of these dialogues reached partial agreements, but the confrontations continued. Only in 2016 did the government manage to sign an agreement with FARC, the oldest guerrilla group in the country. This marked a decisive step towards abolishing war, and for the first time a final peace appeared imminent. However, almost half the country was against it, and there were many demonstrations to prevent the agreement from being signed. Even the government that replaced the one that signed the peace deal sabotaged the agreement from the beginning, preventing it from being carried out, and among the population hatred and the desire for revenge and the prolonging of an absurd war continued to fester.

After decades of raw violence, it was shown that nothing was achieved through fighting. Instead, hundreds of thousands of precious lives had been lost and the country was left plunged in desolation. On the other hand, the countless resources that were wasted supporting this useless war could have been invested in education, health and employment, which could have reduced the social gap caused by poverty, and built a more just society.

With the signing of the peace agreement with FARC, a commission was created to clarify the truth with the objective of trying to understand the atrocities that were committed over all these years. The purpose of the truth commission was to clarify how we had been able to live with this violence as something normal and why as a country we had not done anything to stop it.

Based on the investigations, for the first time in many years, we Colombians began to open our eyes to a painful reality, and the country was able to glimpse the barbarism that for so many years had been justified as a resource toward ending the guerrilla warfare. But the violence was not limited to political ideologies or to fighting among the guerrillas, the paramilitaries and the army. Adherence to radical ideologies had led to violence and intolerance by some groups towards others. The ideas triggered emotions like fear, hate, and anger, and cruelty toward one another became normalized. This spread through various levels of society, and the abuses that were committed were justified on the grounds of racism, aporophobia (rejection of the poor), classism, homophobia, and in general, on the grounds of the rejection of everything that was different.

The priest Francisco De Roux S.J., who directed the Truth Commission, in his speech at the time of the delivery of its final report, said that much of the horror that had been experienced was due to the dehumanization of the conflict. The pain had ceased to have a human face, and that was how the unimaginable forms of horror that were revealed with the statements of the victims and those of some of the perpetrators were justified. Currently, the country is considering the urgency of healing the wounds of so many years of massacres, and many people are wondering how we are going to overcome it. In addition, the imminent need arose to recover the memory of those years of violence and disseminate the facts among the public, including those of young age in school classrooms. It is vitally important not to forget, and at the same time to find mechanisms for alleviating so much pain and resentment.

A TOOL TO HEAL SUFFERING

We can begin to transform our society and help heal so much suffering that the war has left, through kind actions—healthy actions that produce beneficial results. Starting with people who are close to us, we can do simple things, something kind for them.

Then we can extend the act of kindness to strangers. And so, little by little, emitting the radiant light of a kind heart, we can illuminate part of the way for others, so that they find their intimate connection with each living being and can manifest it in concrete actions.

In primitive Buddhism, (Sangaha sutta, *Sutra of the Bonds of Solidarity,* AN 4.32), we find a teaching of the Buddha to create healthy relationships and live in harmony: "Monks, here are four ties that sustain favorable relationships. And what are those four? Giving, kind speech, beneficial action and equal treatment. These are, monks, the four ties that sustain favorable relationships." From the perspective of Theravada Buddhist teachings, the Buddha is inviting us to consider other people in the context of *dukkha,* the Noble Truth of Suffering, and to act in such a way that our actions produce healthy relationships and guide people into the Noble Path that leads to liberation from suffering.

Master Dōgen, however, takes this teaching to the level of our practice itself as bodhisattvas. Beyond creating harmonious bonds and attracting people to the Way, he invites us to carry out these actions as an expression of our vow to free beings. In his *Shishobo* chapter of the *Shobogenzo,* "The Bodhisattva's Four Embracing Dharmas," he invites us to view these actions as expedient means, as concrete actions in life to treat others with respect and compassion, as an expression of our very vows to liberate beings from suffering. Okumura Roshi says that "Dōgen teaches that these four practices allow bodhisattvas to free themselves from the three poisonous states of mind: greed, anger/hatred, and confusion. These practices benefit both the person who practices them and living beings at the same time." When we direct our attention towards others, instead of continuing to satisfy our own desires for gratification, we free ourselves from our egotistical tendencies and free others through conscious actions, taking responsibility for the consequences of our own actions.

Since we started a practice center in 1989, as bodhisattvas we have assumed the commitment to provide tools for alleviating suffering in our society. In 2016, the same year that the Peace Agreement was signed, we held the Third Latin American Zen Encounter in Bogotá. The origin of these meetings dates back to the meeting of teachers held during the celebration in Lima, Peru, of the 110th anniversary of the arrival of Soto Zen in South America. On that occasion it was agreed to bring together teachers, practitioners and the general public interested in promoting the Zen tradition in Latin America, through different disciplines so as to provide alternatives for change, alleviate suffering and help build a peaceful society. Convinced of the benefits of the teachings of our tradition founded by Dōgen Zenji, we wanted to offer our practice in this third version of the Encounter as an alternative for transforming the way we connect with other beings, with nature and with life in general.

As support for our commitment to providing concrete tools to alleviate suffering and bring peace to our country, I would like to reflect on the third embracing dharma of Master Dōgen's *Shishobo,* beneficial action.

It is clear that the more than 60 years of violence experienced in Colombia have fueled a contempt for life, a contempt that turned others into faceless enemies. However, now that we have understood the futility of war and the pitiful waste of countless precious lives, the time has come to review our conduct. How do we treat others? What do we produce in others through our actions of body, speech and thought? Are we aware of how our actions affect others? Master Dōgen says in his *Shishobo* text:

"Beneficial action means creating skillful means to help living beings, whether noble or humble. For example, we care about the near and distant future of others, and we use skillful means to benefit them."

Dōgen Zenji says that we should benefit friends and enemies alike, and benefit ourselves and others alike. It is incredible how a kind action can alleviate the suffering of a person and transform those who perform it. Depending on how we treat others, we will change how we relate to life, and we can try to help alleviate another person's suffering and thus benefit ourselves. Science has shown how a kind action can produce a state of well-being in the person who receives it, as evidenced by the level of neurotransmitters that stimulate areas of the brain that produce this gratification. However, not only the person who receives the action, but also the person who performs a kind act experiences the same well-being as the person who receives it. However, the most incredible thing is that a person who observes a kind act experiences the same condition as the other two. Kindness is indeed contagious.

It has even come to be proven how compassion is not learned through explanations, but through imitation. This can be deduced from the study of mirror neurons, a type of neuron that is activated when an animal executes an action and when this action is observed by another individual. We learn to be kind by reproducing the loving actions performed by others. Thus, we can also positively influence people who observe us acting kindly. Mirror neurons serve to awaken empathy, since when they are activated, we put ourselves in the place of the other. Human beings learn more by observing and imitating the behavior of others than by what is taught to us with words. This is evident in young girls and boys who copy the acts of their parents, rather than following their recommendations.

Given that each individual must assume responsibility for the result of their actions individually, and as a bodhisattva each one must take up the performance of kind actions as an expression of their vow to bring relief to suffering, it is clear that a sangha is a perfect environment for putting this into practice. We have to be careful about the way we treat others. On the other hand, the sangha itself can perform kind actions as an expression of its commitment to providing tools for the building of a supportive, tolerant, respectful and peaceful society. From the expression of the understanding of interdependence, it is possible to produce a repercussion in society, through acts that benefit others in a timely manner.

CONCRETE ACTIONS

It is evident that a small Buddhist community like ours cannot yet have much impact on our society. But if we start with small kind actions that bring some relief, we will be fulfilling our vow. Our question has been: How can we help the most vulnerable?

During the pandemic, seeing the unfortunate abandonment in which the government left the various indigenous communities of the Colombian Amazon, we wanted to help them. Taking advantage of the connections that one sangha practitioner had with Fany Kuiru, a representative of OPIAC (Organization of Amazonian Indigenous Peoples of Colombia), we campaigned to bring them reusable masks and collected some donations for markets in the hope of alleviating the high health risks they were in.

Master Dōgen, however, tells us that kind actions must extend to other living beings, and not just to human beings: "We must have compassion for a cornered turtle and take care of a sick sparrow." This reminds us of how interconnected we are with everything.

Everything exists in interdependence, and what one does affects not only oneself and the people immediately related to it, but also other beings, nature and the entire planet. We must understand that it is not possible to have a country at peace if we continue destroying nature and destroying animal and plant species. Life is an incredible system, but it is also an extremely fragile system.

In our community we have taken a vow to take responsibility for the impact our actions have on the world. This is why we have included in our practice centers the Kasaguadua Natural Reserve located in the Coffee Zone, near the town of Salento, Quindío and a mountain near the city of Ibagué in the Department of Tolima. In these two reserves we have committed to taking care of the native forest and the water, so as to protect the natural environment and the species that live there in harmony. Kasaguadua is a nature reserve with five water sources and has been recognized as a natural park in Colombia. It has the capacity to host guests in eco-sustainable tourism programs. Guests practice zazen in connection, by Zoom, with the other members of the community. During the day there are tours in which tourists can learn how to relate to the forest while producing the least possible impact. There we have a wastewater management system that returns the water used in the toilets and the kitchen, at 100% purity, to the soil that forms a basin providing 3% of the water of the Quindío River, a river that supplies water to a large population.

In Ibagué, we have the Manantial del Dharma Mountain and we are in the initial stage of construction of our rural monastery. There we will have a permanent community to develop a continuous practice and have adequate space for holding sesshins. The monastery will have the same wastewater management system as Kasaguadua; and as part of our commitment to the vital interdependence network, we hope in the not-too-distant future to register it as a nature reserve with the Colombian government, so as to protect the mountain and the species living there.

On the other hand, the community is developing "the Ecological Awareness Sangha" through the Hummingbird program. We develop workshops for raising awareness of the effect that we produce with our own consumption habits. We are currently working on the design of a manual for the responsible management of waste, in order to alleviate the amount of garbage that reaches landfills and the consequent terrible negative impact on nature. The objective of this manual is to provide clear information on waste management. What can be recycled? What can be reused? What can be made use of? The project also seeks to teach the correct way to separate, clean and process this waste so that an appropriate triage can be made for its ideal use. We hope to publish the manual initially in digital format and distribute it widely as a gift from the community to society.

A PRACTICE FOR LIFE

It is clear that our Zen practice is based on the very experience of sitting peacefully and quietly, without seeking any goal. However, one of the big questions that we as practitioners ask ourselves is how this awakening to interdependence and impermanence in zazen can be manifested in our daily life, in the way we connect with other beings, with nature and with life in general. Thus, Master Dōgen tells us at the end of his teaching on beneficial action that "Because beneficial actions never regress, if we attain such a mind we can perform beneficial action even for grass, trees, wind, and water. We should solely strive to help ignorant beings." Ignorant beings are all of us who inhabit this world and who act without considering the consequences of our actions, motivated by the poisons of the mind, eager to find self-gratification, producing suffering. Our practice must extend beyond the zafu, beyond the walls of our practice centers, and demonstrate our commitment to transforming our relationship with life, a commitment that flows out of our bodhisattva vow to help alleviate so much suffering in the world.

Densho Quintero is a missionary Zen teacher of the Japanese Soto school since 2013. He received monk ordination in 2001 from abbot Shinyu Miyaura Roshi in Antaiji. After Miyaura Roshi's death in 2002, he became a disciple of Shohaku Okumura Roshi, from whom he received dharma transmission in 2009. In August 2009, he completed *zuise* ceremonies in Sotoshu's head temples, Eiheiji and Sojiji. He is the current abbot of the Magnanimous Mind Zen temple, Daishinji, of the Soto Zen Community of Colombia. He trained in the official three-month Shumucho Angos in La Gendroniére temple in France in 2008 and in Yokoji, California, USA in 2009–2010. In 2011 he did formal training in Myokoji Senmon Sodo in Fukuoka. He also trained in San Francisco Zen Center and in Shogoji, Kumamoto, Japan, as well as at other temples in Europe and the USA. He is an active member of the Soto Zen Buddhist Association of North America. He is the translator into Spanish of *Opening the Hand of Thought* by Uchiyama Roshi, (Kairós, 2009), *Heart of Zen: Practice Without Gaining Mind* by various authors (CSZC, 2012) and *Living by Vow* by Okumura Roshi (Ed. Nous, 2022). He is the author of several books: *Conciencia Zen, reflexiones para la vida cotidiana* (Alhue,2006); *El Despertar Zen, el camino de un monje colombiano* (Intermedio

Editores, 2012); *Zen, un camino de transformación* (Ed. Kairós, 2016); and *Dudar de la propia comprensión* (Destiempo libros, 2018). He was also a contributor to *Boundless Vows, Endless Practice* (Dōgen Institute, 2018) and co-author of *Budismo y Cristianismo en diálogo* (San Pablo-UPJ, 2018).

Beneficial Action in Real Time

ONRYU KENNEDY

INTRODUCTION

I ACKNOWLEDGE I AM ON HOMELANDS of the Dakota and Anishinaabe Nations. I continue to learn the truth of genocide and racism and how this karma is alive today. I am not separate from this past. I am committed to going through it in the present, and pivoting this karma to my capacity.

I offer homage to the Buddha and other ancestors from India. I offer homage to Japanese, Chinese, Korean Buddhist ancestors. Through their generosity and compassion, I am able to study and practice Buddhism today.

I am honored to have an opportunity to share practical ways I embody the teaching of beneficial action. My learning has taken place at Tassajara Zen Monastery in California, Toshoji Zen Monastery in Japan, South Dakota, Alabama, and Minnesota where I currently live. South Dakota and Minnesota are some of the places of Indigenous genocide, and Alabama, the site of both genocide and slavery of Africans. I have witnessed the horror and cruelty on these lands, and I wish to be a part of healing action. My bodhisattva vow includes untangling the twisted karma of settler colonialism in relation to Indigenous Nations and Turtle Island, a name used by them to refer to North America.

I am grateful to Shohaku Okumura Roshi for the invitation to bring my humble voice into this circle of practitioners. I am honored to share what I have learned in the practice of engaged Buddhism in relation to beneficial action.

LEARNING TO PRACTICE BENEFICIAL ACTION

My practice includes both zazen and the engaged practice of beneficial action. I consider zazen—the formal sitting practice—as an integral action that grounds the practice of beneficial action. Dōgen Zenji's Four Embracing Actions of giving, loving speech, beneficial action, and identity action are not separate from engaged Buddhist practices. Engaged Buddhism was a phrase coined by Thich Nhat Hanh. Engaging the Buddhist practices of zazen, compassion and wisdom, support our capacity for generosity, kind speech and discerning what is action that is mutually beneficial for everyone. These practices are engaged in social, environmental, political and racial injustices. These four actions are interpenetrating each other in each arising and disappearing condition. Each action supports and strengthens the other actions. Each is an offering for how the Buddhist practice is endlessly engaged in the present moment. It is my responsibility to enliven my bodhisattva vow in engaging this practice in the flow of life.

Much of my learning has been through the innumerable mistakes I have made along the way. These mistakes are places of practice and insight for me. Learning to acknowledge mistakes, apologizing, and repairing is the practice of softening into humility. This practice connects me more deeply to all beings. It has not been a linear path, step by step, backward, forward and in a spiral. What is an appropriate response to conditions that are fluid? Conditions include racial injustices, climate crisis, pervasive poverty, and innumerable suffering for all beings. I ask: what is my dharma position in changing conditions as a white, female Zen priest? A step forward for me is to acknowledge the unacknowledged genocide of Indigenous peoples. With a sense of gravity, I acknowledge that I too have both benefited and been harmed by the suffering of genocide.

I have been blessed with many Indigenous teachers who have taken time to share their teaching. Because of their generosity and patience with me I came to understand many things that I was ignorant about. In particular, I want to describe the insight I gained about the intersectionality of Indigenous leadership and engaged Buddhism, and how to practice untangling the collective and individual karma related to genocide and white colonialism. The historical past of genocide and slavery manifests in this present moment as our karma. This moment is connected to both the past and future. And because of this connection and awareness, we have the ability to pivot in this moment with freshness. With awareness of how the past is present and alive, there is possibility of untangling the karma that leads to transformation and healing.

The lessons are not easy to integrate. Learning to deconstruct self creates capacity to bear witness to what is actually happening in this moment. Many times, my egocentricity has to be laid bare. I face my vulnerability. It is the vulnerability that helps me to know clearly that I am not separate. I am connected to all beings through this suffering. Out of this seeing arises compassion and loving kindness towards others, and myself. It supports softening the heart and flexibility of mind.

Development of my spiritual capacity has taken place through my formal spiritual practice and through my professional work where I encountered pervasive suffering in extremely difficult conditions. Integration of spiritual practice is not separate from activities in our daily lives. This integration is essential to engaging ourselves fully in this moment. Staying aware of arising conditions and the beings who appear in front of us is an endless practice.

I attend to this human, lived experience. I practice composting my egocentricity in order to show up in a skillful way. I practice remaining upright in dynamic and complicated conditions. These practices enable me to develop a spiritual capacity for more challenging and stressful conditions. Many peoples and beings have been and are experiencing these high intensity conditions. Conditions of extreme heat, fires, flood, hurricanes and starvation have affected innumerable beings already. Each of us have experienced a loss of someone or something we dearly loved. This is a shared human experience and is interpenetrating our daily lives.

THE THREE TENETS

Bernie Glassman Roshi's Three Tenets provide a framework for cultivating beneficial action. The tenets have been a significant way of training my spiritual capacity by bridging my zazen practice and engaged Buddhism. The Three Tenets support and strengthen my practice to stay present in difficult and challenging conditions. Going inside to settle the mind the mind and stay present, we respond from compassion and wisdom to what is unfolding in the moment. These tenets are a path through the fire of arising conditions. Our spiritual stability is cultivated through this practice. The tenets are alive and live in the power of this moment. They are seamlessly intersecting and simultaneously co-existing. They are circling around each other, and are not sequential or linear. Like Indra's Net, they are reflecting each other, arising and dissolving endlessly.

First Tenet: Not Knowing

This is about relaxing the mind by stilling it and deeply listening. I practice letting go of how I construct the self in relationship to families, communities, and the Universe. I recognize my view for what it is, and I release it. In this way I enter not knowing. Not knowing can be unsettling. Okumura Roshi calls entering not knowing "opening the hand of thought."

I am aware of the vast network of interconnection with all life. I face my reactivity while staying present to myself and all beings. This creates space for the possibility of pivoting away from habit patterns to a fresh way of responding. There are innumerable conditions that shock and destabilize us. We don't turn away from these conditions. These are the very conditions and places of practice. Everything is changing, nothing is static. The practice of zazen provides spiritual stability in the midst of this groundlessness.

Second Tenet: Bearing Witness

This is the call to bring as much presence to the arising conditions as I can summon. I bring full attention to the joys and suffering of my life and the world. I turn towards the arising conditions, and I notice my response to what I am facing. The first tenet of not knowing supports the capacity to stay in the moment. I let go of my egocentricity and I bear witness to the suffering. Zazen offers the possibility of thinning my egocentricity. This thinning of self deepens my capacity for compassion. Compassion naturally arises in response.

Third Tenet: Compassionate Action

Our connection to compassion is always present. It is our egocentricity that hinders our capacity to serve all beings and ourselves in a way that is helpful. Compassionate action emerges from deep listening and presence of bearing witness. It enables us to respond to the call with skillful action. Because we are connected, our hearts are open.

BEARING WITNESS IN HIROSHIMA

While I was practicing at Toshoji Zen Monastery, Seido Roshi, the abbot, brought all of us, twenty monks and nuns to bear witness to Hiroshima, the site of the atomic bombing in World War II. We were from Europe, USA, South America, and Japan. We walked silently together to the Hiroshima Memorial site. On our way, when we stopped and witnessed the remaining structure that survived the nuclear bomb, it took my breath. I felt weak. I could hardly move. I was part of this destruction and cruelty. I was a citizen of the country that had perpetrated this violence on this place and the people who lived here. I was not separate. I was a perpetrator standing in the midst of this horror with Japanese brothers and sisters with whom I had been practicing together for three months. They are dharma siblings I have come to love. This truth went into my bones and penetrated my marrow.

When we arrived at the memorial site in Hiroshima, Seido Roshi placed the incense burner on the site. He then offered incense and we began to chant the *Maka Hannya Haramita Shingyo.* As I was chanting, I felt an extreme sadness. I felt as if I was breaking apart, chanting at times in only a whisper. As I continued to chant, a strength filled me in those broken spaces from the ground up. This strength was in connection to the ground and the connection to the community of monks and nuns and the place we were standing. I felt the great suffering of the twisted collective karma as a citizen of the country who dropped an atomic bomb on children, mothers, fathers, elders, plants, animals, and all the innumerable beings who lived on this land.

My broken heart turned into great love for Seido Roshi and my Japanese brothers and sisters. Their great compassion towards me and others who had perpetrated this horror still resonates within me.

UNTANGLING MY WHITENESS

In Japan, my dharma position is a white, female, Zen priest who is a citizen of the USA. While in Japan it was important for me to be a good guest and take care of what was before me. In the U.S., my dharma position is similar, though my relationship to Indigenous Nations is different. Indigenous Nations are sovereign Nations. When I meet Indigenous peoples I am meeting people who are citizens of sovereign Nations. My dharma position is that of a guest on their land. This is important for me to remember.

Before we went to Hiroshima, there was a monk who taught the history of Japan. He was knowledgeable about the history of World War II, and the United States' role in dropping the bomb and the horror that ensued. He said that the U.S. government knew about radiation sickness but did not share this information with the Japanese government. When Japanese people were sick with radiation poisoning, people thought it was contagious and needed isolation. Thousands and thousands of Japanese died from radiation sickness.

This new knowledge deepened my ability to bear witness. Similarly, living in the U.S., I have been learning about the relationship between Indigenous Nations, the colonizing of their land, and the genocide, including in Minnesota where I live. I was never taught the historical truths until I began my own study and listening to Indigenous peoples. My learning informs my practice in an important way.

My practice emerges from daily living, from interacting with all things and all beings. It was sparked while working with young Indigenous, Black and People of Color and their families. In the beginning of my professional training, I worked in an urban community center in a multi-cultural neighborhood. I would visit families in this community with the intention of building relationships and supporting them. There, I learned to ask the question, "How can I help?" and the importance of discerning what my dharma position was within specific contexts. This particular learning emerged from a conversation with an Indigenous grandmother who said to me, "You are a nice person, and I cannot trust you, because you are white." The lesson was coming to understand why this Indigenous grandmother does not trust a white person who is nice on the surface. Learning about my whiteness as a cause of their mistrust has been a lifelong koan for me. If I don't understand the place in which I stand, if I don't bear witness to the experiences of Indigenous people who have lived and are living on this land, that is ignorance. Ignorance makes us untrustworthy. Ignorance creates suffering for me and all beings.

I practice untangling the karma of my whiteness, including the collective and individual karma in relationships and to the land.

This untangling can only happen within my Buddhist practice. With a spiritual grounding, I have a chance of walking with presence. This Indigenous grandmother was inviting me to become a fuller human being. It ignited within me a desire to learn what was not trustworthy about my whiteness, what was not trustworthy about me.

This journey of becoming a fuller human being is long, messy, and full of mistakes. Beneficial action is an endless practice in depth and breadth. As a young white person working in a diverse community, I was ignorant of my white settler colonialism. I was ignorant that the place I was standing on was stolen land and I was benefiting from this ignorance. Usually, Indigenous peoples don't offer their view unless it may be used in a good way, to benefit others and community. The Indigenous grandmother saw in me a potential to transform the ignorance of my white privilege so that my actions can benefit all beings.

The grandmother's teaching continues to live within me. It eventually took me to Wounded Knee Memorial in South Dakota to bear witness to the massacre site of Lakota men, women, and children. The experience gave rise to a vision to coordinate a Bearing Witness retreat at Fort Snelling in Minnesota. Fort Snelling was a site of a concentration camp of thousands of Dakota women, children, and elders in the winter of 1862. Continuing to learn the history of the land I live on deepened my experience and the opened the possibility of pivoting the karma. I do not visit these sites of massacre and genocide as a tourist, nor do I expect to make personal gains other than learning about the twisted karma of which I am a part.

NOTHING TO GET, NOTHING TO GAIN

Beneficial action excludes commodifying and extracting, or what Okumura Roshi called "being a merchant." A merchant keeps a record of what was given, what was received and what was the outcome. When we go to places to bear witness, we are not acting as a merchant. There is nothing to get and nothing to gain. It is happening within the present moment and then is gone. There's nothing to hold on to. We are in alignment with our vow. The nourishment of the raw experience supports the life force of all beings and cannot be quantified. This is the manifestation of the bodhisattva vow. The practice of beneficial action has also included participating in Bearing Witness retreats at Auschwitz/Birkenau and a street retreat in San Francisco. Each of these experiences have supported my development as a human being and as a Zen priest.

Auschwitz/ Birkenau was profound in opening this mind and this body complex experiencing both the victim and perpetrator that lives within me. Sitting on the selection platform where life and death for the day was decided by the Nazis. I could smell burning flesh, and I could feel the ashes in the back of my throat. I can still remember these visceral sensations. I am Birkenau and Birkenau is me. Swallowing the ashes was the dragon swallowing the Universe. Acknowledging the victim and perpetrator within oneself opens up the possibility of transformation to becoming a fuller human being in a world where suffering and joy co-exist. It supports finding the middle way between the two extremes of victim and perpetrator. It cultivates a deeper compassion and kindness for all beings. The middle way and the extremes are on a continuum and fluid. Beneficial action is like this too. It is not a bypass, it is a way through and includes everything, and includes acknowledging, "I don't know."

I was a participant in a street retreat in San Francisco. Beneficial action exposes and deconstructs the discriminating mind. Though I attempted to enter the retreat with a don't-know mind, the mind was full of fear, and anxiety. Would I have the strength and courage to actually face my fears and anxieties to show up in a mature way. I needed to acknowledge them; only then, could the fear and anxiety be released. This is like zazen: I don't realize how full my mind is until I sit down in silence and the thoughts are everywhere. This seeing of the mind helps me to settle it. This settling is what Okumura Roshi calls, "opening the hand of thought," letting go of clinging as the mind begins to settle itself on itself.

This is the same in beneficial action. I am committed to not knowing and not concerned with looking good. I have done the homework to my capacity, and I trust that I am in alignment with my vow. With a quiet mind, I can see clearly, and compassion naturally arises.

During the street retreat, full of energy and many feelings, I had the experience of plunge. Plunge is Bernie Roshi's word for going into places one has never experienced before. Like a diver, diving into the ocean from a cliff, these places have high intensity conditions.

From the street retreat, I learned that it takes tremendous energy to live on the streets. Walking is often the only way to get from place to place like getting meals, finding shelter, and resting spots. Certain objects become sources of comfort. I never thought about how valuable cardboard could be. It provides a barrier between the body and the concrete at night. People who are without a home and live under buildings and walk everywhere are often more generous than the ones in suits and heels. I received food, information and a blanket from people who were doing what they could to live in a good way without a secure home. This was my greatest lesson in beneficial action. Outside appearances mean nothing.

Towards the end of the street retreat, I was tired and just walking. A man came up from behind me and said, "Don't worry you will find a place to live. I just did and you will too." My egocentricity was blown into pieces by his kindness.

This deconstructing of the mind is not a one-time event. It is a continuous process. The ego's ability to re-construct itself is tenacious. That is why it is good for me to sit in zazen and to go into spaces of not knowing. This gives me a chance of responding to conditions with integrity and dignity. Also, the experience of receiving kind words from a stranger who has suffered and yet can still be generous and caring is a powerful antidote to my habit of centering the self.

DECENTERING SELF

Decentering this self is pivotal work as a white, Zen priest. Whiteness is often centered here in Minnesota, knowingly and unknowingly. In climate actions that are Indigenous led, it is important to know my dharma position. Deeply listening and asking, "How can I help?" is skillful action. I have participated in actions at Standing Rock, against the Dakota Access Pipeline in response to a call from the Lakota and hundreds of other First Nations. I joined the actions against the Line 3 Pipeline in response to the call from Anishinaabe Nation. More recently, I attended a march in Washington, D.C. against fossil fuels in support of the Indigenous leadership.

On the first day of the march in DC, one hundred attendees were detained and fined, including myself. This arrest and the subsequent fine were a condition I chose to accept before I left for DC. On the second day my friend and I were at a coffee shop, trying to figure out a plan for the day. Three people entered the coffee shop and told us that they were on their way to the jail to pay their fines. They offered me a ride to the jail and I accepted it. When we arrived, there was a very long line extending outside the building, but I decided to stay and pay the fine. After several hours, I noticed an Indigenous woman coming towards the long line. I jumped up and invited her to take my place. Initially she declined and after encouragements from others in line, she accepted. I went to the end of the line to start over.

Eventually, my turn came and I got inside. The person in front of me only had a large bill to pay the fine. The attendants would only accept the exact amount of the fine. Several of us began digging in our pockets to offer what we could to her. I gave all I had except the money for my fine. She was able to pay her fine. She was very grateful for the kindness.

After paying the exact amount of my fine, I walked outside only to realize I had no money. I had no way back to the plaza. Not knowing what to do, I sat on the curb at the end of the sidewalk. I heard a voice behind me, asking, "Do you need a ride?" I turned around. It was the Indigenous woman to whom I had offered my spot! I smiled and said, "Yeah." She said, "What goes around comes around." Ordinary mind cannot conceive how life unfolds in beneficial action. The mind lets go and the Universe responds in a way that is beneficial for everyone.

Many people's kindness made my participation in the march possible. I had a place to stay in DC because a Buddhist friend's brother and wife opened their home to me. They are the embodied expression of the Bodhisattva vow. Beneficial action is unfolding all the time, one moment after another.

WATER IS LIFE

I have learned to honor water as a source of life. This pivot has been uplifted through my involvement with Indigenous-led movements. There is a saying in the movement, "mni wiconi," Water Is

Life. Protecting water and saying thank you to water is beneficial action. Water nourishes and refreshes all beings without discrimination. I began taking frequent walks at the river. As I walk along the river, I bear witness to many beings that appear at the river's edge for a drink. Their paw and claw prints are everywhere. I could even sense a beaver's presence in the gnawed trees, the work not yet completed.

Last summer, I experienced deeper gratitude for water. It was an unusually hot summer in Minneapolis, which is actually becoming the norm. Many heat records were broken because of extreme temperature. A friend asked if I would help deliver ice to the Indigenous encampments. These encampments have emerged in response to the lack of affordable housing for Indigenous peoples. Where an Indigenous encampment once stood, there is an artwork that expresses Indigenous genocide, "Never Homeless Before 1492."

I accepted the invitation to help deliver ice. We started out the next day, purchasing several pounds of ice and delivering it to the encampments. I was immediately humbled by people's gratitude. I was the one who was receiving their gift. Their presence and gratitude washed over me. I felt naked from experiencing it. Maybe this is what Uchiyama Roshi, the author of *Opening the Hand of Thought* and Okumura Roshi's teacher means when he wrote, "Life before it is cooked, raw."

Dōgen Zenji speaks about dropping away of the body and mind. When this experience happens, one is in relation to all beings and the boundless world. It is a raw experience, beyond language. The whole world is wholly functioning and one is within this wonderous web of life.

I continued to volunteer at Indigenous encampments in Minneapolis, running errands and helping in other ways. Once I took a sleeping bag to the laundromat to wash it. I put the sleeping bag in the washer and went outside to wait. I was just hanging around when an Indigenous woman approached me.

"How are you doing?" she said. Her smile was bright and big.

"Fine, and how are you doing"? I replied, trying to meet her greeting.

"You don't remember me do you"? she said. I quietly responded, "No," realizing my attempt had failed.

"You and your friend delivered ice to where I was staying," she said.

I immediately remembered her. She was radiating so much light and joy that day. I was embarrassed not to remember her.

"I have something I want to give you," she said, and she pulled out a book. It was the book I had been wanting to read.

"This is for you." she said, handing me the book. I thanked her profusely and asked if I could hug her. No amount of thank you could reach the depth of love I felt for her in that moment. She was the embodiment of Avalokitesvara bodhisattva. She had her suffering — and I had mine, and together we were healing energy for each other. This is the power of beneficial action.

BENEFICIAL ACTION IS NOT ABOUT SAVING PEOPLE

Beneficial action is not about saving people. As a converted Buddhist from Catholicism, this is karma that I have been diligently untangling. The concept of saving is egocentric and patronizing. The relationship of giver and receiver arises because of mutual respect and compassion. Giver and receiver are not fixed and are fluid within the arising conditions. We are all receiving and giving moment by moment. This is the essential nature of beneficial action.

In the beginning of my career as a youth counselor, a respected colleague would often remind me, "Saving is a racist concept and serves no one." The idea of white savior is a delusion. It emerges from white supremacy. I needed to untwist the karma of white supremacy for myself to become a person who is serving in a good way.

Untwisting whiteness comes from reading and studying about white supremacy and the experience of bearing witness to genocide and racism. They take place everywhere, and where I live. The largest mass hanging in the U.S. took place in Mankato, Minnesota. Thirty-eight Indigenous men were hanged on December 26, 1862.

Healing only happens if one is aware of the cruelty that has happened. There is a site in Mankato memorializing the thirty-eight Indigenous men who died the day after Christmas. At the site, there is a bench made of granite, engraved with the words, "Forgive everybody everything." Forgiveness is remembering. Learning about a place and developing a memory of place is important in being in relationship to the land and all beings. We must remember and say their names. Healing begins with learning what has happened while moving in a circular way of not knowing the way forward, one step at a time. It is only through learning the history that can we remember. Ignorance has many forms and no forms. Learning history is an antidote to individual and collective ignorance. It's not the history I was taught in school, but history learned through the teachings of Indigenous, Black and people of color. Listening deeply to their voices and experiences is a powerful antidote for untwisting karma.

Raphael Lemkin coined the word "genocide" in 1942 and inspired a movement in the United Nations to outlaw the crime. Lemkin was a Polish lawyer who responded to the Nazi policies to exterminate the Jewish people. One of the five criteria of genocide is forcibly transferring children of the group to another group. Indigenous children were being forcibly removed from their families and placed in boarding schools at alarming rates. The trauma of the boarding schools has only begun to be investigated and brought to the public attention. The Pope visited Canada this past summer to offer an apology to Indigenous Nations for the Catholic Church's participation in the boarding school system and the genocide it perpetuated. The suffering of the Indigenous peoples in this country meets the United Nations' five criteria for genocide. Yet, the genocide of Indigenous peoples is not acknowledged by the US government. How is this possible?

In the 1990s, while I was working as a social worker in the largest county in Minnesota, my supervisor asked me if I would be a social worker in the ICWA (Indian Child Welfare Act) Unit. This was a new unit that would only work with Indigenous families who met ICWA criteria. ICWA was put in place to support and strengthen Indigenous children and families. This law was enacted because Indigenous children were being removed from their homes and communities at a much higher rate than non-indigenous children. For ICWA to be made into a federal law demonstrates the gravity of dehumanization of Indigenous children and families.

When I agreed to join this unit, I stepped off the 100-foot pole to be part of a collective body unraveling the karma of genocide in relation to Indigenous children and families. By stepping off the high pole, I was trusting in what I had learned from Indigenous teachers and others. This trust supported unraveling the patterns of my habituated white privileges. It opened me to inconceivable possibilities for pivoting karma. I continue to learn and practice.

As a white social worker in the ICWA unit, I was responsible to the Indigenous families from sovereign nations. Listening and following through with how they wanted their families to be helped was critical in demonstrating my commitment to ICWA both in action and in spirit.

My work was not separate from my Buddhist practice. Digesting and metabolizing my white privilege and acknowledging the cruelty and horror that existed in the lives of Indigenous children and families brought me to my knees. I believe my Buddhist practice supported my ability to unravel my white privilege and egocentricity in a way that strengthened my capacity to serve Indigenous children and families.

ANCESTORS

Investigating my historical karma included unraveling my position as a white settler. I investigated where my family was from; what country they left to come to the US; what language they spoke; how they dressed; what kind of spirituality they practiced, and what suffering caused them to leave their homeland. My Irish ancestors on my father's side, and my Scottish ancestors on my mother's side, both sides of my family have suffered great losses. The loss of culture and homeland is trauma and suffering. Their grief was transmitted to me. Insight into this trauma and grief creates the possibility of healing. I cannot heal if I don't understand my family's history. I cannot transform what I do not know.

I have had the privilege to travel to Ireland and the balm of coming home to my Irish ancestors. The coming home was medicine for the suffering. It connected me to all beings who grieve the loss of their homeland. It allowed me to see how the perpetrator and victim were embodied in the understanding of my family's loss. Such insight, seen with compassion, can unravel the karma and is liberating for all beings, including me. This connection helps me to be a good guest on this stolen land.

My friend and I visited the South recently. We followed the civil rights journey from Birmingham to Salem to Montgomery. We believed the experience of genocide and racism in the South is connected to the North. This connection included the Mississippi River, which was used to traffic Indigenous, Black and People of Color for enslavement and dispossession of their land.

Throughout the bearing witness experience, my friend and I asked each other, "Who and where are the Indigenous peoples whose land we are on?" It wasn't until the day before departure from Alabama we found some clue. We stopped at a Starbucks and my friend went to the restroom. She came back from the restroom and said, "I saw a poster for a Pow Wow in Moundsville." I said, "Let's go." My friend googled Moundsville, Alabama. We were on our way to the home of the Mississippian Nation.

When we arrived, we saw many beautiful mounds on the land. There are many theories to explain the significance of these mounds, and to me they do not meet the full meaning they had for the Mississippian Nation. The largest mound was a short distance from the Warrior River. Bearing witness to the mounds and the river, we experienced the timelessness of this place. We could feel the vibrancy of these ancestral homelands of the Mississippian Nation and the Poarch Creek Nation. We learned that the Poarch Creek Nation was hosting the Pow Wow, but not for another week. Even though we couldn't stay to attend, we were very grateful to have had such a powerful experience of being on these ancestral homelands

We remained diligent and we went beyond our first view. If we had not been persistent, we would have missed this sacred experience. This effort is important for one to have the possibility to see what is actually here and now. Ancestors support us to be in the present. In this way, we take care of ourselves and support the next generation. Supporting the next generation is beneficial action.

Developing Fearlessness

Developing fearlessness is a part of beneficial action. This begins with becoming aware of one's fear. We sense the embodied experience of fear and how it constricts our ability to see what is here and now. We can lean into what is triggering the fear and be compassionate towards the fear. Facing fear is a practice of bearing witness to it. This supports capacity to moving into and through fear to the other side, transforming the energy of fear into fearlessness. Fearlessness creates innumerable actions that are beneficial to both the giver and the receiver of the action.

The scent of fear, when Seido Roshi asked me to be *shuso* (head monk) at Toshoji Zen Monastery in Japan, still lingers for me. To say no was death and to say yes was death. This death was a death of how I viewed my constructed self and capacity. As a white, American, woman, Zen priest practicing in a Japanese monastery, I wondered: What could I offer this international sangha? Could I honor Roshi's request through my practice? Could I have compassion for my humanity and the humanity of the sangha I was entering into? I faced my fears, metabolized them, and accepted the invitation to be shuso.

This experience was and continues to be life changing in many ways. Seido Roshi is a Buddha. He uplifts each being and all things with integrity and dignity. He is an ultimate example to me. How do I, as shuso, uplift each monk and nun in relation to the collective body? My egocentricity is continuously challenged through arising conditions. The shadow side of my personality is repeatedly revealed to me. Will I respond to my egocentric needs, or will I respond in a beneficial way for the person in front of me and the sangha? The seduction of power is present too. Can I acknowledge the responsibility that goes with the power of position with kindness, and respond to the monks and nuns in a manner that supports their abilities?

This beneficial action of facing my fears was liberating. When I am liberated, all beings benefit. When all beings are free, I am free. The self connects to something larger than itself, and spaciousness is created. This is liberation from the constriction of the ego. My sangha is no longer limited to a small community. The world has become my sangha.

TAKING CARE OF SELF IS
CARING OF ALL BEINGS

Beneficial action is cultivated in many manifestations of taking care of oneself and all beings. I had a chance to practice this when I had the honor of walking with the Treaty Walkers.

The Treaty Walk is an Indigenous-led, two-week, 240-mile walk to uplift what Indigenous people know, that we are all "treaty people." We, especially the white people, are called to investigate the true meaning of making a treaty. The US government signed treaties with the federally recognized Indigenous tribes, as nation to nation, not as individuals or organizations. Article Six in our Constitution states, "Treaties are the highest law in the land." This is why we are all treaty people. How do we live in a good way as treaty people?

As a white, Zen priest I align myself with my vow and respond to the conditions. Conditions can be dynamic and complicated, full of unexpected turnings. How do I find food to deliver to the Treaty

Walkers? A car breaks down in the midst. Where would I sleep and how would I get there? These were the conditions that arose for me and my friend on the Treaty Walk. With a not-knowing mind, moving step by step. It was beneficial action arising, presenting and dissolving endlessly. In the end, everything worked out, dynamically working in a way the mind couldn't have imagined.

Our Vow in Daily Life

Roshi Joan Halifax of Upaya Zen Center has said, "Buddhism is not apolitical or neutral." The Buddha always engaged his practice with all beings and all things. He actively taught until his death. He demonstrated through actions how to engage this practice with the world, with embodied life.

Transformation does not take place in a vacuum. When we are engaged with the suffering in ourselves and the world, the possibility of transformation can occur. We actively participate in the healing of ourselves, each other, and all beings. This is the wonder of living in connection with the vastness of the world. The practice of zazen does not end on the cushion. Zazen and beneficial action are interpenetrating and affecting each other continuously. This is the strength and the power of spiritual practices. Transforming the suffering in the world is endless, and beyond the thinking mind's restriction. And yet, it does happen.

Each of us has gifts to offer to meet arising conditions. The suffering world needs everyone's gifts and skillful actions. Empowering each other is a beneficial action. It is empowering to hear different voices included in the circle. The circle is strengthened when all are invited.

I have found it is important to honor one's capacity and the capacity of others. Arising conditions challenge us at times to go beyond what we thought was our capacity. I am committed to meet the challenge, as well as to respect the need for rest when it is needed. I am also committed to taking care of my historical karma. This means I go towards, and investigate, habituated activity, composting what is not skillful. I commit myself to showing up again and again to engage with the suffering world with care.

I have been blessed with many teachers from all over this great earth. I continue to educate myself of past actions towards Dakota and Anishinaabe Nations, whose land I live on. I don't turn away from the cruelty of the past. I practice bearing witness to how the past continues to manifest in the present. Buddhist practices are not separate from the genocide of Indigenous peoples, the use and abuse of water, the extinction of species and the climate crisis. We acknowledge this suffering and we are willing to engage in actions. Each of us, individually and collectively, will need to decide how we move into actions. There is an urgency. We need to move without hesitation.

A great learning has been that I am not separate from the natural world: I and all beings are interwoven, and the natural world permeates me. The connection to earth nourishes me as I aspire to nourish the space I walk. When I take steps along the river's edge, I am walking with all beings. All are nourished in the flow of the river, the brilliance of sunlight and the breeze that gently touches all beings. I receive these gifts and smile with gratitude and love to the river and the natural world for this moment. Dōgen Zenji writes, "Beneficial action includes all, friends, and foe. Grasses, trees, water." This is living in vow.

May we respond to the joy and suffering experienced by all beings and all things with beneficial action, including ourselves in this precious circle.

Onryu Kennedy lives in Minneapolis, near the Bdote, on Dakota homelands. She received transmission from Rev. Byakuren Ragir in October 2018 in Katagiri Roshi's lineage and from Rev. Eido Reinhart in January 2021 in Okumura Roshi's lineage. She participated in zuise at Eiheiji on January 11, 2023 and Sojiji on January 14, 2023. She trained at Clouds in Water Zen Center, Hokyoji, Tassajara Zen Monastery and Toshoji International Zen Monastery. In addition, she participated in genzo-e at Sanshin Zen Community. In February 2022, she completed a year long study of Engaged Buddhism at Upaya Zen Center. She participated in Bearing Witness Retreats at Wounded Knee, SD and Auschwitz/Birkenau, and a street retreat in San Francisco. In 2016, she coordinated an interfaith Bearing Witness Retreat led by Indigenous Nations. In 2019, she coordinated the Winyan Awanyankapi: Protecting the Lifegivers Conference. This conference was Indigenous led with white allies offering logistical support.

Kennedy has worked as a social worker for over 30 years with children and families and has an MA in counseling psychology. She is committed to beneficial actions on behalf of all beings. This emerges from the relationship with Indigenous Nations around climate and racial justice issues. Also, she is committed to supporting the next generation of dharma practitioners continuing to deepen our connection with our Japanese dharma relatives.

Practice for its Own Sake

SHŌRYŪ BRADLEY

ONE THING I FIND SO COMPELLING about this part of Shobogenzo
is that it seems Dōgen Zenji openly reveals to us his tender heart,
saying it is tenderness itself that is the center of his teachings and
the essence of the Dharma. I find it especially endearing that he
uses stories about these two gentle, ordinary creatures, a tortoise
and a sparrow, to illustrate the attitude we adopt when practicing
beneficial action. It shows us in a simple and beautiful way what
it means to practice the Dharma for its own sake. Many times I've
pulled over from one of our winding mountain roads in Northwest Arkansas to take a box turtle out of harm's way. I'm not sure
my motivation to help a turtle at these times is always completely
pure; if I analyzed it I might find some underlying desire to feel
I'm a good person doing a good deed, for example, and I think
it's important to make an effort to recognize how we can get off
track in this way. But I believe the initial impulse to simply stop
and help, before thinking too much about it, is just life expressing
itself. In that instant, picking up a box turtle and moving it to
safety seems as natural as if I myself were stepping out of the path

of traffic; there's no time or need to hesitate or doubt my motivations or actions.

The Compassion Koan

Birds, like turtles, also often stir my heart to tenderness in these wooded mountains, and I feel a deep connection with them. For many years my zazen has been filled with the plaintive cries of pileated woodpeckers, the cacophonous caws of crows, or the hurried chirrups of scarlet tanagers, to name just a few. I know summer has officially arrived when I hear the bouncy notes of indigo buntings staking out their territories, and in the fall the excited *kyeer! kyeer!* of the northern flickers remind me to focus on preparing for the coming winter.

But when I first arrived at Gyobutsuji, all too often I heard the sickening thump! of a warbler or robin flying into a window or sliding glass door. Upon hearing that sound I would jump up to see if the bird had fallen to the ground beneath the window, and often my heart would sink to see some beautiful, delicate little body lying there. Every so often, to my relief, the bird would revive after some time and fly away. I was always filled with joy when that happened, but I was later told that these birds often die later because of internal injuries sustained in the collision. These days placing stickers on some of the glass about the temple seems to help, and I even hesitate to wash the windows often, since the collisions seem to happen more frequently after I clean them. Every time my presence here at Gyobutsuji is the cause of the death of some other sentient being, I think of the story I heard my teacher tell about the time he was digging a well while living at Valley Zendo in the 1970s. He said he felt he was working to help establish the Dharma by taking on the arduous task of digging a well on the temple grounds, until he found that a skunk had fallen into the well and drowned one night before the digging was completed. That made him question whether what he was doing was really beneficial action or not, and I have had similar feelings many times since I began living at Gyobutsuji in January of 2012. I try not to interfere with the lives of other beings here, but sometimes it's not so clear what action is the most beneficial when I encounter them. To nurture my vow to offer a place to practice zazen, which I think is beneficial to sentient beings, I all too often have to disrupt the lives of other sentient beings. This is an ongoing koan for me. I want to have a tender heart that offers compassion and respect to all beings, but sometimes the needs of human life and the needs of other sentient beings seem to be at odds.

Left unchecked, rodents can be a major problem on the property, for example, and they can be destructive in many ways. For some reason they find expensive wiring in automobiles to be very tasty, for instance, and their appetites have caused me many headaches and cost hundreds of dollars. I believe my neighbors think I'm a bit crazy for doing it, but I use live traps to catch the critters and take them far enough away that they won't return. (One uniquely marked mouse returned after traversing half a mile of our drive; I trapped it a second time and took it much farther away!)

But after some years of doing this many more times than I would have liked, I began to question how beneficial this practice really was. I caught rodents so often that I felt I didn't have enough time to walk them far enough away, so I began driving them down our county road. But then I realized how much extra fossil fuel I was burning to do this, and of course we know that is not so beneficial to the sentient beings of this earth. Nowadays I try to take the rodents away when I am making a supply run into town, but that sometimes means keeping them confined for days in a container, something I'm sure causes them additional stress. (When I told my neighbor about these "mouse hotels," complete with healthy meals of oats and lettuce, he just laughed!) Even with all of this effort, every once in a while a mouse will still die before I can check a trap. I'm also sure many mouse pups have perished after their mother was caught and taken away.

Nyojo Zenji said, "Buddhas and ancestors do not forget or abandon living beings in their zazen; they offer a heart of compassion even to an insect. Buddhas and ancestors vow to save all living beings and dedicate all the merit of their practice to all living beings."[1] Over the years, I have had to rethink what "offering a heart of compassion, even to an insect" really means. I've tried to avoid harming all sorts of beetles, centipedes, roaches, crickets, grasshoppers, spiders, ants, bees, hornets, etc. etc., but I found I just can't always do it. A case in point is my relationship with wasps. I've always been fascinated with the communities and structures these industrious pollinators create. I think I could watch them building and maintaining their paper nests for hours. I've often thought of how you can clearly see that a wasp community on one level functions as a single organism, and you can also clearly see it as a collection of individuals. In any case, when I first began living at Gyobutsuji, the "live-and-let-live" approach to wasp nests worked. There would always be several nests around the main building, but the wasps just did their thing as people at Gyobutsuji went about their business, and all was fine.

But the nests around the main building kept increasing in number and size, and one year it suddenly seemed wasps were everywhere. Something also changed in their behavior; I remember several people were stung, including me—seven times! These stings happened in the summertime, when wasps are nurturing their larvae, having become more protective and aggressive. (I have since learned that sometimes wasps also become more aggressive in the late summer from becoming intoxicated on fermenting wild fruit—it seems they are mean drunks!). That summer we were preparing for a Jukai (precepts receiving) ceremony, and someone who planned to attend was allergic to wasp stings. After a resident was stung relatively far away from one of the wasps nests, I knew my live-and-let-live approach to this situation had to change. We reluctantly made the decision to knock down the nests around the main building of Gyobutsuji.

These are just two examples of how beneficial action has often appeared as a sort of koan to me. I use the word koan here in the sense of a paradox that can't be understood using our usual, discriminating mind. With the wasps, something beneficial to one group of beings was harmful to another. As a human being, it seemed apparent that I had to reduce the risk of someone suffering from an allergic reaction, but of course this activity was a source of death and destruction for entire communities of other beings. It might seem it was a no-brainer to make the choice I did, but I think it's very important to clearly understand this decision was made in accordance with a limited human perspective and not the "correct" decision in some ultimate sense.

Making such a decision should involve repentance, in my opinion. Repentance in this case means understanding we have created suffering, even if we think we were doing the best we could in our practice. Then we have to return to our intention and effort to express our vow for the benefit of all creatures. How often have we human beings created immeasurable difficulties for ourselves by assuming our limited views and values are of ultimate concern, without considering a broader perspective that includes other forms of life?

BENEFITING SELF AND OTHER

In Okumura Roshi's commentary on Dōgen Zenji's teaching on beneficial action, he explains how Dōgen Zenji used well known traditional stories about a cornered turtle and sick sparrow to illustrate how beneficial action, when done for its own sake, actually benefits the giver immeasurably. One ancient Chinese story tells of how a man becomes governor in return for releasing a captured tortoise back into the wild, and another tells of how a man's descendants prospered for four generations in return for his nursing a sick sparrow back to health. Today we may find the magical worlds of these stories beautiful and intriguing, but of course we don't really believe that an animal we encounter by chance like this can really transform our lives in such a deep way. But I'll go on record saying that I have encountered the power of an animal to exert a deep, transformative influence on my life.

One hot August afternoon in 2012, about eight months after I had moved to these remote woods of Northwest Arkansas, I saw an SUV making its way down our steep unpaved driveway, and to my surprise I also saw what appeared to be a small dog clumsily loping down the drive behind it. A lady from the local assessor's office got out of the car and greeted me, telling me she was making a routine visit on behalf of the county, and she apologized for leading the dog onto our property. Upon looking at the dog more closely, I could see he was just a puppy, probably some kind of shepherd or collie mix. He was panting profusely and looking up to the lady in what seemed to be an exhausted desperation, watching her every move. Occasionally he would look to me as well, as if he were searching for some sign from one of us that he would be accepted.

The lady told me she had encountered the puppy on the road and given him a drink of her bottled water, and he had then followed her to our property. She again apologized, but asked whether I might want to keep him. She said she had owned several herding dogs like him and they had made excellent companions.

Before the lady had finished speaking about the puppy, I knew I "couldn't" take him. Gyobutsuji was to be a monastic practice place, and we couldn't have a dog here, after all, barking during zazen and distracting people who might come to practice. There was also the vet and food expenses; at that point I wasn't even sure how I was going to support my own practice. There was just no way I could have a dog here. I was sure of that. When I told my visitor, she said she understood and was sure the puppy would follow her on her way out. She was right about that, and after her brief visit I watched him again loping after the SUV in the opposite direction. As I saw them disappear in the distance, I noticed a funny feeling in the pit of my stomach, and I couldn't get the sight of the puppy's bright, intelligent and pleading eyes out of my mind. I'd never encountered a dog quite like him; I don't really know how to explain it, and it may sound silly to try, but it was as if I could feel some kind of depth and yearning for connection that I had never felt in the presence of an animal before. In those moments I felt some kind of space opening up in my mind and heart, and I began to wish I had taken the puppy in. What would become of this beautiful being? Would someone take him in before the coyotes got him or he died of thirst? How could I have been so hard-hearted and fixated on my own ideas of the way things "had" to be?... As I walked with these thoughts whirling around in my head, my heart felt heavier with each step, but suddenly, to my surprise, the puppy appeared by my side. He must have found his way back after he could no longer keep up with the SUV. He looked up desperately and imploringly, as if searching my face for some signal that would allow him to stay. I said to myself, "Well, let's give this a try. This is truly a being in need."

I named him Monty, and as it turned out, I'm not sure who needed who more in this relationship. The gangly puppy grew to be a lovely, sensitive and incredibly intelligent dog who is, as I later learned from a border collie breeder, a purebred border collie, likely imported from Scotland. How he found his way to these dusty rural roads of Northwest Arkansas only he knows, but I am deeply grateful he did.

Far from being a distraction from practice, Monty's presence at Gyobutsuji has been a gift. He rarely barks, and usually when he does, I feel he's just doing his part to protect our property. It took very little effort to teach him not to enter the zendo, but in a way he participates in our sesshins by patiently and quietly waiting-out each five-day period in the adjacent room. He greets all of our visitors with unabashed joy, and most of them end up loving him before they leave. I imagine he makes most of them feel more welcome and relaxed than any human could, and he seems to truly love everyone he encounters. I have learned much about bodhisattva practice from this amazing being, and he has shown me so many things about love, affection, discipline, commitment, companionship, jealousy, compassion and more. One reason I love him so much is that it seems Monty is always just being Monty, and often in doing so, he reveals to me my own heart and mind.

I remember a time, for instance, when he showed me just how fragile my emotional composure can be. For years when I first moved to Gyobutsuji, I think I tried to keep myself convinced that I was content in my solitude as long as I could sit zazen. Of course I wanted to offer sesshin practice to others, but few people joined me in those days. Regardless, I would get by fine without companionship, I thought—I had my practice and my aspiration, and that would be enough. I resolved to just keep sitting and to avoid letting the occasional bouts of loneliness distract me.

During those early days, I would leave Monty outside on the property when I went into town for supplies. I understood that others in the area had done the same with their dogs, and I was certain he would stick close to home while I was away. But one late afternoon as I drove down our driveway after returning from a town trip, he didn't show up to greet me, as he always had before. I thought it was odd, and again an uncomfortable feeling in the pit of my stomach began to grow as I approached the main building. I got out of my car and called him. No Monty. I called and called again, but still no Monty.

As my heart began beating faster, my mind raced, wondering where he could be. I called for a while longer and then sat down to think. Why would he leave? Could it be possible someone had come to the property and taken him away? No, of course that was unlikely. Probably he had caught the scent of a rabbit or armadillo and strayed into the woods. Then I realized if someone did happen to find him, they couldn't notify me, because it just so happened during the previous day he had somehow lost his collar while running through the brush. My thoughts went on like this until I decided to try to alleviate my growing anxiety by driving the county road to look for him. But I had no luck. He was nowhere to be found.

That evening after the sun had gone down I could think of nothing but Monty. It had been hours since I had returned home and I was certain he couldn't survive a night alone in the woods—the coyotes were sure to get him. I shuddered at the thought and tears began to roll down my face. I had trouble sleeping that night, and

I could only weep when I thought of Monty facing the coyotes. My little friend was gone. I hadn't known how attached I had become to him.

The next day I went looking again on the county road, though I wasn't hopeful. As I drove, I decided to stop at my neighbors house and ask if they had seen him. I figured it was a longshot, but to my surprise, my neighbor said he thought he had seen a collie chasing his neighbor's truck the day before. He suggested I go check with him. As I approached his house, I saw a dog tied up in the yard, and I knew instantly it was Monty. He started wagging and whining when he saw me, and I couldn't remember feeling more overjoyed and relieved. I was so happy to be reunited with my little companion. He must have followed my car onto the road as I drove out to get supplies. When the driver of the truck hadn't found a collar on him, he assumed he was a stray and took him in.

With this incident, Monty had shown me who I was, that I had been pretending to myself to be someone else. I wasn't an iron monk who needed nothing but zazen. He showed me how easily my world could be turned upside down. These days I even wonder if I would have been able to endure the many dark, solitary winter nights without Monty. In those early days he was more than just a companion: he was a living being I could care for when I wasn't connecting much with others. He gave me something tangible to nurture and love.

OKAY, NOT-OKAY, OKAY

Over the years I've found that zazen practice offers us something precious. It's a simple but profound offering: the chance to see ourselves and the world around us with the eyes of acceptance. When this acceptance comes to me, often after a sesshin, it's clear it's a gift. I don't feel I've done anything that makes me deserve it. These days I think of this acceptance as wisdom—it's not my wisdom but the wisdom of reality itself. In fact it is reality itself. It's the reality of the *Heart Sutra* that says, "Everything's ok and you don't have to fret and worry; the suffering, strife and conflict you and other beings encounter is not real in the way you think it is." Feeling connected with this reality inevitably splits my heart wide open and leaves my mind at peace.

Of course I don't walk around feeling this way all of the time. No feeling lasts forever. But I think there is a way this wisdom of reality colors a person's experience eventually if they commit themselves to practice. It's a kind of ground upon which to build one's life, and it offers support and comfort to one's thoughts and emotions. Sometimes we might feel we lose our connection to this foundation, but it is always there for us when we return to it in practice, and the more often we return to it, the more we develop a kind of faith that it continues to support us, even during difficult times when we feel lost. But I've noticed an interesting experience connected to this gift. I'll call it the *okay, not-okay, okay* experience. I gave it this name thinking of something I heard my teacher point out about the *Diamond Sutra.* He said the sutra uses a logic that is very different from the standard logic used in human thinking. Here is an example:

"And how so? Subhuti, if someone should claim that the Tathagata speaks of a view of a self, or that the Tathagata speaks of a view of a being, a view of a life, or a view of a soul, Subhuti, would such a claim be true?"

Subhuti said, "No, indeed, Bhagavan. No, indeed, Sugata. Such a claim would not be true. And why not?

> Bhagavan, when the Tathagata speaks of a view of a self,
> the Tathagata speaks of it as no view. Thus is it called
> a 'view of a self.'"
>
> The Buddha said, "Indeed, Subhuti, so it is [...]"[2]

Okumura Roshi presented the *Diamond Sutra's* logic as something like this: A, not-A, therefore A. This of course is nonsense from a usual, logical standpoint. But this I think illustrates the koan of our practice life as bodhisattvas, and this is what I'm speaking of when I talk about the *okay, not-okay, okay* experience.

For me, the experience goes something like this: the more I truly understand that I and the world are ultimately alright because everything is empty (okay), the more I am able to see beyond my own self-centered views and be moved to address the suffering of others (because suffering is not-okay). But the more I am moved to help, the more I must practice to avoid reifying beings and attaching to the preferred outcome of my actions, since these things and everything else are empty (okay). So the experience keeps circling back on itself, because it becomes clear that every aspect of it is an alternate expression of every other aspect.

I think this is one way to talk about the fact that we can only really truly offer beneficial action for its own sake. We can't really act to "help others," because "others" and the idea we can help them is ultimately a kind of fiction. And if we cling to a certain outcome of our action, we are just making the offering in the service of our own ideas and our own egos. Yet if we don't make the "mistake" of offering our practice to others, we lack compassion, and wisdom without compassion is not really wisdom at all. So we can never really pinpoint a motivation for beneficial action that holds up to the reality the *Diamond Sutra* teaches; there's nothing to do but simply follow the path of an open heart and do it for its own sake.

I really began recognizing the nature of this koan four or five years after I began living at Gyobutsuji. I had come here to develop a place that would offer our unique style of sesshins, and I was very grateful to be in this beautiful setting and to live a life centered on this way of practice. I found doing these sesshins each month to be deeply meaningful, feeling their gift of acceptance entering more and more into my life. As I said, as this feeling increased, a desire to make some positive impact on the world increased with it. But it was difficult in those days to feel I was having much influence on others' lives since I mostly lived here with Monty as my only companion. Eventually I began to question if I was really making an offering of my life or not.

It was around this time I began studying what is called the *Jijuyuzanmai* section of Dōgen Zenji's *Bendowa*. It tells us that the benefit to all beings of one person's zazen is immeasurable. I had long been inspired by this teaching, but at this point in my practice it seemed more relevant than ever. Studying this text, in combination with doing monthly sesshins, really helped me to keep going during those years of so much solitude.

But during this time I was also compelled to keep studying seemingly "non-Zen" subjects such as issues around climate change and racial injustice. It again seemed strange that the more I felt able to accept this world as it is, the more I felt motivated to learn how to lessen its suffering. I had believed for years that all societal problems are really rooted in a misunderstanding of the nature of the self and of the nature of our shared lives. Part of the reason I established Gyobutsuji was to bring some understanding of the true nature of our lives into this world by expressing it in practice. It seemed it was the most important work one could do. But sometimes it just felt like what I offered was less than a tiny drop in the ocean of reality, especially since relatively few people came here to practice. I began to think more often of leaving Gyobutsuji to offer my life to some kind of beneficial work that would have a more tangible impact on people's lives.

This tension really came to a head in the summer of 2020 when there was so much visible unrest and conflict in our society. This was the height of the COVID-19 pandemic, and there were racial justice protests happening across the world. At times I wanted to just leave everything at Gyobutsuji and lend a hand in some concrete way. Why should I be entitled to my settled life in the wooded mountains when there was so much suffering and strife going on out there? I grappled with this question often, thinking of how I might be able to keep offering sesshins here while at the same time doing some kind of activity that would directly help society.

But the tension was relieved to a large degree through some communications I was having with a longtime friend of mine who is a physician and a Zen priest. I was stunned when she told me how grateful she was for what I was offering at Gyobutsuji and how inspired she was by my efforts. It amazed me that this was coming from a person who seemed to be doing such deeply meaningful and important work as a physician during a global pandemic. She told me of how she longed to be able to devote her life to living the way I was living, and I told her of how I had longed to feel I was making a real difference in people's lives, as she surely was. At that time a light went off for both of us, I think. Of course we need people working actively within society to directly address people's suffering. Of course we need people devoting their lives to doing regular sesshins and offering regular teachings about the

Dharma. We need both forms of practice, and they depend on and inform each other. They are manifestations of the same vow that offer different, yet essential expressions. Compassion is expressed uniquely according to the qualities and contexts of each individual being, and it can't be limited to any particular form of practice.

That experience reminded me again that I had long believed that the work of offering ourselves in service to society must be anchored in the "flexible mind" and compassionate heart of zazen, as Dōgen Zenji said. Otherwise, we risk the danger of our engagement becoming a cycle in samsara, done in the service of our own egos. Also, settled practice in a quiet place such as a wooded mountain temple must not become overly disconnected from society. We need to make an effort to keep our practice inclusive and to share our experiences and insights. Otherwise, this practice becomes only an escape for a small group of people with no relevance to the larger society.

I remember my teacher speaking on this subject many years ago, saying these two ways of practice have informed and supported each other since the early days of Buddhism. That was part of what inspired me to establish Gyobutsuji, and over the years I have seen directly how important it is for both aspects of our tradition to support this kind of interdependence in our practice.

OFFERING BEYOND OUR LIMITED VISION

Practicing with the hope that we benefit others is an essential part of our vow, of course, but I found that practicing with the hope to see that I benefit others is a trap, and that is another aspect of the compassion koan. It's natural for a human being to seek meaning in life by making an offering to others. When we settle down into our practice, we see the reality of our shared life, that everything from the air we breathe to the language we use to the food we eat, is a gift. We see we couldn't survive without receiving the offerings of other things and beings, so we are naturally moved to give back and do our share in this vast web of interconnection. Yet if we don't continually return to our understanding that even our ability to make an offering is empty and itself a gift, we might end up making an offering in the service of ego rather than in the service of vow.

I've never had the expectation that a large number of people would come to Gyobutsuji on a regular basis. It's located in a remote, rural area, and our style of practice doesn't have wide appeal. It almost feels miraculous when people do join me for a sesshin, and I'm happy to feel I may play some part in supporting their practice. Back in 2020 when the pandemic prevented many people from going to a local Zen center, we started offering online practice, and I began to give regular dharma talks as part of that. Ironically, the closing of our temple doors ended up creating conditions that made me feel more immediately connected to other people through this online practice. But I found as time went on, I had to make a more concerted effort to offer this practice for its own sake. I sometimes saw the tendency of my mind to stray into some way of trying to measure the "success" of my practice in terms of the number of people who are regularly engaged with Gyobutsuji. But this of course is a recipe for samsara. I often found that just when I felt we had established a foundation of regular practitioners, things would change and attendance would decrease. Then in some weeks or months numbers would again increase. So trying to measure the benefit I was offering in this way was like a roller coaster ride, as the saying goes.

Attempting to measure my worth as a monk or a teacher like this is trying to find fulfillment outside of the self, as Uchiyama

Roshi said, and I think Dōgen Zenji is pointing to this reality when he says we should do beneficial actions for their own sake. That's another way of saying we must meet everything we encounter as the self. Doing beneficial action to see some benefit is trying to find fulfillment outside of ourselves, and it creates stress and suffering.

It might be difficult to understand the profound teachings of *Jijuyuzanmai* that say our zazen practice resounds throughout the past, present, future and all space, but we can easily feel how we are at the same time released from our suffering and connected to others when we truly make some offering for its own sake in the present moment. Making an offering for its own sake is the way we open the hand of thought in our lives beyond the zazen cushion.

I can pretty easily see when I am veering from my vow when I give a dharma talk, for example. When I realize in some moment that I'm fixating on how I think I'm being perceived by my listeners, I know that is a moment of straying from my intent to make an offering to others rather than an offering to my ego. At these times I have to let go and settle back down into the moment and remember my real intention. I find when I can sincerely engage with my real intention in this way, I enjoy myself and I'm released from my judging mind. For me, doing something for its own sake involves doing something joyfully. It's not some kind of ascetic practice that we do grudgingly; it's actually the way we are released from our own suffering.

Shōryū Bradley grew up in Central Texas and was ordained in 2002 by Seirin Barbara Kohn at Austin Zen Center. In 2004 he moved to Bloomington, Indiana, to study with Shohaku Okumura Roshi and Sanshin Zen Community. He also trained at Tassajara

Zen Mountain Center and Sotoshu International Training Monastery angos held in the US and Japan, and in 2010 Shōryū received dharma transmission from Okumura Roshi. Since January of 2012 he has lived and practiced at Gyobutsuji, a small monastic practice place he established in the Ozark Mountains of Northwest Arkansas. Practice at Gyobutsuji is centered around monthly sesshins done in the style of the Sanshin lineage.

Is "Beneficial Action" A Means of Attracting Followers or Non-dualistic Altruism? An Etymological Exploration

Dōju Layton

THE PHRASE "BENEFICIAL ACTION" sounds straightforward enough. It just means "do good things," right? When Dōgen uses this phrase in *Bodaisatta Shishōbō,* he tells us that we should not be motivated by some reward, but instead that we should be "motivated solely by beneficial action itself." Dōgen is well known for his teaching that we practice the Buddhadharma solely for the sake of the Buddhadharma, and his presentation of beneficial action is no exception to this. We should thus "do good things" for their own sake, not as a means to an end. Because there is no separation between self and other, the same goes for the doer of the beneficial action and the receiver. It therefore does not make sense to think of one party benefiting at the other's expense as we might normally think. This is a basic idea that Dōgen wishes to convey in *Bodaisatta Shishōbō,* and more broadly in the *Shōbōgenzō.*

However, whenever we read Dōgen, we have to take into account that he is drawing on over a millennium of Chinese Buddhist tradition and textual material. He did not write in English, and if we read a translation of his work without having this fact in mind, it is easy to misunderstand what his writing is doing. His words are merely the tip of a vast iceberg, and he takes for granted that his audience knows this. Dōgen's fame as a writer is due in large part to his subversion of language. He takes some phrase or word whose meaning none would question, and then proceeds to utterly transform it into the realm of the non-dual. Although *Bodaisatta Shishōbō* is not the most famous example of Dōgen's use of this technique, the very phrase *shishōbō* ("four embracing actions") was uttered by Buddha himself and scores of subsequent monks and nuns before Dōgen ever used it. It was thus ripe for transformation in Dōgen's eyes, and that is indeed part of what Dōgen seeks to do in this fascicle. It is thus worthwhile to explore what "beneficial action" and "four embracing actions" meant in their earliest contexts before Dōgen got ahold of them. In this chapter, I'd like to briefly explore the history of these two terms, looking at the original Indic phrases and then the Chinese translations that Dōgen adapted in *Bodaisatta Shishōbō.*

Both of the terms that come down to us as "four embracing actions" and "beneficial action" appear in the Pali suttas (the body of sermons said to have been presented by Śākyamuni Buddha himself and treated as authoritative by the Theravāda tradition). In my limited research I was able to find three such suttas where these phrases occur. The first is in a sutta called the *Saṅgītisutta* ("The Recital"), which is found in the *Dīgha Nikāya,* or *Long Discourses* (DN 33). This sutta is very dry, and aside from a brief introduction, it is literally just a long list of 230 other lists, one of which is our "four embracing actions." The Pali text for it is as follows:

Cattāri saṅgahavatthūni—dānaṁ, peyyavajjaṁ, **atthacariyā,** samānattatā.

The first two bolded words are our "four embracing actions," the last bolded word is "beneficial action," and the three unbolded words are the other three embracing actions which I won't discuss here. Let's start with the first bolded phrase, cattāri saṅgahavatthūni. Cattāri just means "four" and is certainly our least controversial word and the easiest to translate. It is the inflected form of catur: in Pali and Sanskrit, words have to have their endings changed to indicate what part of speech they are, just like in Latin or German, so cattāri indicates that this "four" is nominative (part of the subject of the sentence) and plural (numbers other than one are obviously always plural). You may also notice that catur sounds like Spanish cuatro (four) or catorce (fourteen), and this is of course because Pali and Spanish (and English) share a common ancestor.

Anyway, to get back on topic, we next have the mouthful saṅgahavatthūni, which is actually two words smushed together: saṅgaha and vatthūni. In this only vatthūni is inflected, and its base form is vatthu. The Pali dictionary defines vatthu as "object; thing; reason; ground; story." The root of the corresponding Sanskrit word, vastu, means, "to dwell, live, stay, reside." You may be thinking that none of these options seem to correspond to either "embracing" or "action," and you would be correct. In this case, vatthu means "ground" in the sense of "foundation," hence the connection with dwelling, since houses are built on foundations. This is the word that ends up as "action" in our English translation, but we'll have to look at the intermediate Chinese translation before we can fully understand why that happens. Saṅgaha (in Sanskrit saṃgraha) is the more crucial word, however. It means, "collecting, gathering, accumulation, comprising, inclusion, classification." You can probably detect some relationships here with the idea of "embracing," but it's also not quite the same concept. So all together we might settle on a brutally literal translation like "four grounds for collecting."

Next let's look at atthacariyā, the source of our "beneficial action." Again we have two words stuck together: attha and cariyā. For attha, the dictionary gives us, "interest, advantage, gain; (moral) good, blessing, welfare; profit, prosperity, well-being," while for cariyā we find, "conduct, behavior, state of, life of." A Pali epithet sometimes used for the Buddha is atthassa ninnetar (in this case attha becomes atthassa due to grammatical inflection), which means "bringer of well-being." So for atthacariyā we literally have something like "well-being-conduct," and more loosely and accurately in English this would be "conduct that brings about well-being."

Fortunately we can do better than my mechanical dictionary translations since the Pali suttas have been translated into English by a number of different scholars. Here are some of the translation choices that have been used along with our full Pali sentence from above, and how this sentence would look using Okumura Roshi's translation choices. I have put our terms of interest in bold text:

Cattāri saṅgahavatthūni—dānaṁ, peyyavajjaṁ, **atthacariyā,** samānattatā.

Four embracing actions: giving (*dana*), loving speech, **beneficial action**, identity-action (Okumura Roshi)[1]

Four ways of being inclusive: giving, kindly words, **taking care**, and equality (Bhikkhu Sujata, 2018)

Four grounds of popularity, to wit, liberality, kindly speech, **justice,** impartiality." (T.W. & C.A.F. Rhys Davids, 1921)

Four bases of sympathy: generosity, pleasing speech, **beneficial conduct** and impartiality." (Maurice Walshe, 1987)

Four means of sustaining a favorable relationship: Giving, endearing speech, **beneficent conduct,** and impartiality. (Bhikkhu Bodhi, 2012)[2]

The first thing to note here is the range of possibilities. Indeed, the only word that is consistent between all of these is the number "four." Also of interest is how the translations of *cattāri saṅgahavatthūni,* especially that of the Rhys Davids and Bhikkhu Bodhi, seem to suggest a means of bringing others into the Buddhist fold. Whereas Okumura Roshi's "embracing actions" suggest four bodhisattva activities done for their own sake, the Pali suggests something more like a means to an end. Here we get our first sense of what Dōgen might have been trying to subvert, for, as we recall, he implores us to perform embracing actions only for their own sake.

This sense of "embracing" as a means to an end in the Pali becomes more obvious when we look at another *sutta* where the four embracing actions are found, namely the *Dutiyahatthakasutta,* which is found in the Aṅguttara Nikāya, or Numbered Discourses (8.24). This *sutta* is brief, so I will quote it here in full:[3]

On one occasion the Blessed One was dwelling at Āḷavī at the Aggāḷava Shrine. Then Hatthaka of Āḷavī, accompanied by five hundred lay followers, approached the Blessed One, paid homage to him, and sat down to one side. The Blessed One then said to him:

"Your retinue is large, Hatthaka. How do you sustain this large retinue?"

"I do so, Bhante, by the **four means of sustaining a favorable relationship** taught by the Blessed One. When I know: 'This one is to be sustained by a gift,' I sustain him by a gift. When I know: 'This one is to be sustained by endearing speech,' I sustain him by endearing speech. When I know: 'This one is to be sustained by **beneficent conduct,**' I sustain him by beneficent conduct. When I know: 'This one is to be sustained by impartiality,' I sustain him by impartiality. There is wealth in my family, Bhante. They don't think they should listen to me as if I were poor."

"Good, good, Hatthaka! This is the method by which you can sustain a large retinue. For all those in the past who sustained a large retinue did so by these same four means of sustaining a favorable relationship. All those in the future who will sustain a large retinue will do so by these same four means of sustaining a favorable relationship. And all those at present who sustain a large retinue do so by these same four means of sustaining a favorable relationship."

Then, after the Blessed One had instructed, encouraged, inspired, and gladdened Hatthaka of Āḷavī with a Dhamma talk, Hatthaka rose from his seat, paid homage to the Blessed One, circumambulated him keeping the right side toward him, and departed.

Then, not long after Hatthaka of Āḷavī had left, the Blessed One addressed the bhikkhus:

"Bhikkhus, you should remember Hatthaka of Āḷavī as one who possesses eight astounding and amazing qualities. What eight? (1) He is endowed with faith. (2) He is virtuous, and (3) has a sense of moral shame and (4) moral dread. (5) He is learned, (6) generous, and (7) wise. (8) He has few desires. You should remember Hatthaka of Āḷavī as one who possesses these eight astounding and amazing qualities."

The Buddha's question to Hatthaka is about what means he uses to "sustain" such a large following. If you recall that Bhikkhu Bodhi uses the translation "sustaining [a favorable relationship]" instead of Okumura Roshi's "embracing" when translating *sangaha,* it should come as no surprise that the "sustain" used in the Buddha question is *sangaṇhāsī* in Pali, which is simply a conjugated verbal form of *sangaha.* Every subsequent use of "sustain" in the sutta is likewise this same Pali word. In this particular story's context, even if we replace "sustain" with "embrace," it would still be clear that the Buddha's question is about attracting and maintaining a group of followers, rather than a non-dual sense of "embrace." We can thus conclude that Dōgen's four embracing actions as an expression of non-duality were instead in the Buddha's teaching four means for attracting and sustaining a group of followers, which is of course dualistic.

How then did these Indic language teachings manifest in the Chinese language, which is ultimately what Dōgen and Okumura Roshi relied upon? Before we proceed, I need to briefly explain a relevant feature of the Japanese language as it relates to Chinese. We often think of Dōgen as a Japanese writer. Although much of his writing was actually in Chinese, the *Shōbōgenzō* and *Bodaisatta Shishōbō* are certainly in Japanese. However, it's actually possible to include words, phrases, and even full sentences from Chinese in Japanese writing without doing any "translation." This is a bit hard to understand for us English speakers, but I'll do my best to explain it.

The English language, despite being a Germanic language, owes the bulk of its vocabulary to Norman French and ultimately Latin. In the same way, the lion's share of Japanese's vocabulary comes from Chinese rather than actual Japonic roots. However, the relationship between written Chinese and Japanese has an added feature that goes beyond this comparison. This is because of the fact that Chinese characters represent ideas rather than the sounds represented by an alphabet. As a result, the same written phrase can be understood by both readers of Chinese and readers of Japanese even though they would pronounce it differently. This feature also allows readers to read very old texts without too much difficulty. We English speakers have a very hard time with Chaucer, and reading Old English is impossible without special training. This is because the pronunciation of words or even the root language of the word has changed, and we cannot understand it phonetically. However, in Chinese written texts the pronunciation is not the basis of the writing system, so this problem does not exist. This means that the phrase "four embracing actions" in the Japanese version we find in Dōgen, the version a modern speaker of Japanese like Okumura

Roshi would use, and the original phrase in very old Chinese translations of Indic texts are all identical despite the time and space between them.

Why point this out? This feature of Chinese and Japanese is what allows someone like Dōgen to pick up a written phrase that has been used for centuries, use it in his own writing, and, in his case, transform it. A case in point are our phrases of interest. In Dōgen's *Bodaisatta Shishōbō,* "four embracing actions" is 四攝法. In modern Japanese this is pronounced *shishōbō,* while in Mandarin Chinese it *sì shèfǎ,* but again, the meaning is identical (it can also be perfectly intelligible in Korean as *sa seopbeop* and in Vietnamese as *tứ nhiếp pháp*). Although Dōgen used this phrase in the 13th century, an early appearance of it in the Chinese language is in a translation of the ninth sūtra of the *Dīrghāgama* (known in Chinese as 長阿含經, meaning "long discourses"). That collection was translated by Buddhayaśas and Zhu Fonian between the years 412 and 413, more than 800 years before Dōgen used it.

Let's now look at how the process of translation from Indic into Chinese might have changed its meaning. As you might recall, the Pali sentence we examined above came from the *Dīgha Nikāya,* which, like the *Dīrghāgama,* is also translated as "long discourses." Many of the texts found in these two collections correspond to one another, and this is the case with ninth sūtra of the *Dīrghāgama.* This sūtra is called 衆集經, or *The Numerically Assembled Sūtra,* which is very similar to the *Saṅgītisutta* we looked at above. In the *Saṅgītisutta* we explored the sentence, "Four embracing actions: giving (*dana*), loving speech, beneficial action, identity-action." The corresponding sentence in Chinese (with the Japanese phonetic readings) is:

四摂法：惠施、愛語、**利人**、等利
(*Shishōbō*: ese, aigo, *rinin*, tōri)

In the first compound, the character 四 (*shi*) is again uncontroversial and just means "four."

The second character, 摂 (*shō*), is a crucial one and will explain why Okumura Roshi used "embracing" rather than some of the other choices for the translations of the Pali we saw above. For this character, the dictionary gives us, "to hold, to grasp, to manage, to take in, to attract, to be squeezed in between," among other options. The left portion of this character, 扌, means "hand," and lends the character its sense of embracing, holding, or grasping. With this range of appropriate meanings, you can see why the translators Buddhayaśas and Zhu Fonian would have selected it, but we can also guess they may have had the definition "attract" in mind given what we learned from the dialogue between the Buddha and Hatthaka above. Dōgen instead interpreted it in the sense of "to take in," however, and this explains why Okumura Roshi chose "embrace."

The third character, 法 (*hō;* note it becomes *bō* in *shishōbō* due to rules about combining sounds in Japanese) in this case means something like "method" or "means." It also means "law," and in this sense it is used as the standard translation for the Sanskrit *dharma*. In an earlier translation of *Bodaisatta shishōbō*, Okumura Roshi translated this phrase as "four embracing dharmas" rather than "four embracing actions." However, we've examined the Pali, and we know the word in question was *vatthūni* and not *dhamma* (the Pali for *dharma*). Okumura Roshi made the same discovery and changed his translation. This is a good example of how ambiguity can be introduced in the process of translation. In the Pali, we saw that the word *vatthu* meant "ground" or "foundation." The

Chinese translator may have used this word 法 (*hō*) because it has the sense of an ironclad law, in the same way that a ground or foundation is a solid base, but 法 itself cannot be used for "ground" or "foundation."

Moving on to the phrase "beneficial action," the Chinese translation in *The Numerically Assembled Sūtra* is 利人 (*rinin*). The first character 利 (*ri*) means "benefit, profit, favorable." This character originally depicted a grain plant on the left and a knife on the right, representing a farmer harvesting grain and thereby benefiting in the process. The second character 人 (*nin*) means person or people (plural forms are not usually indicated in Chinese and Japanese), and as you might be able to see, this character depicts a person in a sort of stick figure form. This Chinese translation thus literally means, "to benefit people" and is thus a loose translation since it does not include the "conduct" portion of the Indic original.

So how then did Okumura Rōshi get "beneficial action" rather than "[do things that] benefit people"? In *Bodaisattashishōbō*, Dōgen actually quotes a different Chinese translation of the list of the four embracing actions. Instead of the 利人 (*rinin*) used by the translators Buddhayaśas and Zhu Fonian, Dōgen's text has 利行 (*rigyō*), while the name of the actual list, 四攝法 (shishōbō), is the same in both. Another interesting feature of the Chinese Buddhist canon is that many Indic texts were translated by a variety of translators over many centuries. Just as we saw in the diverse English translations of the Pali above, the Chinese translations of Buddhist texts have a similar diversity. It's tempting to think that there is a one-to-one relationship between a given Sanskrit or Pali Buddhist term and its corresponding Chinese/Japanese version, but that is unfortunately a gross oversimplification. For these reasons, it's difficult to pinpoint which earlier Chinese text or texts Dōgen

would have drawn his exact language from in *Bodaisatta Shishōbō.*
Whereas Buddhayaśas and Zhu Fonian have:

四攝法：惠施、愛語、**利人**、等利

(***Shishōbō:*** *ese, aigo,* ***rinin,*** *tōri)*

Dōgen has:

四攝法：布施、愛語、**利行**、同事

(***Shishōbō:*** fuse, aigo, ***rigyō,*** dōji)

Perhaps Dōgen's most quoted and beloved sūtra is Kumārajīva's
translation of *The Lotus Sutra,* which was completed in 406 CE and
includes the phrase 四攝法 *(shishōbō)* exactly once. It occurs in the
twelfth chapter entitled *Devadatta.* However, the contents of the
list are not laid out, and it is only mentioned in passing. Kumārajīva does, however, enumerate the list using the same words for each
item that Dōgen uses in his 404 CE translation of the 25,000 verse
Mahāprajñāpāramitā-sūtra. This was an important Mahayana text
that Dōgen likely studied. The same version of the list was also used
in many later translations and commentaries, and it is likely that these
essentially copy from Kumārajīva, whose work was highly influential. At any rate, in the 利行 *(rigyō)* that Dōgen uses, the second
character 行 *(gyō)* originally depicted a street intersection. Related to
that, its primary meaning is "to go" or "to walk," but it can also mean
"behavior" or "conduct," and in this sense has essentially the same
meaning as the Pali *cariyā* that we saw above. Okumura Roshi's
"action" for this character is of course quite similar.

The Chinese translation of this list of four is thus more ambig-
uous than the Indic, which allowed writers like Dōgen to take it in

a different direction. As mentioned above, Dōgen is well known for taking some word or phrase that is clearly meant in a dualistic sense and transforming it into something non-dual. The same process is going on in *Bodaisattashishōbō,* although perhaps more subtly, and it is especially hard to detect in English translation since we cannot detect the ambiguity of the Chinese characters. In its original context, the "four embracing actions" were presented in a dualistic fashion. We saw Hatthaka on the one hand using these four types of behavior in order to attract and maintain his retinue of followers. For Dōgen, there is no "in order to." We perform the four embracing actions because they are the activity of a bodhisattva; there is no gain to be had, and there is no inside and outside of the actions.

In its original Pali context, the phrase "four embracing actions" were better understood as "four means of attracting [followers]." It's hard to imagine Dōgen being able to apply his non-dualistic word transformation if he were writing in Pali, at least if the sentence we examined above were the one he had to work with. It was the process of translation of Buddhist texts into Chinese, and then Dōgen's playfulness with the Chinese language as a Japanese writer, that provided the conditions for his virtuosity with words that we celebrate today. To truly understand what Dōgen is doing in his writing, however, we have to go back and investigate the words he uses to appreciate how he subverts and alters them.

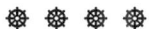

Dōju grew up in the Washington D.C. area. He received an undergraduate degree from the College of William and Mary and a master's degree in Ecological and Evolutionary Biology from the University of Missouri-St. Louis. While in the latter program, he began practicing zazen at the Missouri Zen Center in St. Louis after deciding against an academic career but facing uncertainty about his direction in life. Inspired after reading Kōshō Uchiyama's Opening the Hand of Thought, in 2015 he moved to Sanshinji in Bloomington to practice under Okumura Rōshi, who ordained him as a novice priest in 2017. To supplement his priest training, Dōju studied Buddhism at Indiana University, receiving a master's degree in Religious Studies in 2021. He is interested in the intersection of practice, ecology, and politics, and how to engage with these topics while being true to the Buddhist tradition. In this vein, he currently combines his background in biology with his vows to help all beings by working as a land steward for the Sycamore Land Trust in Bloomington where he protects and restores wildlife habitat.

Identity Action

Total Functioning

Myoho Kendall

> The cosmos is all there ever is ever was or ever will be.
> – *Carl Sagan*

Clouds form, the wind blows, the sun shines without humans controlling or managing its functioning. Even our own bodies breathe on their own and we do not have control over the way our genes express, how our cells operate, or how our bodily functions keep us alive. If this total functioning did not exist we would not be here. What is it we can learn from this total functioning that is beyond our control? How can seeing life from this perspective help inform our practice?

I remember watching a 2018 TED Talk given by the co-founder of Google X, Tom Chi, in which he showed how science has proven that we are all interconnected. Within three short minutes he explained that we are a continuous flame of inter-becoming and 98% of all atoms within the body cycle out within a year. He calculated that each human body cycles out 7% of its total mass (roughly the size of one's arm) of solids, water, and air on a daily basis and cycles out a full body's mass within two weeks' time. So what I think of as me, is not actually me. I am made up of elements and nutrients that the planet and sun freely gives to this body. Keeping this in mind, when we look at ourselves in comparison to others, we see that we are all the same. We all breathe, eat, sleep, and have physical systems that contribute to the functioning of our bodies and are a part of the larger functioning of the environment in which we live.

With everything we have going on in our daily lives, it is easy to get caught up in the illusion that our lives are separate from others; however, when we look at things from a larger perspective we see that this is not the case. NASA recently came out with a video that portrays our planet earth as a living being that breathes in during the spring and summer months and breathes out during the fall and winter months. Being able to see the planet for the first time from space in 1968 forever changed our perspective and the way we see ourselves and the place we call home. Our perspective changed from "me" in my home to "us" on this planet. When we realize that we are all in this together, we can see more clearly how to take care of our lives, each other and the only place we call home. We are all right here, right now spinning around on this tiny blue dot within this unfathomably vast universe.

When I took an online course offered by astrophysicist Neil deGrasse Tyson, he stated that if an asteroid were to crash into earth and end all of life, fragments of earth would be expelled in every direction throughout the universe until they eventually came to land on a habitable planet. He said that even a speck of dust would contain all the information needed to recreate life as we know it in new forms. Whether or not my individual self continues on after death seems irrelevant when compared to life continuing on in the universe after an apocalyptic event. Perhaps a question to consider is: how do my individual actions contribute to the benefit or suffering of myself, other living beings, and the planet?

For example, I now know the plastic I throw away may end up in the ocean, killing a fish that can't digest it, or as waste on a beach halfway around the world. As an individual, I think I am dealing with my waste by throwing it away, but when I look more deeply into how my waste is processed at the local, state, and national level, I see the larger view. When I realize my waste is creating problems for others and our environment, I can make better choices. I started by recycling my plastics and eventually limited purchasing products that contain plastics and moved to more biodegradable materials. When we understand how our individual actions impact the larger whole, we can make choices that cause less suffering to ourselves, others, and the planet.

INTERCONNECTEDNESS

What if flowers decided they did not want to open and share their pollen with insects? What if bees decided they did not want to collect pollen because it was too much work? Plants over time have developed relationships with fungi and other insects that allow them to take care of themselves and other living beings at the same time. Larger trees that grow tall and provide a forest canopy soak up most of the sunlight from smaller plants that also need the sunlight to grow. Through study and observation we know that forest trees and plants form a symbiotic relationship with the mycelium of fungi. This relationship develops a vast underground network that provides the nutrients for smaller plants and trees to sustain their lives in the spring and summer months. When the taller trees lose their leaves, the smaller coniferous trees in turn feed their taller neighbors during the winter months. There are numerous beneficial relationships that exist all around us. We can look to these naturally occurring relationships to help inform our own lives. How does my life connect with nature and other living beings and how can I live in a way that benefits all?

To further examine this concept, we can look at how people behaved during the beginning of the pandemic. We were all encouraged to stock up on supplies and only leave our homes when necessary. This created a sense of panic that resulted in shortages of certain products that some of us would consider necessities, like toilet paper. At the time, it felt like a big deal to make sure we all had enough toilet paper to "survive." I know some who would purchase the largest package they could find that under normal circumstances should last a household for six months. I had neighbors that stockpiled pallets of supplies in their garages out of an abundance of caution so that they wouldn't go without. During this time I noticed my own reaction to what I perceived as items I couldn't live without and decided to start checking out alternative options. I ended up purchasing cloth toilet paper and reusable cloth tissues to show myself that I didn't need to rely on these single use items that I had grown so accustomed to using. While it did take some getting used to, I was able to change some of these ingrained habits of consumption.

It's not just about toilet paper. There are lots of other items that continue to be in short supply, whether it's yeast for making bread, certain kinds of cereal, or pet food. As our supply chain continues to be affected by the pandemic and our relations with other countries, we can ask ourselves the following questions. How is stockpiling supplies affecting the larger whole? If I take more than I need now, there will be others that go without. Am I okay with that or do I want others to have what they need also?

Self and Other as Suchness

Growing up, I observed and experienced the importance of caring for others. My birth mother had a mental illness and could not take care of any of her children in the long term. I was the last of six children to be born and the only one to be adopted within the family. I had the opportunity to know my birth mother while being cared for by my grandma, and my aunt and uncle who adopted me. I saw how my whole family would come together when my birth mother got sick and make sure she was safe and properly cared for. I observed how my adoptive parents took care of their neighbors by shoveling snow and mowing lawns, and also took care of their own parents as they became elderly. I carried this forward in my life and sought out opportunities to help others in need. I volunteered at a nursing home, sponsored women overseas, delivered meals to homebound older adults, and volunteered at a crisis center. When I was ordained as a Soto Zen priest, I still felt like I needed more experience and knowledge before I would be able to be of any help to others. What made the most sense to me at the time was to further develop my own practice and understanding with the hope I would eventually see more clearly how to help others.

I first completed training to engage in Buddhist outreach within our state's prisons. I remember feeling scared the first few times I visited the men, but quickly realized there was nothing to be afraid of. I could have just as easily been in their situation given the same set of circumstances. I remember thinking, *what is it that I can bring to them that they don't already know?* What I came to realize is that it wasn't what I said that was helpful or even useful. It's that I was showing up for them. Just coming and practicing with them was enough. Looking back on it, I saw that they are the ones who provided me with teachings: how to practice zazen even while lying down, how to stand up for oneself without anger or conflict, how to take responsibility for one's actions, how to let go of what one thinks life should be, and how to appreciate and be content with what one has.

I then had the opportunity to be a Buddhist representative on our local inter-religious council. This was a very informative experience and helped me see the commonalities among religious traditions and humanistic ways of thinking. I remember being a part of a panel where we discussed the idea of "treating others as you would want to be treated." While some may believe Jesus was the first to come up with this idea, there is evidence in almost every religious tradition of these teachings. Even the Buddha in the Udanavarga 5:18 was reported as saying "Hurt not others in ways that you yourself would find hurtful." I learned so much from the other religious leaders and representatives through this experience. It felt like we were a microcosm demonstrating to the larger community how we can live in peace and acceptance of others.

I also spent a year as a volunteer chaplain and became the first Buddhist to go through our hospital's chaplaincy training program. Since I grew up as a Catholic, it wasn't foreign to me to pray to God and Jesus. I just approach life with a different perspective now that I'm a Buddhist. I remember before one of the training sessions I was alone with one of the other chaplain trainees who asked, "What are you doing here?" I considered the question, looked up and said, "Buddhists also have compassion for others." What I quickly came to realize is that what I think or believe has no relevance when it comes to providing spiritual support to those who are gravely sick or near death. Being a calm presence without saying a word is a universal way to ease another's suffering. In a lot of cases, the people I visited didn't identify with a religion or spiritual practice – they just didn't want to be alone.

I remember being called to a hospice room where a man had been taken off life support and his body was starting to shut down. I had been involved in a similar situation the week before. The body will do all it can to keep itself alive. The lungs make a very loud and abrupt rattling noise and forcibly move the entire body as it gasps for air. It can be a scary and unsettling experience to witness. When I arrived on the hospice floor, the man's family was sitting outside of his room. I gently asked if we could all move into the room to be with their dying loved one to provide him with love and support as he passed. They agreed but didn't know what to do. I explained that the body was working in overdrive trying to keep going so I imagined that it might feel good to have a cool washcloth on his forehead, to hold his hand and just sit with him. They called other family members to come and be with them and before I knew it the room was filled with family and friends. They all laughed and cried as they shared stories of their loved one. Each taking turns holding his hand and dabbing a cool cloth on his forehead to help bring him comfort.

It's all about changing our perspective and treating others how we would want to be treated. This is how we can best care for ourselves and others. How would I want to be treated or cared for if I was in the same situation? If we all live our lives from the perspective of others, we naturally do not steal, kill, harbor ill will, etc. We recognize that others are just like me. Think of how the world would be if we all lived with this perspective in our hearts. Now, realize that we don't have to wait. We can live with this perspective right now; it's a matter of choice. Life is like a blooming lotus flower or ripening persimmon. We are all opening and ripening at different speeds due to the causes and conditions in which we were born and live. Some of us are ready to live in a way that benefits self and others while others are still a bit astringent and are not yet ready. When we see others struggling to see and experience life from a larger perspective, we can offer them our compassion and patience. Our practice of zazen allows us to let go of our individual perspectives. When we let go of our individual perspective, we can experience self and others as suchness.

PRACTICE IS ENLIGHTENMENT

When I turned six years old, I began taking piano lessons and first had to learn what all the notes were on the white and black keys starting with middle "C." I had to play using my right and then left hand separately. It took a year before I had enough coordination to use both hands playing different parts at the same time. Learning a new song was always hard at first. I had to really concentrate, first looking at the notes on the page and then putting my fingers on the right piano keys. It was slow going and took hours of practice to learn a new song. It took even longer to memorize a song and trust that my fingers would develop the muscle memory to carry me through the entire song. Once muscle memory had developed, my mind was able to focus on other things, like the tempo and how loudly or softly I played each of the keys. I began to notice that it is only when I let go of my mental chatter that I could start to express the feeling of the composition and connect with the audience. This is the point when the piano player, the listener and the composition come together as music.

I wanted to use the example of practicing the piano because I see it as similar to the way I practice with the bodhisattva vows. When I began studying to take the precepts, I first needed to learn what the precepts were and how to practice with them in my daily life. For example, when I read the precept about not stealing, I thought, "Well, this is an easy one. I'm not a thief." The opportunity then came along for me to see that I do have the capacity to steal. I was ignorant of my behavior because until this point I had not had a reason to examine my actions with this level of detail. I remember I was in my office at work and was looking through my desk to find a pen. When I opened my drawer I noticed there was a pen that I didn't recognize as being my own. I remembered it belonged to one of my co-workers, who had let me borrow it during a meeting. I was able to return the pen, say thank you, and apologize for not returning it sooner. While this seems innocent, there are countless ways we can hold ourselves privately accountable for not stealing, whether it's not speaking up when we notice the cashier gives us an extra $10 in change, or taking a parking spot when we know someone else is waiting for it. Once we begin to see how the precepts can inform our lives and relationships with others, we continue to learn and grow with them and our practice deepens.

When I first ordained, I didn't feel qualified to help others. I thought I needed to focus on my own practice and understanding. I had this idea that I needed to be more and that my existing knowledge and experience was somehow lacking. It was only through my interactions and practice with others that I came to realize who I am and that what I have to offer is enough. There is not some other person I need to be in order to help others. What I thought of as my individual practice turned out to be connected with others in numerous ways. I realized I also receive benefits when helping others, and the giver, receiver and gift are all one.

I remember how I used to be concerned with saying the right words and acting in the right manner in all situations. I would rehearse conversations before they would happen or go over and over what they said or I said and what it all meant. This is our discriminating mind that is constantly judging our thoughts, words and actions. When the discriminating chatter quiets down, we begin to see how our vows and practice are supporting us. When our practice is one with how we live and we trust that in any given situation we will give what is needed, we use kind speech and respond with beneficial actions. This is how we are wish-fulfilling gems that take on the beneficial form or identity that is needed to save all beings.

SPIDERS AND MORNING GLORIES (A POEM)

One day I found that a yellow and black garden spider had made a web using the leaves of my morning glories for support. I was in awe of its size and beauty.

The next day I found it had dropped from its web and died. I had thought of putting its body in with the flowers as a resting place, and then noticed the ants were making a good meal out of it, so I left it alone.

A few weeks later, I noticed that the same morning glories in which the spider once made its web were now blooming. I was in awe of the two colors that spun themselves together to form its bloom. In a week they will also be gone.

Cheers to life and all its splendor. Cheers to death and letting go so new life can happen. What seems like a lifetime apart is one and the same function.

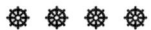

Myoho Kendall lives in Cedar Rapids, IA. She was ordained as a novice in 2017 by Zuiko Redding at Cedar Rapids Zen Center and practiced and trained with her there for several years. She now practices with Shōryū Bradley of Gyobutsu Zen Community in Kingston, AR. Her areas of special interest are prison outreach, yogic studies and online Buddhist classes.

Living Together, Dying Together

Issan Koyama

I USED TO LIVE IN WASHINGTON HEIGHTS in New York City, which has the highest elevation on Manhattan Island. On top of the hill is a beautiful historic park, Fort Tryon Park. Although the elevation is merely 100 feet above sea level, because the park faces west, there is a sweeping view from this park. Under the sharp cliffs, you can see the Hudson River. Across this immense body of water is New Jersey, another sharp cliff of the Palisades, and a view into the vast American continent.

I loved to take walks along the beautifully planned English flower gardens of this park particularly around sunset. As the sun set over the continental horizon, the last ray of sunlight hits the flower garden horizontally. With the clarifying last ray of the day, everything is completely exposed. There is no shade, no hidden spot. All are exposed by the strong light. All the flowers, plants, and trees then look so different, revealing every detail to us.

After a long day of work at hospice, which was often exhausting both physically and mentally, this felt like a beautiful clear metaphor of our lives and was very healing for me.

Among those of us who are engaged in the end-of-life care, it is often said that at the end of life, all the issues of our lives we have neglected dealing with and somehow kept pushing aside for various reasons tend to be explosively exposed and made obvious, and we have no other choice but to face them and come to some sort of resolution and reconciliation. This is how we come to understand what has happened in the course of our lives and what it means to us.

The year 2023 marks the 20th year anniversary of Sanshin Zen Community. It is also the 40th anniversary of my arrival in the United States.

After graduating from college in Japan, I got a job with an American-owned international media company as a newspaper and TV reporter. This job first brought me to France in 1981. Then, in 1983, I accepted a position at their headquarters in New York City. My job was to report on the arts, entertainment, lifestyle, and fashion. My office was in Greenwich Village, Manhattan. At first, the job I was assigned for sounded fun, glamorous and exciting.

However, it didn't take me much time to realize that I had just landed right in the epicenter of the early AIDS epidemic. Working with the progressive artist communities of downtown New York in the 1980s, I was diving head first into a tragic and chaotic time for New York City.

I used to have the habit of going through my Rolodex to remove cards I no longer needed. By 1986, I was pulling nearly one quarter of the cards out to throw them away. One year I went to a few funerals and then the next year I was going to a funeral every month and my calendar was dotted with memorial services all over the place. Every day I would see beautiful young men and women start to deteriorate and die in front of my eyes as if documentary films reviewing their lives were suddenly playing on fast-forward because of some terrible mistake.

This inevitably made me think seriously about issues of life and death and what I was doing for work. I was part of a highly commercialized promotion machine which kept on spinning out beautiful illusory visual images of eternal beauty, youth and sensual desires, while in reality, I was surrounded by the stark undeniable reality of impermanence, incurable illness, physical and psychological suffering and death.

When I looked to world religions and spiritual practices for solace, I found that Buddhist teachings offered the answers I was seeking. I started a serious practice of zazen and study and became a volunteer at an AIDS ward. My interests in life and my understanding of how to make the best use of my time in this world started shifting drastically. By the beginning of the millennium, I found myself abandoning my work in media entirely to become a full-time hospice chaplain for the nation's second-largest healthcare organization in New York City.

When a huge earthquake occurs in one part on the world, the ripple effects propagate outward from the epicenter until the entire globe feels the impact. In this way, throughout the vastness of Indra's Net, whenever an event makes a strong impact in one particular place—such as in the case of wars, catastrophic accidents, or natural disasters—the ripple effects eventually shake up every part of Indra's Net. They travel to every part of the network of interdependent origination and no matter how far away a place might be from the original event, it feels the reverberations. However, we are often unable to see or acknowledge this fact. Instead, we believe that isolated events that take place far away have nothing to do with our lives.

One of the most interesting things about end-of-life care is that we are the last recipients of these waves created by the merging ripple-effects of countless events; and the last wave shows us most clearly what exactly all these events have done to us—just like the last rays of sunlight mercilessly (or mercifully) expose every detail of the flower gardens in Tryon Park without leaving anything hidden.

In time, another generation reaches "hospice age." During my lifetime, I have witnessed the prolonged suffering and harm World War II did to people. I have also learned about the traumas experienced by the people who were involved in the Korean War and Vietnam War. Some people were never able to find the resources they needed to heal themselves and ended up living very hard lives until their entry into hospice care. One after another, as we encountered these people entering end-of-life care, we were forced to face and acknowledge the true reality of what these devastating wars had done to individual lives and to society as a whole.

The hospice organization I worked with had an inpatient unit in a large hospital in East Village, which is home to a community of Ukrainian immigrants. New York City is also home to many Russian Jewish immigrants as a result of antisemitism in Soviet Russia.

From the beginning of the millennium and into the 2010s, we experienced a curious phenomenon. Our hospice began receiving a series of new intakes who had been affected by the Chernobyl nuclear power plant accident.

The "inpatient unit" for hospice care is a place for emergency medical interventions. When a patient experiences an acute condition that cannot be managed elsewhere, they are brought to the inpatient unit until the crisis is resolved. Though some can go back home after a successful re-assessment of symptom management, very often death occurs while patients are still in the inpatient unit. The atmosphere of the inpatient unit is often both somber and panicky.

I was a part of a three-person team of chaplains who covered the inpatient unit at the hospital. We worked in rotation, and I went there two days a week, including Fridays. In its heyday, this inpatient unit had been an AIDS ward taking up an entire floor of the hospital building. At this time, however, the number of people dying of AIDS had drastically decreased and the hospital had converted half the floor into a maternity department. After spending many somber hours on the hospice side of the floor, I would always spend some time looking at the newborn babies through the large glass window before going home. This would bring back a wholesome sense of balance and widen my perspective to include the entire spectrum of life.

One Friday, I started my day at the northern tip of Manhattan's East Side, visiting patients' homes one after the other from uptown to downtown. It was a particularly demanding day. Each visit took a little longer than usual. By the time I finally arrived at the inpatient unit downtown it was already nearly 6 pm and the caregivers' team was shifting to the night team. As I checked in at the nursing station, the receptionist told me a patient's daughter was requesting to see a chaplain and had been waiting for me to arrive.

The patient's room was toward the end of the corridor, one door away from the exit leading to the maternity department. As I entered the dimly lit room, I saw there was a man in the hospital bed who appeared closer to middle-age than old. The man was lying still. From his characteristically erratic breathing, it was obvious the man was actively dying. There was a young woman sitting in a chair beside the bed. She sat slightly hunched towards the patient as if she were paying close careful attention to him. From the back, she looked petite and demure, almost like a young child.

I called out softly, introduced myself as the chaplain and inquired about the reason for her request. The young woman turned around to face me, still in the chair. I was wearing my name tag on a chain dangling from my neck at the level of my chest so the name tag was the first thing she saw. I sensed her looking intensely at the name printed on the tag: Rev. Hajime Issan Koyama. Then she stood up with a look of surprise and asked, "Are you Japanese?"

I always freeze for a moment when someone asks me this question. In this hugely diverse city, it is inevitable that some people will love certain ethnicities and hate others for a multitude of historical and cultural reasons. In my work, I have met patients who refused my visits due to my ethnicity based on events that took place between their ancestors and my ancestors decades, or even centuries ago. After all, the present time contains all that has happened in the past, so in our work, of course, we respect patients' preferences. But to be honest, this type of interaction always generates thoughts and emotion that can be rather uncomfortable. So, I timidly answered, "Yes."

This produced a surprising response from her. She grasped my hand with both of hers and thanked me for being Japanese, profusely and emotionally. This was the first time I had ever been thanked for being Japanese. I was quite surprised. What she told me afterwards, however, explained it all.

Her father, the patient, had been at the Chernobyl Nuclear Power Plant at the time of the accident and had been exposed to radiation. The family was of Jewish heritage. Since religion was not "allowed" by the communist regime, the daughter had no knowledge, information, or experience regarding her family's religious traditions. Oppressed by the strong antisemitic tendencies of Soviet society, the family eventually immigrated to the Unites States. During the time following the Chernobyl accident, it was very difficult for her to obtain any accurate information concerning what exactly had happened to her father and what would happen to him as a result.

After settling in the US, a strong wish to provide the best possible care for her father made her decide to go to school to become a medical professional. In addition, she made every effort to collect as much information about the consequences of exposure to nuclear radiation as possible so that she would be able to take appropriate measures to care of her father. It was difficult and time-consuming to search for this information. Then, one day, she discovered the detailed accounts left by those who had suffered from the radiation released by the Hiroshima and Nagasaki atomic bombs. The information included a documentary film produced immediately after the bombings which had been kept secret by the American military for over 20 years before being returned to Japan. The documentary featured unbearably graphic, close-up images of the ravaged bodies of the victims—one after another.

I knew this documentary very well. I was in elementary school in Japan when this controversial documentary was returned to Japan by the US, and in the middle of summer vacation, students were urged to gather in the school auditorium for a special viewing of the film. I believe it was shown on August 6th—on Hiroshima Day. The intention of the school administrators was to show the devastating consequences of the war to the young so that they might grow to be adults who support world peace. But the film was way too much for 12-year-old me. It was chilly scientific observation and graphic raw footage of unimaginable injuries, extreme burns and scars, and destroyed flesh, bones and organs. After the screening, I was so scared that I had to sleep with the lights on for many weeks. The memory of the film stayed with me so vividly that I intentionally avoided the memorial sites and museums of Hiroshima and Nagasaki for a long time despite my frequent visits to Japan. While the patient's daughter spoke about her discoveries, my mind took me back to my own past.

She continued to talk about her discovery of the many life stories left by the hibakusha. Hibakusha is a globally recognized term for all those who have suffered from exposure to radiation from nuclear weapons. Their detailed reports describe the progression of their ailments, the keloid scars covering their bodies, the discrimination they suffered when ignorant people mistook their wounds for contagious diseases, their sense of despair and fear, and above all, their courage, bravery and determination to keep on living and to let the world know what happened to them so that future generations might recognize the horror of nuclear weapons and appeal for world peace.

With this information came a deep sense of resignation as well as determination. She understood her father's situation. She knew about the ailments that would afflict him as he approached death and what could be done to mitigate his suffering. She also experienced a strong feeling of empathy for those who had suffered in Hiroshima and Nagasaki and was comforted and encouraged by their bravery.

Whatever has happened has happened and can't be undone, but instead of spending time and energy cultivating resentment and anger, why not utilize this experience to learn how to help others who come after us? The Japanese people featured in the documentary film and the hibakusha who carefully recorded their life stories all knew that their days were numbered, but they still tried to let the world know what they had experienced so that we could learn from their suffering.

At this point, she knew her father was very close to the end of his life, but because of the efforts she and her father had made to care for one another, she had a strong sense that they had done their best and beyond, and that there was nothing to regret.

However, there was still one thing she was concerned about. A while ago, she had accidentally caught sight of her father coming out of "that building." She was searching for a word and when I suggested "Synagogue," she said "Yes." Shyly, she told me that even though she and her father had never spoken about his religion, she wanted to respect his heritage and she wanted to know if there was anything specific that needed to be done for him as a Jew.

When I mentioned that she needed to speak with a rabbi, I found out she didn't even know the word "rabbi." And, furthermore, it was now after sundown on a Friday and she didn't even know that it was the Sabbath or what that meant.

Now it was my turn to go into action. The hospice I worked for was originated as an organization dedicated to the support of Jewish immigrants at the end of 19th century. Even now, there was a strong Jewish element in the hospice and I had a long list of rabbis I could call in case I needed Jewish-specific spiritual and religious support.

But this was the Sabbath and many observant Jews would not be taking phone calls. I started calling one number after another from the top of the list to the bottom and met with one answering service after another. Then, I remembered a rabbi I knew in my neighborhood, Rabbi Stephen. Washington Heights traditionally has a large Jewish community. Among the many rabbis I had worked with, Rabbi Stephen had particularly impressed me with his attitude that "for compassionate needs you can change the rules and regulations spontaneously." I called Rabbi Stephen. I got his answering machine, but I kept on speaking and explaining the situation. The rabbi, who was monitoring the machine, decided to pick up and answered the call. He agreed to travel from the northern tip of Manhattan all the way down to the East Village despite the hour and the Sabbath.

Sitting quietly with the patient's daughter at his bedside, I waited for the rabbi to get there. When Rabbi Stephen arrived and started talking with the daughter, I felt that it was all right for me to end my visit and leave the patient and his daughter in the trusted hands of this kind and generous rabbi. By the time I left the inpatient unit, it was already 9 pm.

The last chapter of The Bodhisattva's Four Embracing Actions is about 同事 (doji), which Okumura Roshi skillfully translates as "Identity Action." Do means "same" or "together," and doji refers to the action of an individual self that identifies with all beings as parts of one interdependent reality. "Identity Action" can take place when the individual self and the Universal Self are not viewed as different things. In my mind, doji, or Identity Action, is synonymous with another expression that appears in Zen literature: 同死同生 (doshi dosho), which means "dying together, living together."

Whether we recognize it or not, whether we are aware of it or not, we are always living and dying together with all things in Indra's Net. Our individual being is so small and limited that no matter how "enlightened" we may feel we are, we are never able to perceive our connections with all the myriad things all of the time. But sometimes, the unimaginably immense network of interdependent origination creates a wondrous "crash" of events that enables us to see the reality of "living together and dying together" very clearly.

The people of Hiroshima and Nagasaki in August 1945, the people of Chernobyl in 1986, 12-year-old Issan spending sleepless nights in 1970s Japan, and the young daughter of a Chernobyl accident survivor discovering records left behind by survivors in Hiroshima and Nagasaki in 1990s and coming to a strong compassionate resolution… Although on the surface these appear to be separate events occurring in different places at separate times, all these incidents and individuals ended up coming together when a dying man's devoted daughter encountered a Japanese-born hospice chaplain in the East Village of New York City in the 2000s, thus enabling us to recognize that we are actually all related and inseparable. All these events somehow wondrously brought us together and allowed us to recognize that we are always living and dying together. With that recognition, what can we do together right here and right now?

The image I have now is one of a pond of perfectly still water. Then a stone is dropped into the pond. Starting from the point where the dropped stone hits the water, waves are created which propagate outward. When a wave finally reaches the shore where I stand, how shall I receive the wave? As the wave hits the shore, it does not disappear. Instead the shore sends the wave back towards the epicenter. In the same way, we can receive the wave, transform the quality of the wave and send a wholesome wave back to the source of the wave. Depending on what we do with it right now, the meaning of a situation or series of events can be transformed. That is when healing becomes possible.

Doji or Identity Action is an action affecting this individual me. This individual me is acted upon and formed by the action of the whole of existence. But at the same time, this individual me can act wholesomely together with the whole. As a matter of fact, we are always being acted upon and acting upon others, receiving waves and sending them back simultaneously, all the time, moment by moment.

The years I spent in the realm of end-of-life care generously and graciously offered many wonderful opportunities for clarifying the true reality of the world. For those moments, when Dōgen's teachings were clearly manifested in real life experiences and actual events, I am truly grateful.

Afterword: I wrote this essay on December 24th in Nagasaki, Japan. On this day, I visited the Nagasaki Atomic Bomb Museum for the first time in my life. Later I went to visit Urakami Cathedral to join their Christmas Eve Mass. Urakami Cathedral was the largest Catholic church in Asia in 1945. It stood about 500 yards away from the epicenter and it was instantly destroyed by the atomic bomb on August 9th, 1945. The cathedral has been rebuilt from scratch and is now the center of the world peace movement. The special prayer chapel for hibakusha built nearby was lit with the colors of the Ukrainian flag.

Rev. Issan Koyama is a Buddhist priest and disciple of Shōhaku Okumura Rōshi. He is originally from Japan and came to USA as a newspaper and TV journalist. In the early years of the AIDS epidemic, Issan volunteered for end-of-life care in New York City and subsequently became a professional care giver. While working as a full-time hospice chaplain in the USA, Issan co-established and managed a residence and medical facility in Japan that hosted geriatric/palliative patients and family clinics. His work was featured in both American and Japanese mainstream media such as *The New York Times, Asahi Shimbun, PBS Morning Edition,* and StoryCorps' book *Callings.* Issan currently divides his time between the USA and Japan, focusing on Dōgen study.

No Identity-Action Without Identity-Action Towards Myself

Jisho Takahashi

I came across zazen and the teaching of Buddhism through the struggle to live. When I became a home-leaver in September 2017, my hope was to resolve this struggle. Yet for the next five years, I have continued to struggle in muddy water. I lost my hope as a priest and found myself in darkness. Finally, more recently, my feeling has changed. I have realized that I am enabled to live by others. And so it is as if I've now been re-ordained.

In April of 2018, half a year after I was ordained as a priest, I knocked on the door of Aichi Senmon Nisodo and spent the next two years there for ango. Even when there was a long break during the ango, I could not visit my own teacher's temple. Instead, I would visit Shundo Aoyama (青山俊董) Roshi's temple, Muryo-ji (無量寺), to help out with Obon and New Year's ceremonies in order to learn more about life at a temple. Even when priests who were living there were busy, they focused their utmost attention on cleaning, flowers, tea, calligraphy scrolls (掛軸 kakejiku) and incense, and even attending to unexpected visitors. In between the temple duties, they worked in the field to grow fresh vegetables as offerings to the Buddha during the memorials. Zen is not just sitting, but all of the activities that shine light on our lives. At the temple, they showed me how to practice as a priest in everyday life. Even though the practice at the temple was hard on my body, it was fulfilling to me.

During the second winter of ango, the abbot, Daisen Roshi, had asked me, "If you are leaving the nisodo by next March, would you be interested in coming to Muryo-ji?" The vice-abbot there, Joko Roshi, had lost mobility in her legs, and Daisen Roshi had been working hard by herself. I thought perhaps for the time being I would do so, and decided to go help out at Muryo-ji, starting in the spring of 2020. But from then on, so many things happened that were beyond my imagination.

Muryo-ji is located in Shiojiri, Nagano, which is equally distant from the Japan Sea and the Pacific Ocean. The temple is surrounded by nature, and from there you can see the northern Japanese Alps. In the spring, you can harvest mountain vegetables, in the summer vegetables, in the autumn grapes, and in the winter apples. Throughout the year, people visit the area for hiking, skiing, and hot springs.

In the latter years of Kosho Uchiyama Roshi's life, he lived in Shiojiri during the summer to escape the heat in Kyoto. Aoyama Roshi and Uchiyama Roshi had a connection for many years, so she would invite him here. Back then, this area was a quiet countryside, but nowadays a major freeway runs nearby, factories of major corporations were built, and the fields have been replaced by newly-built apartment complexes. The roads are constantly congested, and you cannot even locate where Uchiyama Roshi used to reside.

In 1627, during the Edo era, Muryo-ji was built by Ensai (円西) Osho of the Jodo Sect. During the abolition of Buddhism in the Meiji Era, the temple was vacant for about 30 years, merely existing as a building. In 1904, Bairin Shuzan (梅林周山), a nun who was an aunt of Aoyama Roshi, re-established the place as a Soto sect temple. She lived with her cousin Senshu Ryokan (仙周亮寛), who was also a nun. Together they would do service every morning throughout the year, while they lived a self-sustaining life through taking care of silkworms and weaving fabrics, and doing farming and reforestation.

Aoyama Roshi came to Muryo-ji when she was five years old and was raised by Shuzan and Senshu. She learned how to chant the Heart Sutra, while also learning different forms of livelihood such as how to care for silkworms and how to deconstruct and clean a kimono. When she was fifteen years old, she was ordained as a nun, started training at Aichi Senmon Nisodo, and also went to Komazawa University. After her studies, she went back to Muryo-ji, deciding not to focus on the danka (檀家) system,[1] but instead teach tea ceremony and ikebana to the local people. Also she began giving Dharma talks twice a month. It was because she wanted the temple to be "a place for people who are alive, not dead." Even to this day, she teaches as many as 70 students of tea ceremony and flower arranging; and about 30 people come regularly to the Dharma talks.

Currently, there are four female priests living at Muryo-ji: Shundo Aoyama Roshi, a 90-year-old retired abbot; Joko (浄光) Roshi, an 82-year-old vice-abbot; Daisen (大仙) Roshi, a 70-year-old abbot; and me, a 42-year-old priest. Joko Roshi became unable to walk without a walker, gradually became easily exhausted, and experienced pain during her sleep. When her family told her to move into a care home, she became very depressed and tried her best to prevent that from happening. However, as the days went by, she became less capable of doing things and experienced increasing pain in her foot. It was a lot harder than I'd initially imagined to live with her, since I couldn't truly understand her pain.

Daisen Roshi seemed far from being sick, although she did have a prior medical condition, because she was carefully maintaining her physical conditions and diet. However, in September 2020, she had an unexpected stroke, and as a consequence, she experienced a speech impediment. Right after her stroke, she could not remember her own name and address, or simple nouns like "flowers" and "cats." Although she recovered to the point of being able through rehabilitation to have a daily conversation, it became difficult for her to chant by herself, and sometimes she completely forgets some vocabulary items. While I can sense her stress and sorrow from being unable to speak, the only thing I can do is patiently try to understand what she is trying to say.

Aoyama Roshi had gone through a stroke, myocardial infarction, and shingles, and we had to keep an eye out for any relapse. Since the spring of 2020, because COVID-19 cases increased, she stopped her public appearances for lectures. Maybe COVID was ultimately good for her body, she joked. Yet by the summer of 2021, she was diagnosed with colorectal cancer and immediately taken into surgery. Ten days later, she experienced heart failure and was treated with cardiac massage and a pacemaker. By the summer of 2022, she had liver metastases and was treated with radiofrequency ablation. Even currently, her condition is under critical watch. There are limited forms of medical treatment for the life of someone like Aoyama Roshi, who would like to prioritize her time with her students and training priests. There are even fewer things that I can personally do for her.

Through my first-hand experience of the great Eastern Japan Earthquake in 2011, and also losing close friends to suicide and cancer, I aspired to become a priest as well as a hospital chaplain, learning about spiritual care for those who are going through old age, sickness, and grief from disaster. Yet the place for such learning was not in a hospital or disaster locations, but here and now. Being with those people who are experiencing such pain 24/7 was the most difficult challenge for me. It was a teaching for me that anywhere could be a place for learning to be together with people who are experiencing emotional pain. It was not easy to be with those experiencing different sicknesses and pain. Along with the usual temple duties, I took care of the three people at Muryo-ji all by myself—taking them to the hospital and shopping, and coming up with their dietary plans.

Fortunately, they could take care of themselves in terms of using the bathroom and bathing, and they could walk by themselves if they used a cane or a walker. Hence we didn't hire a professional caretaker, and instead, I am on my own to take care of them. I've looked into heat treatment and diet therapy in hopes of helping them. Yet as half a year went by, I started to get exhausted and felt like I was sacrificing my own time. I had no time to sit zazen or quietly read books. I would wake up at 5:00 am every day and work in the kitchen until 10:00 pm. I had no time or energy to study and would go straight to bed. When we had major ceremonial events back-to-back, I was completely burnt out. I cried, thinking, "Why me?" and "I want to leave here."

When my elder saw me in such a condition, she asked me, "Are you happy right now?" I couldn't say "Yes." She advised me, "If I were you, I would leave here. You need to become happy." But what is happiness? I didn't know what happiness meant to me. In my mind, there was no option to leave those three behind and go somewhere else. I am suffering, yet those who need someone else's help are suffering more. This held me back from going elsewhere.

In the Shobogenzo fascicle Shoji (Life-and-Death), it says: "If you seek the Buddha outside of life and death, it is like looking south to see the North Star. You will gather the cause of life and death more and more – and lose the way to liberation." If I sought a place other than here, it would be like looking for the North Star in the southern sky.

In a letter, Okumura Roshi told me, "Instead of reading books, please focus on your action at this very moment, believing that it's a study of the real Buddhist sutra. Remember at this moment, you are in the midst of the Buddha's Way. Uchiyama Roshi also focused on taking care of Sawaki Roshi, from the time he retired from being an abbot at Antai-ji to when he passed away. He said we should actively seek for the opportunity to volunteer to take care of those who are getting sick and dying. This is because it's an opportunity to learn about the reality of old age, sickness, and death." His words dissuaded me from wanting to escape.

However, even when I reflected on his words, my body was screaming, my mind was becoming depleted from exhaustion, and I spent a lot of time blaming myself. I was getting frustrated, I couldn't honestly accept any requests and sometimes ignored them in rebellion. I was becoming miserable. I couldn't accept anybody's words of advice. I spent a lot of time in seclusion and isolation. Even if I wished that a person would be a certain way, it wouldn't come true. That is just my own ego, and my perspective. When I have a feeling like this, I won't be able to understand another person's feeling. And even if I wanted others to understand me, it would be impossible. I was ashamed of myself that up until then, I had never been able to consider the feelings of those caregivers and what they had suffered through in caring for their elders and sick ones.

When I read Standing at the Edge by Rev. Joan Halifax, I realized how harmful and dangerous my current situation could be. In that book she writes,

> The Edge States are altruism, empathy, integrity, respect, and engagement, assets of a mind and heart that exemplify caring, connection, virtue, and strength. Yet we can also lose our firm footing on the high edge of any of these qualities and slide into a mire of suffering where we find ourselves caught in the toxic and chaotic waters of the harmful aspects of an Edge State.
>
> Altruism can turn into pathological altruism. Selfless actions in service to others are essential to the wellbeing of society and the natural world. But sometimes, our seemingly altruistic acts harm us, harm those whom we are trying to serve, harm the institutions we serve in.
>
> Empathy can slide into empathic distress. When we are able to sense into the suffering of another person, empathy brings us closer to one another, can inspire us to serve, and expands our understanding of the world. But if

we take on too much of the suffering of another, and identify too intensely with it, we may become damaged and unable to act.

Integrity points to having strong moral principles. But when we engage in or witness acts that violate our sense of integrity, justice, or beneficence, moral suffering can be the outcome. Respect is a way we hold beings and things in high regard.

Respect can disappear into the swamp of toxic disrespect, when we go against the grain of values and principles of civility, and disparage others or ourselves.

Engagement in our work can give a sense of purpose and meaning to our lives, particularly if our work serves others. But overwork, a poisonous work-place, and the experience of the lack of efficacy can lead to burnout, which can cause physical and psychological collapse.... There is humility, perspective, and wisdom that can be gained from our greatest difficulties.[2]

Upon reading these words, I felt a glimmer of hope. As time went by, the situation changed, and there were some moments when my heart was saved. When I was told about the risk of surgery, I hoped that their surgery would be a success. When Aoyama Roshi, Daishin, or Joko had a biopsy, I would pray that their result would be negative. Every time I go to the hospital with them, I get nervous with a sense that life is limited, and death is constantly looming over us. If the test results are good, I feel relieved. Because I have faced the fear of losing someone, I face this present moment and cherish the fact that we are still together, and our relationship becomes renewed.

I was raised by many people—my parents, siblings, relatives, teachers, and friends. Further on, there will also be a time when I will need someone else's support to go through old age, sickness, and eventually death. I realize that I am no exception in being someone who needs someone else's support to live. The fact that I am taking care of someone is a reminder that one day I too will need help from others, and it's not a matter of when. Even now, I am supported by everyone and am not living alone.

Aoyama Roshi often tells us, "If you change, the entire world will change (私が変われば、世界が変わる)." For me to change, I need to know myself. In order to know myself, I interact with others and realize that nothing goes according to how I feel. Aoyama Roshi also says, "Being together with other people is the most important practice." After I left the Aichi Senmon Nisodo, I had the option of living in a vacant temple or house, sitting zazen, and living by *takuhatsu*. Yet by spending time with others, I truly feel like it shone a light upon myself. When Uchiyama Roshi uses the phrase "all beings (衆生)," it means not beings that are separate from ourselves, but refers to the attitude of meeting our own life everywhere. I can only exist within the relationship between myself and the person in front of me. To thoroughly face each of those moments is identity-action.

However, in my own experience, practicing identity-action was very difficult. Even though I thought that I understood it in words, words are just words. I still get frustrated with things not going the way I'd hope for. Because I have not yet experienced old age and sickness first-hand, I cannot say that I truly understand how they feel, and if I said that I did, it wouldn't be true.

In his poem titled *Ordinary* (あたりまえ *atarimae*), Kazu-kiyo Imura (井村和清), a doctor who died of cancer while leaving a young child behind, said:

> . . . Being able to inhale a lungful of air.
> Being able to laugh, cry, and scream.
> Being able to run around.
> These are ordinary things.
> No one feels joyous about such wonderful things.
> Those who know how wonderful these are
> Are those who have some disability.
> I wonder why.
> So ordinary.[3]

If I, with my able body, could wholeheartedly put my hands together in gratitude, would my frustration and haste completely disappear?

In a passage from *Tsurezuregusa* (*Essays in Idleness* 徒然草), Kenko Yoshida, a 14th-century Japanese monk, poet and essayist, lists "young people" and "able-bodied people without sickness" among the "seven types of people who it is bad to be friends with." It is because they don't understand what it feels like to be those who are old and getting sick. This is inevitable. Yet we need to accept the fact that we don't understand, be humble, and maintain the attitude of hopefully learning from the old age, sickness, and death of others.

The other day someone gave me a calligraphy by Doyu Ozawa (小沢道雄) Roshi (1920–1978), also known as the "legless zen master (脚無し禅師)." He was adopted and raised at a temple, went to war when he was 20 years old, and returned at age 25. Due to getting severe frostbite on a battlefield in Siberia, his legs had to be amputated. Although his life was full of difficulty, he became a traveling priest, sustaining life through *takuhatsu* (托鉢). The calligraphy I received reads "enabled to live (恕されて生きる)." Ozawa Roshi explained about "being enabled to live" in his book as follows:

> I was enabled to live by the Buddha. Therefore, I must cultivate a strong sense of gratitude. With gratitude I must offer service to society for the sake of the Buddha. Ordinary people are capable of immediately putting this into action. But because I am missing my two legs, it makes it difficult for me to repay my gratitude. So I've vowed to do the following four things: always keep smiling, listen to people openly, be kind, and never become angry. Throughout my life, even 8 years after four amputation surgeries, I've continued to travel with my disabled legs while supporting myself by *takuhatsu*. . . . I am here today because of my ancestors, parents, and society. In other words, my life consists of indebtedness. I must repay my gratitude.[4]

I interpret the title "Today I Was Born" to mean that Ozawa Roshi felt that after the amputation of his legs, he was "reborn" as a legless being. So now without legs, he had no way of comparing who he was before with who he was now.

It is hard to imagine how he must have felt when he made these vows, while missing his legs and enduring pain. He truly went on carrying out *gyoji hoon* (行持報), the continuous practice of expressing gratitude for the kindness [received from all beings].

His continued practice, despite his physical difficulty, reminds me of the three practitioners at Muryo-ji. Even after a major surgery, even when they are experiencing great pain, and even when it's difficult for them to speak or write, they do the best they can. Setting aside their concern for tomorrow, they are determined to do what they can now, for the sake of the dharma. So many times I've witnessed those three tirelessly expressing their way of life, which they've cultivated since they were younger. I am awed, while receiving the greatest teaching from them. Compared to them, I am not disabled. Yet I complain, become lazy, and struggle if things don't go according to my will. Still they are tolerant, without scolding, and spend another day with a lazy person like me. Even when I act like I am living independently, I am supported by everything around me.

With humility, I must consider this fact: I am supported by all relationships, including my ancestors, parents, and society. To exist here and now, I am supported by total dynamic functioning, the protection of the Buddha. The light of Buddha shines upon me. By realizing this, I renew my vow to do everything I can do.

"Enabled to live." This phrase gave me courage. It seemed to be telling me that even someone who is immature like me is enabled to live. At that moment, my mind was freed from the environment, and I felt like I had met myself. I've realized that until now, I was always thinking about carrying out identity-action towards others, but not towards myself. What I needed the most was not a helper, nor comforting words, but identity-action towards myself.

"If you cannot take care of yourself, you cannot take care of others." This is a common saying among hospice workers. It means that if you cannot meet yourself, you cannot meet others. "Meet" in other words, means identity-action. Through this opportunity to write this chapter, I've gotten a chance to meet myself. If anyone asks me now "Are you happy?" I will be able to answer, "Yes, I am." My desire to escape from here and now has faded away naturally.

Ozawa Roshi also wrote: "Living itself is *takuhatsu*. If I become sick, sickness is *takuhatsu*. If I am dying, death is *takuhatsu*."[5]

Even the difficult time had given me an opportunity for a realization. Putting my hands together and accepting here and now as *takuhatsu* is my first step toward identity-action. For me, identity-action is not just the active aspect of supporting others, but also the passive aspect of being supported by others. I feel that this is like the Buddha's light, and I would like to continuously live the Buddha's way.

I'd like to acknowledge the kind assistance of Jikei Misaki Kido and Seigen Hartkemeyer in the writing of this chapter.

Jisho Takahashi is a graduate of Tokyo University with a Master of Arts degree. She practiced in Japan at Aichi Senmon Nisodo for two years and has been at Muryo-ji in Nagano prefecture since 2020.

Afterword: Embracing the Community, Sanshin Style

HOKO KARNEGIS

> Bodhisattvas do not avoid unwholesome activity
> out of fear of punishment and they do not engage
> in wholesome activity out of expectation. They do
> so because their behavior is in itself awakening to
> the true reality of interdependent origination.
> — *Shohaku Okumura*

AS OUR 20TH ANNIVERSARY APPROACHED and Okumura Roshi prepared to move from a day-to-day leadership role to the position of founding teacher, one of my most important undertakings was to look very carefully at what he'd been trying to do here for the last two decades. What exactly was it he'd been engaged with and that now he was handing to the next generation of leadership and practice? It looked straightforward enough—do a lot of zazen, study Dōgen Zenji's teachings, carry out a particular kind of sesshin schedule, and generally keep things simple. But how were we to make decisions going forward about what activities to include in the life of Sanshin? How were we best to prepare new teachers and leaders? What did a healthy community look like in this style of practice, and how were we to build and sustain it? Most importantly, how were the various elements he was demonstrating as part of his own practice connected, and what was the underlying thread?

Over the years, practitioners had made a lot of assumptions about what they saw when they visited Sanshin and why we did what we did. For many, the attraction was Okumura Roshi's ability to make Dōgen's teachings a bit less opaque. For others, it was the chance to challenge themselves with many long hours of zazen. Bloomington is a relatively small town, and most of those who took an interest in Sanshin lived somewhere else. Their introduction to Sanshin came in the form of Okumura Roshi's books, or those of his teacher, Uchiyama Roshi. When asked why they wanted to practice here, they frequently said that these books "resonated" with them or that they "connected" with these teachings. Something about the way our family explained the dharma seemed to make sense, and they wanted a little of that for themselves.

These days, I'm glad when such folks make the effort to actually come to Sanshin to see how we practice, because it's not at all obvious from the books. Our practice activities include a lot more than listening to Okumura Roshi take apart translations of the *Shobogenzo,* and a lot less variety than most other Western dharma centers. Visitors sometimes arrive assuming that they'll be participating in various rituals and ceremonies, spiritual direction or mentoring, Japanese cultural activities, or other things. Not long ago, an out-of-town practitioner arrived for sesshin and, after dropping his belongings next to his bed, went sailing past me toward the zendo with an oryoki set in his hands. "Where should I put this?" he asked. "Next to my cushion?"

"Back in your suitcase," I said, glancing up from whatever I was doing. "We don't use them for sesshin." He stopped, dismayed, and returned to his room, a victim of assumption. I imagined the internal dialogue. What do you mean meals are taken buffet style with ordinary plates and forks? Okumura Roshi spent a whole chapter in *Living by Vow* delving into the meaning of the meal chant! I was looking forward to demonstrating how well I know the process. Anyway, *everyone* uses oryoki for meals during sesshin – it's part of the practice!

With so many practitioners being short-term visitors from out of town, appearing for a few days of sesshin or genzo-e before disappearing again for another year or two or more, it was easy to lose sight of the real purpose of Sanshin: *to investigate inter-connectedness as it manifests in community.* All of these sesshin, retreats and other events were carried out by pop-up communities, individuals that came together briefly from all over the world in order to have a certain kind of experience for themselves and never had time to really gel as a group before breaking apart and going home again. It was difficult for participants ever to move beyond feeling like guests who were reliant on others to carry on the actual sesshin while they watched from the sidelines. Investigating community is possible under these circumstances, but it's not easy.

It became clear to me that residential practice needed to move to the core of this organization if we were going to deeply understand Sanshin style. The container of residential practice, intensified regularly by participation in sesshin, is one of the most effective opportunities to investigate community. The stability of doing the same things in the same place with the same people day after day moves practitioners beyond feeling and behaving like guests standing along the periphery of Sanshin's life and allows them to fully engage. That in turn gave them the space to fully encounter the reality of community.

SANSHIN'S STYLE OF PRACTICE

There's a reason that Sanshin Zen Community includes the word *community* in our name. You might think that the most important thing we do here is study texts by Dōgen, or sit 50-minute period of zazen after 50-minute period of zazen. According to Okumura Roshi, those things are important, but that's not it. Buddha and dharma are essential, but not more so than sangha, which is a vast dharma gate into the exploration of interconnectedness and thus also into emptiness. The simple act of showing up in the zendo to practice with others turns out to be the real key. The community itself is the ground for building a deep and concrete understanding of interconnectedness. Figuring out what community really is means studying what selflessness really is. Our zazen, work and study are all ultimately connected to this investigation of interconnectedness.

In the first chapter of this book, Okumura Roshi wrote, "The goal of our practice is to find a way we and other beings can live together without causing suffering to each other." You might have found this surprising. Aren't we always hearing in this dharma family that zazen is good for nothing, and that we should let go of clinging to our ideas about what we're getting out of practice? How can there be a goal? And yet, without some aspiration or direction, we'd never engage in practice at all. There's a difference between "zazen is good for nothing" and "zazen has no result." We approach the cushion without any expectation of reward to use as a yardstick to evaluate our success, but nonetheless we may notice that when we practice we become wiser and more compassionate, less in the grip of our preconceptions and better able to move through the world as bodhisattvas, with clarity and equanimity.

Here at Sanshin we undertake this investigation into being able to live with others without causing mutual suffering from a particular point of view. We call it Sanshin Style, and it's a continuation of the approach to practice that we've inherited from Kodo Sawaki and Kosho Uchiyama through Shohaku Okumura. We've made just enough adjustments to make it possible for a small, mostly lay sangha to carry it out in the American Midwest. You can read more about it in our booklet *Understanding Sanshin Style,* available for free download from our Dōgen Institute at *https://dogeninstitute.podia.com.*

There are some key themes that run through Sanshin Style practice. The main one is *non-reliance,* or connection without dependence. Non-reliance is an exploration of this question: *what is it that drives our practice?* Over and over again, Sawaki Roshi, Uchiyama Roshi and Okumura Roshi point us back to the need to give up our habit of relying on something other than our own awakening in every moment-by-moment activity of our lives. What happens at Sanshin only makes sense in the context of non-reliance as we encounter our teachers' admonishments not to rely on:

- the calendar to tell us what ceremonies to do
- teachers or officers to push us to practice
- a system to manage our training
- our ideas about anything
- goals, objectives or rewards to motivate us
- creating separation to maintain our identity
- things to make us happy
- doctrines to tell us what to believe or how to think

It might seem that not relying on these structures and expectations would make our practice a free-for-all that arises solely from our own opinions and preferences. Without the regular evaluation of a teacher, without a curriculum that indicates what to study next, without a liturgical calendar that tells us what services it's time for, how can we manage our practice?

It's true that if you're someone who needs a lot of direction and correction, Sanshin is probably not the place for you. You have to be willing, even as a beginner, to engage in your own investigation of the practice. That means you take advantage of instruction, ask questions, pay attention to what other practitioners are doing and how they're conducting themselves and maintain a spirit of inquiry about this one unified reality in this moment and place. There's no system to carry you along, no checklist of milestones or stages to pass through, no one watching and monitoring your "progress." If you choose not to practice, that's up to you. Teachers and sangha friends are here to welcome you when you come, but if you don't come, they're not going to go looking for you to drag you back to the zendo and onto a cushion. You can only rely on your own bodhicitta for that.

Of course, the danger in relying on ourselves is our tendency to treat our opinions and ideas as if they were the One True Way. If no one is telling me how to practice, then whatever I want to do is good no matter whether others like it or not, right? If we're not relying on the teacher to step in and manage our practice, how does this dynamic get resolved? How do we not just run roughshod over other sangha members and the larger community in the name of Sanshin style? Is there a way to reconcile not being reliant on sangha with being completely interconnected with sangha?

It's true that at Sanshin, there is no construct that looks like "teachers" "training" "students." There is simply a space for everyone to pursue practice together, wherever they are on the path. Some with more experience may serve as examples or resources for others, but the emphasis is not on moving people along a trajectory or timeline toward a particular state of being or understanding. Teachers simply do their practice and welcome those who want to join them in that. Sanshin is a community of people practicing together in our family style rather than an organization which is striving to "spread the dharma." It's an opportunity to investigate the real meanings of community, interconnectedness and emptiness in a practical, concrete way.

It would seem that an emphasis on non-reliance is incompatible with a focus on the investigation of community. However, not relying on others to drive our practice doesn't make us oblivious to how well we're upholding the harmony of the community. It's just the opposite—we take responsibility for the health of the interconnected network because we and "our" awakening are integral to it. If something harmful or helpful is happening, we take notice for ourselves and either continue the wholesome things we're doing or reverse the unwholesome things to which we've fallen prey. We don't wait for someone else to point out that we're making mistakes or that we have the opportunity to help liberate others from suffering. We're aware of these things because of our own awakening and we practice not to avoid punishment, or because someone else expects us to, but as an expression of the reality of interconnectedness. Non-reliance makes our practice genuine and authentic.

We could also assume that not being reliant on something to give us an identity or on someone to drive our practice is the same as not being connected to that thing or person. When you and I meet in the space of awakening, we both see with the eyes of Buddha and we don't need to tell each other what to do or cling to ideas to create an identity for these five skandhas. We recognize that we are and always have been completely interconnected with everything else, but we're not reliant on any of it to determine our actions or understanding for us. We see the same reality the way Buddha sees it, and what we need to do in order to create and maintain a wholesome community right in the midst of both non-reliance and interconnectedness becomes clear. We're able to see one reality from two sides and express two sides in one action.

We might think of non-reliance as the concrete manifestation of emptiness—what we *do* based on how things *are.* Approaching our lives on the basis of non-reliance is a practical gateway to the study of the larger and more abstract aspects of community. We can ask ourselves about the basis for our relationship with all the dharmas we encounter. What do I expect from my relationship with the things around and inside me? Am I relying on them to build my identity or motivate me to practice?

Not relying on things doesn't negate their existence or our relationship to them. The true existence of things is not the product of our relationships with them, just like the true self is not the self we fabricate out of our ideas. The problem is our habit of clinging. Clinging to anything creates suffering, so when we realize we're suffering we can ask ourselves: on what am I relying for my comfort or happiness or peace of mind? What's really driving my practice?

We might rephrase Sanshin's practical investigation of interconnectedness as it manifests in community as an investigation of what it means not to be dependent on sangha while being completely interconnected with sangha. As Okumura Roshi has said, "Independence is important, but isolation is not necessary."

Intersecting non-reliance and the four embracing actions

What happens when we look at the four embracing actions through the lens of non-reliance as part of our investigation of community? In order to find a way to live together with other beings without causing suffering to each other, we have to deeply understand what community is. How can non-reliance help us understand these four actions more clearly, and vice versa? What can it show us about interconnectedness and emptiness?

At the core of our intensive practical study of interconnectedness within the context of community are residential practice and sesshin; these form the basis of our investigation and provide the purest way to manifest our understanding. From there our practice spreads outward on a firm foundation to include householder practice and engagement with the larger community. When we can successfully practice within the sangha, we can continue to have the same attitude toward home life or work or the larger community. Thus Sanshin includes two kinds of day-to-day practice situations. Some practitioners are residents, living on campus and participating in full days of zazen, work and study. Others are householders, commuting to Sanshin as their lives permit to participate in practice. Each of these circumstances offers its own opportunities for investigating particular aspects of community.

Inside the temple: residential practice

It's not possible to simply sit zazen from morning to night every day and survive as a temple or community, so other activities are necessary on a practical level as well as serving as important dharma gates. These day to day functions support the temple community as a miniature network, with each person's practice supporting the practice of all the others. This network of activity includes everyone from leaders on down, so in addition to individual practice, there is also only one action—the action of the community as a whole. It's not unlike chanting during liturgy; we all have individual voices, but when we put them together there is only one sound.

Living and practicing with the same people on the same schedule day after day is a concentrated experience in seeing patterns and connections in both oneself and others. It's a means of studying how to be together with zabutons, groceries, tools and other practitioners, and an opportunity to engage in the practical study of *sanshin,* the three minds about which Dōgen teaches in the *Tenzo Kyokun:* magnanimous mind, nurturing mind and joyful mind.

THREE MINDS AND FOUR EMBRACING ACTIONS

Cultivating the three minds is critical to our ability to engage in the four embracing actions. Manifesting nurturing mind (*roshin* 老心) within a residential community means making a shift from wanting to be looked after to wanting to look after others. Rather than focusing on whether we're receiving offerings and loving speech, and whether others are adapting themselves to our needs, we see the larger picture and naturally act for the benefit of everyone, including ourselves. As Okumura Roshi has written elsewhere, "The inner attitude of the caregiver is very different from that of the one who expects to be cared for. This difference determines the quality of the community. A place where people want to be taken care of is very different from a place where people care for others. We should understand that this small difference in our inner attitude has very large effects on the world around us."[1]

Of course, sometimes it's a lot of work to care for others and to do all the things we need to do simply for the community to exist and function. One day when I was in a training temple in Japan and most of the trainees were out doing ceremonies or *takuhatsu* (alms collection), my friend and I talked together about how much day-to-day work it took just to live as a community in a temple. Someone had to clean the bath and heat the water, someone had to cook and clean up after meals, someone had to carry out the three daily services, and that wasn't to mention simply answering the phone, signing for deliveries, or burning the trash. When you're down to only a few people remaining in the temple, you can only take care of the most basic functions—and even those take up much of the day. The next day, we started all over again.

Without joyful mind (*kishin* 喜心), it would be easy to become discouraged and resentful in that kind of circumstance. It's pretty hard to avoid snapping at people, resisting doing that one more task, or seeing absent members as abandoning or taking advantage of those staying behind. Instead, our practice is to continue carrying out the four embracing actions, understanding that wherever we are, we're all carrying a small piece of the total dynamic functioning of this moment. We can let go of our feelings of martyrdom and desire for escape. Okumura Roshi reminds us, "If we do things for our private gain or personal benefit, then no matter how hard we work, no matter how much we achieve, it will come to an end. Instead, we dedicate our work to all beings. That is our attitude toward work and toward other people. That is joyful mind."[2]

Magnanimous mind (*daishin* 大心) is closely related. "We should not think that to prepare a meal for one or two people is easy or that to prepare a meal for many people is heavy or difficult. We take the same careful, attentive attitude in either case," Okumura Roshi writes. Dōgen says that magnanimous mind is neither biased nor contentious. It's spacious enough to see beyond the immediate demands of the small self without ignoring them altogether, putting things in context without getting stuck in a narrow view.

These three minds are necessary in removing the obstacles to practicing the four embracing actions. That's why we understand residential practice at Sanshin as focusing on investigating and cultivating them. Without nurturing, joy and magnanimity, there's no chance for the community to remain healthy and skillful. As Dōgen points out, engaging in the four embracing actions allows bodhisattvas to be free from the three poisons (greed, anger and ignorance), benefiting both themselves and all beings. We can see how cultivating the three minds and practicing the four embracing actions are mutually reinforcing.

Practicing in a community has been likened to putting potatoes into a bucket of water and agitating them together to knock off the dirt, or putting rocks into a rock polisher to chip off the rough edges and make them smooth. If practicing in a community is the study of interconnectedness, and if community is the central aspect of Sanshin's life, then practicing here cannot be a curriculum for individual self-improvement, a mystical spiritual quest, or a personal project of any kind aimed at achieving a goal or gaining anything at all. The point is immersion in the total dynamic functioning of the universe, and nothing more.

Living in the intersection between non-reliance and the structures of communal practice is an opportunity for deep investigation. On one hand, we're told not to rely on roles, teachers, calendars or other things to drive our practice. On the other, we give up a lot of personal choice when we enter into a practice community and agree to go along with what's being done. Antaiji's website reminds potential arrivals, "Life at Antaiji is based on shared practice where it is not possible for individuals to make their own schedules. You will be expected to work together with everybody else and perform shared tasks at set times." Sanshin's life is also like this: different people with different karmic circumstances all engaged in the same activities. Residents sit, study, work and eat together, taking responsibility for themselves and their practice within the network of community.

That shared practice life points us back to interconnectedness moment after moment. As Uchiyama Roshi has written, "In a monastery, no matter how weak our determination may be, we have to get up at four o'clock in the morning when we hear the wake-up bell. No matter how tired we may be, we have to go to the zazen hall to sit. Even in July or August during the hottest time of the year, we have to wear various robes, Japanese kimono, Chinese koromo, and Indian okesa, and sit in zazen. Since all monks in the assembly do the same things in the same way, we have to always work together in harmony with others even if we don't like the work or the people. Somehow we can do it. This is the so-called divine power of the assembly."[3]

OUTSIDE THE TEMPLE: HOUSEHOLDER PRACTICE

In the same way that living and practicing inside the temple is a gateway to the study of the three minds, activities outside the temple are gateways to the study of the three pure precepts:

- *Shoritsugikai* 摂津儀戒: The precept of avoiding all evil acts or embracing moral codes
- *Shozenbokai* 摂善法戒: The precept of doing all good acts or embracing all good dharmas
- *Shoshujokai* 摂衆生戒: The precept of embracing and benefiting beings

The *sho* (摂) that appears in each of the three pure precepts is the same as the one in *Shishobo,* with the same meaning of embracing and accepting. Householding practitioners engage the dharma by taking care of their families, carrying out their jobs or professions, doing volunteer work in the community or other things. These are concrete ways to apply the precept of embracing all beings—not just the practitioners within the temple, but the neighborhood, society as a whole, and even plants and animals. The dharma isn't just an abstract idea, but something concrete and practical.

THE OUTCOME IN BOTH CASES

When we're spiritually healthy and have some clarity about the nature of reality, we naturally engage in skillful action—action that moves us and others toward understanding two related things: interconnection and cause-and-effect. Interconnection, or non-separation, means that within this one unified reality, nothing is actually disconnected; there is nothing outside of Buddha's way. That sounds nice when we think of it as being supported by all beings. It sounds scary and uncomfortable when we think of it as being unable to escape from the things in our lives that we don't like so much. How can we help ourselves and others to see and acknowledge interconnection? Cause-and-effect is important because it reminds us that what we do has consequences. We don't operate in a vacuum; when we do something, it sets up causes and conditions that unfold across space and time. That means that it's important that our actions in the world—even small actions—are skillful, because whether we're being wholesome or unwholesome makes a difference for others besides ourselves. How can we help ourselves and others to see and acknowledge cause-and-effect?

Transformation of our understanding of interconnectedness is key. We practice giving, loving speech, beneficial action and identity action in the intersection of abstract theory and concrete activity, seeing one reality from two sides and expressing two sides with one action. Sanshin becomes the place to which we return to share our growing understanding, check our perceptions, broaden our awareness, and gain support to wrestle with the tough questions. There will be a diversity of views, interests and experiences of engagement as practitioners identify their bodhisattva paths. What holds it all together is our shared commitment to a healthy network.

In one way, that network is already perfect. This one unified reality is functioning exactly as it should according to cause-and-effect. We might not like what's happening because its making us uncomfortable or not giving us what we think we want or need, but things are always unfolding in the only way they can given current causes and conditions.

In another way, we can improve the health of the network by carrying out the four embracing actions and renewing our vow to liberate beings from suffering. This is what Giun means when he says that to practice *shishobo* is to add flowers of beauty to the golden brocade that is already beautiful. Functioning within an already-perfect universe, we can practice non-reliance and stop being pulled around by delusion without being cut off from delusion. We can recognize suffering and work to help beings without being cut off from beings and their suffering. In the midst of samsara, we are also in nirvana.

Hoko was ordained as a novice by Shohaku Okumura in 2005, and she completed her *shuso hossen* that same year at Kogetsu-an in Shiga, Japan. She received dharma transmission in September, 2012 and completed *zuise* at Eiheiji and Sojiji in November of that year. In January, 2016 Hoko was named vice-abbot and successor at Sanshin, and she took over day to-day leadership there in June, 2023. She previously served as communications director at Hokyoji Zen Practice Community in southern Minnesota from 2013 to 2016 and as interim practice director at Milwaukee Zen Center from 2011 to 2013. She has served as an adjunct instructor at Lakeland College in Sheboygan, WI, where she taught Eastern Religious Traditions in the classroom and online, and later taught Zen as a part of Ivy Tech Community College's lifelong learning program in Bloomington, IN. She is recognized by Sotoshu as *nito kyoushi* (second-rank teacher) and as a practitioner of baika, a type of Japanese Buddhist hymn created by Sotoshu in 1952. She is serving her second four-year appointment from Sotoshu as *kokusai fukyoushi,* or international teacher.

Notes

SHOBOGENZO BODAISATTA SHISHOBO

1 This translation by Shohkau Okumura and Hozan Alan Senauke appeared in
   a series of articles for Dharma Eye, the magazine of the Soto Zen International
   Center, in the years 2003 to 2007. Printed here by permission of the Soto Zen
   International Center. A version of this translation also appears in the book, *The
   Bodhisattva's Embrace: Dispatches from Engaged Buddhism's Front Line*, by
   Alan Senauke (Clear View Press, 2010).

THE BODHISATTVA'S FOUR EMBRACING ACTIONS

1 Dōgen, Taigen Daniel Leighton, and Shohaku Okumura, *Dōgen's Extensive
   Record: A Translation of the Eihei Koroku*, 1st ed (Somerville, MA: Wisdom
   Publications, 2004). Vol. 2 Dharma Hall Discourse 135.

2 Ibid.

3 Translations of Ryokan's poems are from: Abe Ryuichi and Peter Haskel, Great
   Fool - Zen Master Ryokan, University of Hawaii Press, Honolulu, 1996, with
   minor changes by the author.

4 Augustine Ichiro Okumura, *Awakening to Prayer* (Washington, D.C: ICS
   Publications, 1994).

5 Ibid., p. 11. (Translated by Theresa Kazue Hiraki and Albert Masaru Yamato,
   with minor changes).

6 The Awakening of Faith The Classic Exposition of Mahayana Buddhism,
   Asvaghosa, translated by Teitaro Suzuki, Dover Publications, New York,
   2003. This translation was originally published by the Open Court Publishing
   Company, 1900. p. 84-85.

7 Ibid., p. 91-92.

8 Jp. *Aikuo-kyo*, Taisho:50.

9 Mark 12:41-44.

10 Kōshō Uchiyama et al., *Opening the Hand of Thought: Foundations of Zen Buddhist Practice* (Boston: Wisdom Publications, 2004), p. 153.

11 Translated by Gudo Nishijima and Chodo Cross, with small changes, Master Dōgen's Shobogezo Book 1, Windbell Publications, 1996, p. 165.

12 The Sutta-Nipata, translated by H. Saddhatissa, Curzon Press, 1994.

13 Here are some examples: [1-7] harsh words (p.35); [1-10] arguments (p.40); [1-17] defiled words (p.56); [4-10] avoiding careless speech (p.149), [4-13] speaking words which cause enmity between two or more persons (p.156); [5-4] straightforward speech (p.168); [5-7] meaningless arguments (p.171); [5-17] not speaking of the faults of others (p.188); [6-12] listening carefully to others (p.218); [6-17] listening to one's teacher without holding on to one's own views (p.222). Section numbers and page numbers are from Shobogenzo Zuimonki, Sotoshu Shumucho, 1988; translated by Shohaku Okumura.

14 The Zen Fool Ryokan, translation by Misao Kodama & Hikosaku Yanagishima, Tuttle, 1999.

15 Translated by Burton Watson. Columbia University Press, 1977, p.115.

16 The Threefold Lotus Sutra, Weatherhill/Kosei, 1987, p.212; italics added.

17 Matthew 5:43-46.

Bäume und Menschen

1 Deutsche Übersetzung: Meister Dōgen, Shobogenzo, Bodaisatta shishobo, Werner Kristkeitz Verlag 2006, Bd. 3, S. 61ff.

2 Deutsche Redewendung: Sie bedeutet, dass jemand etwas vollkommen Offensichtliches nicht erkennen kann und die nächstliegende Lösung seines Problems vor lauter Auswahlmöglichkeiten nicht bemerkt.

Trees and Human Beings

1 German translation: Master Dōgen, Shobogenzo, Bodaisatta shishobo, Werner Kristkeitz Verlag 2006, Vol. 3, p. 61ff.

2 German idiom: It means that someone can't see something completely obvious and does not notice the closest solution to his problem because of all the choices.

Dana (Offering)

1 The Diamond Sutra, translation and commentaries by Red Pine. Counterpoint, 2001, Chapter Four.

SILENCIO AMOROSO

1 "Loving-speech means, first of all, to arouse compassionate mind when meeting with living beings, and to offer caring and loving words. In general, we should not use any violent or harmful words." (*Shobogenzo Bodaisatta Shishobo*, Trad. Okumura, S., Senauke, A. Recuperado de https://www.sanshinji.org/shishobo.html).

2 Okumura, S. (2022). Vivir guiados por el voto. Una introducción práctica a ocho textos y cantos esenciales del Zen. España: Nous, p. 202.

3 Ibid.

4 Ibid., p. 201.

5 Debo dar crédito a este neologismo: (conversación informal con Reigen Sanjuán) "*Escapachita*": palabra que surge de esa aspiración que se tiene en algunos momentos cuando queremos escapar del mundo y sus agobiantes tribulaciones. Surge de los sonidos que componen la palabra "Bodhichita," que es la mente que aspira al despertar. *Escapachita*, por su parte, es la mente que aspira al escape inmediato.

6 Amaya, J., (2021). Vistiendo un campo de arroz: el hábito y la costura en la comunidad Soto Zen de Colombia. Universidad de los Andes. http://hdl.handle.net/1992/56516, p.22.

7 Amaya, J., 2021, p. 24.

8 Amaya, J., Notas de diario de campo, noviembre de 2020.

9 Palabra que en nuestra sangha se refiere a la persona que está cosiendo, rakusu u okesa, y que aspira a vestir la enseñanza del Buda.

10 Hay que decir que, gracias a mi maestro, Denshō Quintero, pude llegar a esta aproximación de manera más clara: Por eso es la práctica misma de zazen, de solamente estar aquí, del *shikan*, de poner todo nuestro ser en el acto de coser. Por eso es una práctica que se debe hacer en silencio, aunque sea en grupo, se debe hacer en silencio, y pues muy concentrados, porque sí realmente los puntos quedan muy separados o muy irregulares, pues hay que descoser y volver a eso… queda la evidencia del estado mental en lo que uno cosió. (Denshō Quintero, comunicación personal, marzo de 2021).

LOVING SILENCE

1 "Loving-speech means, first of all, to arouse compassionate mind when meeting with living beings, and to offer caring and loving words. In general, we should not use any violent or harmful words." (*Shobogenzo Bodaisatta Shishobo,* Trans. Okumura, S., Senauke, A. Retrieved from: https://www.sanshinji.org/shishobo.html).

2 Okumura, S. (2022). Vivir guiados por el voto. Una introducción práctica a ocho textos y cantos esenciales del Zen. España: Nous, p. 202. Translation of *Living by Vow.*

3 Ibid.

4 Ibid.

5 I must give credit to this neologism (casual conversation with Reigen Sanjuán). "Escapachita": a word that arises from that aspiration that appears when we want to escape from the world and its overwhelming tribulations. It comes from the sounds that form the word "Bodhichita," which is the mind that aspires to awakening. Escapachita, on the other hand, is the mind that aspires to immediate escape.

6 Amaya, J. (2021). Vistiendo un campo de arroz: el hábito y la costura en la comunidad Soto Zen de Colombia. Universidad de los Andes. http://hdl.handle.net/1992/56516, p. 22.

7 Ibid., p. 24.

8 Amaya, J., Field diary notes, November 2020.

9 Word that in our sangha refers to the person who is sewing rakusu or okesa, and who aspires to wear the Buddha's teaching.

10 I must say that, thanks to my teacher, Denshō Quintero, I was able to arrive at this approach more clearly: "That is the practice of zazen itself, of just being here, of *shikan*: putting all our being in the act of sewing. That is the reason why the practice must be done in silence, even when it is in a group, it must be done in silence, and therefore very concentrated, because if the stitches are too separated or very irregular, then you have to unpick and redo... the evidence of the mental state in what you sewed remains. (Denshō Quintero, personal communication, March 2021).

SEEING BUDDHA, SPEAKING BUDDHA

1 Bhikkhu Ñāṇamoli and Bhikkhu Bodhi, trans., The Middle Length Discourses of the Buddha: A [New] Translation of the Majjhima Nikāya, 4. Ed, The Teachings of the Buddha (Boston: Wisdom Publications, 2009). Angulimala Sutta (Majjhima Nikaya 86).

2 Quotations from: "How One Man Convinced 200 Ku Klux Klan Members To Give Up Their Robes," produced by Matthew Schwartz, adapted for the web by Wynne Davis.

PRACTICE FOR ITS OWN SAKE

1 Shohaku Okumura, trans., Hokyoki (unpublished translation).

2 Red Pine. The Diamond Sutra: Text and Commentaries (Berkeley: Counterpoint Press, 2002). Section one, Verse 31.

Is "Beneficial Action" a Means of Attracting Followers or Non-dualistic Altruism? An Etymological Exploration

1 Okumura Roshi translated from the Sino-Japanese text of Dōgen, not from the Pali text; this is adapted from his translation of Dōgen's text for the purposes of comparison.

2 This is adapted from Bodhi's translation of the Saṅgahasutta (Aṅguttara Nikāya, 4.32), which uses nearly identical language as that found in the Saṅgītisutta (Dīgha Nikāya, 33).

3 Bhikkhu Bodhi, The Numerical Discourses of the Buddha (Wisdom Publications, 2012). His translations of cattāri saṅgahavatthūni and atthacariyā are bolded here for context, but not in the original.

No Identity-Action Without Identity-Action Towards Myself

1 "The danka system (檀家制, danka seido), also known as jidan system (寺檀制度, jidan seido) is a system of voluntary and long-term affiliation between Buddhist temples and households in use in Japan since the Heian period. In it, households (the danka) financially support a Buddhist temple, which, in exchange, provides for their spiritual needs." Up until World War II, each Japanese family had a strong connection with a particular temple in the same area. Source: https://en.wikipedia.org/wiki/Danka_system

2 Halifax, Joan. Standing at the Edge: Finding Freedom Where Fear and Courage Meet. New York: Flatiron Books, 2018, p. 3-4.

3 Imura, Kazukiyo. Asuka e soshite mada minu ko e (飛鳥へ、そしてまだ見ぬ子へ / To Asuka and to My Next Child Yet Unseen). Tokyo: Shodensha, 1980. Poem, p.186. Unpublished English translation by Jikei Misaki Kido.

4 Ozawa, Doyu. Honjitsu Tadaima Tanjou (本日、ただいま誕生 / Today I Was Born). Tokyo: Hakujusha, 1976. P.239. See also: https://ja.wikipedia.org/wiki/%E5%B0%8F%E6%BE%A4%E9%81%93%E9%9B%84

5 Ibid., p. 239.

Afterword: Embracing the Community, Sanshin Style

1 Shohaku Okumura, *Living by Vow,* Wisdom Publications. 2012, p. 40.

2 Ibid., p. 38.

3 Eihei Dōgen, Kosho Uchiyama, translated by Shohaku Okumura, *The Wholehearted Way,* Tuttle Publishing, 2011, p. 194.

For more information

Dōgen Institute: www.dogeninstitute.org

Sanshin Zen Community: www.sanshinji.org